HAUTE · COUTURE · EMBROIDERY
THE · ART · OF · LESAGE

Karl Lagerfeld. An eighteenth-century clock of mat gold sequins and gold bugles, the convex face formed by chalk-white sequins. For the back of a black crêpe gown.

originally published 1987 by Editions du Chene

this edition published 1994 by

LACIS PUBLICATIONS
3163 Adeline Street
Berkeley, California 94703,
USA

ISBN 0-916896-36-6

© 1987 Editions du Chene
© 1994 Lacis

printed and bound in France

Chanel (Karl Lagerfeld). Detail. A trompe-l'œil clasp for a suit.

HAUTE·COUTURE·EMBROIDERY

THE·ART·OF·LESAGE

PALMER WHITE

LACIS
PUBLICATIONS

· D E D I C A T I O N ·

French fashion could never have achieved or maintained its unique place as the supreme world arbiter of feminine elegance without its unsung heroes.

These are the designers of fabrics, prints, jewellery, footwear, trimmings and accessories, the milliners, dyers, furriers, suppliers of plumes, photographers and workroom *premiers*, *premières* and seamstresses.

Among these also figure the embroiderers, whose contribution greatly helps a woman to create and maintain her image according to her fancy, individuality, wealth and position.

The most durable, imaginative and innovative Paris embroiderer is Lesage. This house inherited the tradition and repute of an embroiderer who started in the mid-nineteenth century with the first couturier, Charles Frederick Worth. It has served the four major generations of modern Paris designers from Madeleine Vionnet to Christian Lacroix, and is now also enhancing the lustre of American fashion.

Albert Lesage handed down his business to his son, François. But the name of Lesage would never have become synonymous with contemporary Parisian artistry, refinement and luxury had it not been for the support of Marie-Louise, wife and mother.

This book is dedicated to that lovely French lady known as Yo, as well as to the embroideresses in the Lesage ateliers and the world over, united by the underlying warmth and charm of this particular expression of feminine grace.

The Bayeux Tapestry. With the special authorisation of the City of Bayeux. Detail. Harold II, King of England, and his Saxon followers setting out for the Battle of Hastings and death at the hands of William the Conqueror, 16 October 1066. The embroidery exemplifies all the various stitches known at the time and still used today.

CONTENTS

*A*CKNOWLEDGEMENTS 8

*T*RIBUTES 9

PART · ONE · LESAGE, ALBERT

1 STITCHES IN TIME 16

2 THE DAY AND AGE OF MESSRS WORTH AND MICHONET 24

3 ALBERT 29

4 MARIE-LOUISE 34

5 FROM MICHONET TO LESAGE 38

6 LA GARÇONNE 42

7 MADELEINE VIONNET 47

8 ELSA, EMPRESS OF THE THIRTIES 56

9 THE LIGHTS DIM 70

10 A NEW DAWN 77

PART · TWO · LESAGE, FRANÇOIS

11 BIDUL 82

12 A BABE IN TOYLAND 86

13 LESSONS IN FASHION 92

14 YOUTH WILL OUT : THE SIXTIES 106

15 MAY 1968 AND *MONSIEUR* YVES : THE EARLY SEVENTIES 114

16 OF ARAB OIL AND PRINCESSES : THE LATE SEVENTIES 121

17 A GOLDEN AGE : THE EARLY EIGHTIES 129

18 THINGS OF BEAUTY, JOYS FOREVER 142

19 RUE GRANGE 146

EPILOGUE 166

APPENDIX : FRAUDULENT COPYING 167

SHORT BIBLIOGRAPHY 169

INDEX 170

ACKNOWLEDGEMENTS

Without the support of François Lesage, who introduced me into his 'family' of employees, this book would not have been written. The embroideresses, draughtsmen, stockroom workers and their supervisors; the sales, fabrication, accounting and secretarial personnel; the accessories and jewellery designer and his assistants — for months all of them, like himself, remained available and patient.

To these unsung heroes must be added Laura Sinderbrand, Director of the Design Laboratory of the New York Fashion Institute of Technology, who organized the first Lesage exhibition and who believed in me; François Huertas, Art Director, Chêne, and my art designer — his great gifts are everywhere manifest herein; Patrice Stable, responsible for all the Lesage photographs, who repeatedly proved his initiative and eye for beauty; and young Gaël de Dieuleveult, the assistant whom François Lesage assigned to me, obliging, resourceful and tireless, as knightly as his name.

I also wish to pay tribute to the many unsung persons who, in costume centres, institutes, societies and museum costume sections the world over, devote themselves to collecting, preserving and through exhibitions keeping dress alive and vibrant and, in France particularly, to maintaining the social and artistic legacy of fashion.

Not to be forgotten, either, are the international fashion editors and reporters who, beyond the daily, weekly or monthly task, record so penetratingly this phase of contemporary history.

I should especially like to thank the following: *Monsieur* Yves Saint Laurent. Jean Arcache, Chêne; Francine Benhamou, Legal Consultant, Fédération Française de la Couture, du Prêt-à-Porter des Couturiers et des Créateurs de la Mode; François Besse, Chêne; Bill Blass; Marc Bohan, Dior; Eugene Braun-Munk, one thing leading to another; Nadine Briché, Maison Lesage; British Film Institute: Tice Vahinaghi; Gabrielle Buchaërt, Yves Saint Laurent, so constantly helpful; David Campbell, Chêne; Patton Campbell (costume students should erect a monument to this inspired guide); Emmanuel Chaussade, Jean-Louis Scherrer; Cinémathèque Française, Photothèque: Bertrand Delmas; Michèle Coïc, Curator, Bibliothèque Municipale et de la Tapisserie de Bayeux; Jean-Claude Colas; Madeleine Delpierre, Honorary Curator-in-Charge, Musée de la Mode et du Costume de la Ville de Paris, Palais Galliera; Francisque Des Garets, that grand French gentleman; Jean L. Druesedow, Associate Curator-in-Charge, Costume Institute, Metropolitan Museum of Art, New York; Angela Dyer, my forebearing literary editor; Diana Edkins, Permissions Editor, Condé-Nast Publications, Inc., New York; Fabienne Falluel, Curator, Musée de la Mode et du Costume de la Ville de Paris, Palais Galliera; Raymond Felgines, Maison Lesage; Guillaume Garnier, Curator-in-Charge, Musée de la Mode et du Costume de la Ville de Paris, Palais Galliera; Chantal Garrard, in a major art designing debut of great promise; Nadine Gasc, Curator-in-Charge, Department of Textiles and Fashion, Musée des Arts de la Mode, Louvre; Jean-Claude Gerschel, Metro-Goldwyn-Mayer; Hubert de Givenchy; Alain Goldman, Paramount Pictures; David Helman, Maison Lesage; Carolina Herrara; Lucien Jalou, Directeur, l'Officiel du Costume et de la Mode de Paris; Charles Joussellin, a life-giving force; Marie-Andrée Jouve, Balenciaga; Calvin Klein; Christian Lacroix; Karl Lagerfeld; Jacques Le Brigant, Nina Ricci; Jean-François Lesage; Sophie Michau; Monique Millon, Maison Lesage, with special affection to be shared with Jennifer; Françoise Montenay, my Executive Lady whom Schiap would appreciate now more than ever; Erik Mortensen, Balmain; Jacques Mouclier, Vice-Président, Fédération Française de la Couture, du Prêt-à-Porter des Couturiers et des Créateurs de la Mode; Jean de Moüy, President and Managing Director, Jean Patou; Oscar de la Renta; Carolyne Roehm; Jacques Rouët; Juliane Russo, always there; Jean-Louis Scherrer; Dominique Sirop, Givenchy; Françoise Tétard-Vittu, Palais Galliera and Jean Patou; Laurent de Teto, my fine young comrade, and his great-aunt, Raymonde Zehnacker; Susan Train, Paris Editor, US *Vogue*, my friend and guide, with love and gratitude, ever; Gérard Trémolet, Maison Lesage; Emanuel Ungaro; Valentino Garavani.

I also wish to recall, with infinite affection, the debt of gratitude that I owe to those friends who first guided me in fashion: Arletty, André Laug and Madame Poiret.

'It is not generally known that embroidery is still executed by hand today as it was in the eighteenth century. It happens that a gown is covered with millions of sequins or beads, each placed one by one by fingers that, particularly in our machine age, take on the appearance of the fingers of fairies.'

Christian Dior

'We play our role in the realm of the imagination. Embroidery can be a woman's dream come true.'

François Lesage

TRIBUTES

Marc Bohan,
Christian Dior

Madeleine Delpierre,
Honorary Curator-in-Charge, Musée de la Mode et du Costume de la Ville de Paris, Palais Galliera

Jean L. Druesedow,
Associate Curator-in-Charge, Costume Institute, Metropolitan Museum of Art, New York

Guillaume Garnier,
Curator-in-Charge, Musée de la Mode et du Costume de la Ville de Paris, Palais Galliera

Nadine Gasc,
Curator-in-Charge, Department of Textiles and Fashion, Musée des Arts de la Mode, Louvre

Hubert de Givenchy

Christian Lacroix

Karl Lagerfeld,
Chanel

Érik Mortensen,
Pierre Balmain

Jacques Mouclier,
Vice-President, Fédération Française de la Couture, du Prêt-à-porter des Couturiers et des Créateurs de la Mode

Jean-Louis Scherrer

Laura Sinderbrand
Director, Design Laboratory, Fashion Institute of Technology, New York

Emanuel Ungaro

Valentino Garavani

(Translations from French to English by the author)

MARC · BOHAN
(CHRISTIAN · DIOR)

From time immemorial embroidery has been the art causing women to dream about clothes and rendering styles so dazzling. 'Gold', 'moonbeams', 'romantic' or 'risqué floral motifs' — poets have sung the praises of this art and authors have described it endlessly.

With Monsieur Lesage, embroidery is not only adornment and ornamentation, it can be an entire gown. It exists for itself, it is an idea, for it is in itself inspired. A sample, the creation of an artist, is the point of departure for the conception of a gown. From there, the couturier faces the task of pursuing the thread of this inspiration so that, together with the embroiderer, a final harmony may be attained.

Monsieur Lesage's embroideries unite a fabulous technique — constantly renewed, surprise upon surprise — with his vast inspiration and also, this is important, with his quality, inimitable and perfect.

For him, all themes become the subject of admirable variations. The embroideries that he designed for me on the theme of Gustav Klimt would have enchanted the great Viennese painter himself. His 'Chinese partitions' seemed to come straight out of the Taipei Museum with a *je-ne-sais-quoi* touch more of elegance.

The dream can continue for ever, the trompe-l'œil, feathers, flowers of all sorts, 'false laces' — themes that Monsieur Lesage lavishes upon us to inspire fresh styles and give rise to new longings.

Yet another of his gifts is to gather round him the artists who stitch and paint his marvels. What a rare choice of collaborators to attain such quality!

Throughout my collections Monsieur Lesage has always had his part to play, and it is only seemly and right to stress this fact: he is a Master of fashion.

[signature: Marc Bohan]

MADELEINE
DELPIERRE

'**A**dornment makers'! *(Paruriers)*. Under this term so evocative of elegance are grouped the professions which endow dress with additional refinement, 'decoration' *(parure)*. The expressions are practically obsolete, but the crafts, for the most part ancient, are still vigorous.

Worth, confronted with the advance of mediocre ready-to-wear, founded haute couture to ensure the continuation of a de luxe product and drew adornment to it. Often the adornment makers were — are — eclipsed in the eyes of the public by the fame of the couturiers. They did not — and do not — contribute any the less to the success of these couturiers. And such contributions are brilliant.

Like the couturiers, they are Parisians, if not always by birth at least by the manner in which they nurture their imagination with the atmosphere of Paris — even if, moreover, they sometimes employ workers from the provinces and raw materials purchased abroad. For they work in partnership with the couturiers, making proposals to them and receiving suggestions in return.

Matti, who for Worth embroidered the famous 'Byzantine gown' ordered in 1904 by Countess Greffulhe for her daughter's marriage; Albert Lesage, who translated Schiaparelli's innovations so wondrously; Rebé, who in a career spanning fifty years collaborated with all the great couturiers and reached his apogee with Dior — all identified themselves with the spirit of the gowns they were asked to adorn. As to Jeanne Lanvin, who trimmed almost all her models in her own workrooms, she was the very incarnation of embroidery.

Yes, without these 'adornment makers' the most beautiful gowns, so lovely for their fabric and their cut, would be incomplete, like an i without its dot.

[signature: M. Delpierre]

JEAN · L.
DRUESEDOW

Throughout the history of costume design, imaginative elements of applied decoration have been an integral part of the total creative process. An aesthetic evaluation of costume must include a consideration of the artistry and skill evident in the applied decoration and how that contributes to the beauty of the whole.

Costume, as in other decorative arts, is usually the result of close cooperation. Each step in the realization of a design depends on the sensitivity of various artists and craftsmen to the original concept of the piece. Because costume is a complex medium of expression, collaborative effort is of particular importance, and when it is successful it becomes impossible to separate the various elements into distinct entities that are in any way the equivalent of the complete work.

It is in this respect that the contribution to costume of Albert Lesage et Cie is of special significance as an example of the kind of creative cooperation that can result in the very finest realization of the design potential to be found in Costume.

[signature: Jean L. Druesedow]

GUILLAUME GARNIER

Embroidery, fancywork for young ladies? This is an idea to be banished at the approach of a work wholly devoted to the accomplishments of embroiderers of yesteryear and today through the story of Maison Lesage as told by Palmer White.

In spite of the diversity, so limiting, of techniques, materials and ornamental themes, the art of the embroiderer is first an art of synthesis. What an intriguing paradox, this activity which combines the tradition of perfected craftsmanship with innovations achieved through methods constantly being transformed.

Tribute has to be paid to the great Parisian houses and to those creative geniuses who established them. However, we must also recall the careers of several generations of craftsmen and, through them, a profession, a veritable science, animated by its own particular spirit. Very often the ornamental structures invented in the 'laboratory' of the craftsman have contributed to announcing, indeed to focusing the future of fashion.

Embroidery easily assimilated passementerie in the 1880s, the venomous flowers of the Belle Epoque, the Oriental motifs of the time of Poiret. The decorative arts, surrealism, the romanticism of the New Look — these also offered an occasion for a flowering of renewed ornamentation.

Today, have the increasing rarity of materials and the rising cost of pieces depressed the field of activity and the prestige of Paris fashion embroidery? A visit to François Lesage's workrooms would persuade the reader of the contrary. At a time when couturiers are returning to displays of luxury and lyricism, embroidery is in its element.

The time has come for the position between the embroiderer and the couturier to be reversed in order to see the creation of gowns that will *first* be embroideries. Here is adornment, the 'modifier', becoming the 'subject' of fashion.

Guillaume GARNIER

NADINE•GASC

Under the dazzling light of the spots the mannequins parade in rhythm to the music as the models emerge in their established order. Comes the enchanting passage of the evening gowns when the magic of the inaccessible mingles with the spirit of dreams. Finally, the wedding gown appears, while, to the sound of the applause, the couturier steps out to receive the acclaim. The ritual of a Paris fashion collection is over.

In the press and hubbub of the departing crowds are to be glimpsed some figures who collaborated on the collection — silk manufacturers and embroiderers. They remain quiet and unidentified as they gauge the reactions of those who make and unmake fashion. The embroiderer knows only too well the number of hours spent on this frock or that bolero, which a mannequin displayed but a few minutes during the show.

With each season, spring-summer, autumn-winter, this embroiderer prepares several hundred samples which he presents to the couturiers. He has to sense, to anticipate, the direction which a customer is going to take. He knows his personality and his work. He selects his materials meticulously and with insight. Their richness varies infinitely: sequins, beads, rhinestones, braid, ribbons, silk, chenille, raffia and so on. His palette lends itself to all the compositions meant to embellish the fabric and cut specified by the couturier.

Each model is unique. It is executed attentively and patiently by fairy fingers. The apprenticeship is long. Each embroidery involves a particular technique, and the embroiderer has to know its features and limits.

Ever since the emergence of haute couture, museums have included a large number of embroidered gowns in their collections. The labels reveal the name of the couturier. But who did the embroidery? The reply here is more evasive. Such uncertainty should cause twinges of conscience, for this is an injustice.

The objective of Palmer White's book is to bring to the attention of a wide public an art which has only too often remained unacknowledged.

HUBERT DE•GIVENCHY

As I state in the press releases for each of my collections and in interviews when reporters ask me questions about my profession, I am happy to point out the importance of the participation of embroiderers and other suppliers of adornment and accessories in my collections for both haute couture and *prêt-à-porter*.

Obviously, among these artists there are very good ones and inferior ones. I try to employ them all and personally guide each in the execution of the models I have designed.

In particular I work with Lesage and Vermont, as well

as other embroiderers. To my mind, however, Lesage is the finest. Formerly, Rebé also figured among the great embroiderers. Their creativity, the quality of the embroidery and their refinement attain perfection. Often their samples serve as the springboard to creation.

I have worked with Monsieur Lesage for many years. A visit to his ateliers always comes as a revelation to me when I observe the meticulous work of the embroideresses, who are often very young. I am fascinated by their technique and patience.

CHRISTIAN LACROIX

*A*dorn, adorners : these words figure among those I most prefer in my profession because they are magical and because they issue forth from centuries past to summon up the original notion of elegance, as futile as it is sacred.

*S*uch legacies are still intact, but also greatly threatened. So fashion has to make haste and use and abuse all their possibilities to the utmost in order to recover the intoxication of adornment (this does not necessarily mean causing a rumpus) and to resuscitate and regenerate techniques on the brink of oblivion.

*A*nd over and above collaboration, one must achieve complicity — a rare secret in this profession. For technique devoid of feeling is naught.

*L*esage is an accomplice, not only a supplier but a creator. It is difficult to talk about him without employing the truisms common to perfection, for with him one comes close to what are indeed masterpieces.

A Lesage embroidery is first and foremost a true luxury : technique effacing itself before art, time spent unstintingly to achieve the most impalpable of effects, and opulence that is always refined.

*E*ach time Lesage reveals his new collection, it is for me the epicentre of a season, a long-awaited delight, excitement mingled with joy. In each theme his style is, of course, always recognizable : Africa à la Lesage, Antiquity à la Lesage, the Eighteenth Century à la Lesage. There is never any concession to style or styles, as he knows full well that 'to want to be of one's time is to be already outmoded' (Ionesco). His motifs are eternal and eternally renewed.

*O*ne can derive an almost sensual pleasure from the subtle profusion of his materials, from their delicacy without affectation, the canny art of their juxtapositions and their exalting richness.

I might talk about the man, the friend, the master, but that would mean failing to recognize his discretion and also mine. Let me simply say that he is a gentleman who never takes himself too seriously, a man of great heart who honoured me with his sponsorship, and a great talent, for which I need no further proof than his eternal quest for what is perfect.

*M*ay the young witness of forty fascinating and mad years of fashion be allowed to embrace him, with infinite gratitude.

KARL • LAGERFELD (CHANEL)

*F*or me Haute Couture without embroidery does not exist. I am saying it right from the start. Embroidery is practised throughout the world, and it comes in all kinds and at all prices. But if there is one thing unique and inimitable about it, Paris embroidery is that.

*T*he pretty term 'adornment maker' (parurier), so obsolete today, must have been invented for the Parisian embroiderers. The expression evokes so many images and defines so unequivocally the objective of a job, a craft, indeed an art. One tends to accuse 'adornment making' (parure) of being frivolous in our day and age, which shies away from happiness and tries to acquire a clear conscience by commiserating with the innumerable misfortunes which, alas! do exist.

*T*he impression must not be given that embroidery is something sedate designed for museums, not women. Embroidery embellishes. It adorns. It is work placed at the service of an ideal of beauty. Dwelling on it intellectually robs it of life where fashion must be life itself.

*T*he world may well have changed, but there has to remain in it a non-negligible area for things which are meant to be fleeting and superficial. They must not be endowed with a solemn look, if only to be enjoyed unashamedly. One has never to be ashamed of anything in this domain, not even of luxury. Except when it is tasteless, aggressive, flashy and mediocre.

*A*t a time when mass-produced embroidery is more vulgar, and vulgarised, than ever, François Lesage has given letters patent of nobility back to his profession. He is the rare diamond in a sea of rhinestones and sequins. Yet it is with these materials that he conjures up his wonders.

I know that the French did not invent embroidery, but for me it is an essentially French art. At all events, Paris is its holy place and François Lesage its high priest today. In this city of chapels, Maison Lesage is the cathedral of gold and silver thread and braid, of all stitches, and of all beads, jet and sequins.

Most of the fashion designers of the planet — should any exist outside of Paris — come to François Lesage. His fame is worldwide. He represents luxury at its finest and craftsmanship in what is its most illustrious.

Each Lesage sample is a little masterpiece of invention, and the various interpretations of ideas suggested by this or that designer are marvels of the creative spirit.

My collaboration with François Lesage figures among the great joys that I experience in my work for Chanel haute couture. I also like to use embroidery in the de luxe prêt-à-porter, but it has to be employed differently. Yet there too we have come up with gay, amusing and witty pieces together.

François Lesage makes a liar out of Diderot, who said: 'The minute an artist thinks about money he forfeits his sense of what is beautiful.' He is obliged to remain realistic, but he never loses his feeling for beauty because of that. His embroideries have a soul. And if the soul of a diamond is light, the Lesage embroideries are electricity.

Karl Lagerfeld

ERIK · MORTENSEN (PIERRE · BALMAIN)

The first thought that crosses my mind when I consider the suppliers of accessories with whom we work in haute couture is an expression attributed to Napoleon: 'Impossible is not French!' Their importance in the creation of a collection is parallel to that of the couturier himself, for the inspiration and enthusiasm with which both are imbued has to be positively contagious to obtain the finest result.

Well before I started at Balmain, the house had been working with one of the most important of these suppliers, the embroiderer Lesage.

I recall 'Yo', Madame Lesage, François Lesage's mother, coming to show their collections: we sat about a table like children waiting for Santa Claus to show them their Christmas gifts. As the samples passed through our hands, the future names of the models started to float through the air — Chambord, Paris, Oriane. The form of a gown was often directly inspired by the embroidery.

It also happened that, at the end of a presentation, M. Balmain requested special designs for trend models that he had already conceived in his mind's eye.

This is the moment when teamwork, motivated by identical artistic ideas, takes on its greatest significance, comparable to that of a stage director and his principal actor. With Lesage it often came as a happy surprise for us to see the result exceed the basic conception.

In the world of Paris haute couture, considered by some as outmoded and useless, it gives us great pleasure to know with certainty that there are still idealists who defend — marvellously — one of the loveliest of French banners.

Erik Mortensen

JACQUES · MOUCLIER

Fashion is feminine adornment as related to the present day. It is not only a gown, suit or coat. It is also the accessories — that is, whatever completes the feminine silhouette: embroidery, flowers, feathers, bags, belts, scarves, jewels.

Thus it transpires that the craftsman-artist, by means of his technique and experience, contributes to enriching the creations of our couturiers, who gain fame through the subtlety of their designs and the cut of their scissors.

The names of the suppliers of accessories ring pleasantly in our ears: Lesage, Lemarié, Lemarchand, Desrues, Cerny, Guillemin, Anquetil, Péral, Gripoix. Monsieur Lesage is one example among many of these craftsmen-artists who so vigorously help haute couture to maintain its pre-eminent place in the international firmament of fashion.

JEAN-LOUIS SCHERRER

French fashion could not exist without the suppliers of adornment. They exercise a magical craft, an incomparable *savoir-faire* that is part of our heritage and contributes to the prestige of haute couture throughout the entire world.

Embroidery has to look like a fabric incorporated into the model, and it is up to the embroiderer to interpret it according to the personality and vision of the couturier.

I work personally in close collaboration with the makers of adornment and in particular with François Lesage. I admire his talent and have for many years selected the embroideries for my collections with him.

François Lesage is a true magician, who transforms the merest substance into a pure jewel.

Jean-Louis Scherrer

LAURA SINDERBRAND

Throughout history and in all cultures, decoration applied to textiles has served to symbolize and distinguish rank, region, religion and heraldry. Embroidery as decoration has also expressed the abiding compulsions of creativity and individualism.

The need to clothe the body to protect it from the elements and to preserve the cultural edicts of modesty does not require the application of decoration, and yet it is difficult to evoke a time or a society that did not develop the craft of embroidery within its own technical, aesthetic and social context.

Decoration as expression has proven as necessary to mankind as music and dance. It is in evidence in architectural details, the culinary arts, the end papers and embossing of the books we read and, indeed, in applications to the thousands of articles we use each day. If embroidery as a form of decoration is gratuitous to function, it is nonetheless essential to the human aesthetic spirit.

This fact is well illustrated when one views the impressive archives of Lesage et Cie. They are an encapsulation of the history of French haute couture and its influence on American design. The embroidery charts the changing palette, ground fabrics and motifs of Western fashions. The samples document the preference for the romantic florals of the nineteenth century to art deco geometrics of the twenties, the surreal concoctions during the thirties and back again to glorious sprays of garlands and butterflies in the fifties. Psychedelic and aggressive geometrics depict the sixties and seventies and recall the minis and maxis that swept in and out of fashion.

The dynamic and often breathtaking beauty of the beading of the eighties represents the culmination of a workshop and its artisans applying shimmering enchantment to fabric for a hundred and twenty years.

The extraordinary beauty of the comprehensive Lesage archives is matched by the spirit and generosity of the man who guards them. François Lesage greets requests from schools, museums and researchers with graceful magnanimity and enchanting anecdotes which more than anything else bespeak the love he has for the magic he performs.

EMANUEL · UNGARO

Adornment. The word alone evokes the wondrous.

Jean-Jacques Rousseau said: 'Trees, bushes and plants are the garb and adornment of the earth.' In point of fact, pure creation, whatever it may happen to be, is incomplete without decorative finery. Transposed into the world of fashion, trees become diadems; bushes, birds of paradise; plants, multicoloured pampilles.

The magic of the word at once opens out a mysterious world to us. First there is the complicity. The communion between the designer and the adornment-maker, for the cut of a garment no longer determines its elegance alone but in harmony with the decoration.

The ornamental aspect then takes precedence over all the other features, and a continuous dialogue is now established. The adornment-maker interprets designs with an incredible spirit of invention. He juggles with his materials in an almost scientific way: colours that translate his inspiration, sequins sprinkled over the most delicate of fabrics, passementeries enhanced with faceted seed pearls, feathers ornamenting a headdress, gold threads intermingled with polychrome silk threads to conjure up a landscape, little flowering branches, a swirl of arabesques, a dream...

Like a magician, he transforms a garment as conceived in its basic essentials by reinforcing its beauty and lustre with magnificent additions. His fingers metamorphose jet, topaz and mother-of-pearl into so many stars in the subtle compositions where each stitch is a shadow, an éclat.

VALENTINO GARAVANI

My collaboration with Lesage dates back several years now. And even if I have occasionally tried to work with various 'master embroiderers' in other countries, I have always had to bow before his unequalled supremacy.

In haute couture, embroidery is an essential part of creation: here we have the finest expression of craftsmanship. But in the case of Lesage it is a craft that becomes an art. In his work there is not only the perfection of the embroidery, the veracity being so close to the real that his work sometimes resembles a print, but also a creativity, an imagination and a passion for research that is not simple execution. This he confirms as a true creator.

valentino

PART · ONE · LESAGE, ALBERT

1947, Elsa Schiaparelli. A robin redbreast — sacred to the household gods — keeps watch over the white sequin eggs in its nest (a felt jacket pocket) of raffia, silk-wrapped metal strips and feathers.

1 · STITCHES · IN · TIME

How did a cavewoman come to stitch? She had to assemble hides, skins and furs as clothing for her mate, her offspring and herself. As needles she used thorns and fish bones, and later wood, ivory and metal. She made her thread out of animal tissue — reindeer tendons, for example — and horsehair.

Soon men came to feel an imperative need to adorn and decorate themselves and their belongings. First they tattooed their bodies, and later, when they were dressed, they transferred the tattooing to tanned hides and cloth. At that moment embroidery was born, one of the most striking expressions of the need to adorn.

Inland Eskimo women embroidered bear and reindeer costumes with downy feathers. Their Aleutian counterparts, living near aquatic hunting grounds, embroidered the seams of the seal- or walrus-skin parkas of their menfolk with bands of seal gullet and fish intestines. North American Indian squaws showed great ingenuity in executing embroidery of porcupine and bird quills. These were held in place with thread from the manes and tails of caribou and horses and incorporated into skins of otter, deer, sheep and bear, and also into birch bark. Later these early embroideresses added stones, shells, animal teeth, minerals, straw and feathers. Upon emerging from their caverns and grottoes, they embroidered their homes — huts, wigwams, igloos, cabins — and their places of worship. Thus developed a form of artistic expression.

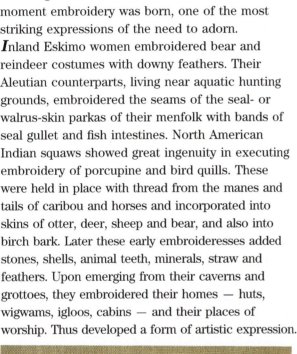

Fourteenth century, Germany. The back of a chasuble embroidered with several kinds of gold thread.

1950, Elsa Schiaparelli. A candelabrum of medieval inspiration to decorate a linen jacket. Bulging gold-thread cord ('bigoudi'). The candleholders of handmade ceramics.

As man's sense of community developed, he revealed much about himself through his clothing. Motifs handed down over the centuries informed the rest of the world where a person came from and to which group he belonged. Immediately responsive to environment and culture, embroidery made it possible for man to express his position in increasingly complex societies, signifying liturgical, economic and social status. It was the first industry of the decorative arts, involving as it did the gathering of fibre, and spinning and weaving of textiles, while encouraging artisanship and the development of tools. The more richly man embroidered his dress, whether prehistoric skins or modern silk, the more it proclaimed his power and achievements. Together with the insignia of authority, this was and to some extent still is true of all the social hierarchies: the kings, emperors, pharaohs, tyrants, czars, khans, sheiks, emirs, rajahs or caliphs; their ministers — mandarins, viziers, magistrates, pashas, satraps or residents; the artistocracy and its ranks — lords, seigneurs, peers, patricians or grandees; public officials, legislators, favourites or eunuchs; pagan and Christian leaders, high priests or Popes and their organizations; military officers, by land or by sea. Embroidery identified and classified them all.

With the dawn of historical times gold thread came into use. Soon it was joined by threads of wool, flax and cotton. Employed in China twelve thousand years before Christ, silk thread was also known in Persia and in Egypt towards the second century BC; the Western world became aware of it only during the days of Julius Caesar.

Embroidery flourished in the fifth century BC in Mesopotamia, Egypt, China and Central and South America. Mention of it preceded painting in the Bible: the Lord ordered the prophet Ezekiel (chapter 16, verses 7, 10 and 13) to remind the ungrateful and disobedient people of Jerusalem that he had bedecked them with 'embroidered work' and 'broidered garments', while Solomon ordered the veil of the Temple to be embroidered. Homer, in the *Iliad*, describes Helen (long before, in the twelfth or eleventh century BC) as reclining on a terrace of the palace in Troy and embroidering scenes of the battles taking place

1987, Lesage. 'Wedgwood' bag and belt. Greek style. for the new accessories line. Chalk-white bugles on mat blue sequins.

below her on the plain stretching into the distance.

Muslim embroidery was highly regarded. Even the most archaic examples were splendid, particularly in Arab Sicily. In the seventh century BC remarkable embroidery for apparel, blankets, upholstery, fabrics, saddles and arrow quivers came from Ottoman Turkey (Anatolia) and Iran. In North Africa more popular articles, but of great refinement, were produced from innumerable workshops in Tunis, Algiers and Morocco — in Tatouan, Rabat, Salé and Fez.

Although Assyrian bas-reliefs attest to the unusual skill of embroideresses in Nimrud (Calah in the Bible), Babylon was the most renowned centre of embroidery between the reigns of Hammurabi and Nebuchadnezzar II, which extended over more than a thousand years. By the end of that time the former Greek colony, Byzantium, had begun to flourish. Its lustre waxed glorious when the Roman Emperor Constantine, changing its name to Constantinople (now Istanbul), inaugurated the Byzantine Empire. Empress Theodora did much to encourage the arts, among them embroidery.

The Orient taught embroidery to the Occident. When, during the Dark Ages, the Byzantine Empire started to decline, embroiderers fled to Ravenna, city beloved of Theodora. From Ravenna their work spread throughout Europe until the twelfth century. Fabrics were heavy, threads unwieldy, designs crude, stitches unvaried. Then from the Near East the Crusaders brought back works both religious and chivalric — chain purses, banners, streamers and banderols bearing coats of arms — which inspired embroiderers to refine their efforts.

Embroidery was not confined, however, to communicating messages of opulence and rank. It also conveyed thoughts of love, faith and hope. Over the millennia embroideresses recorded their lives, male-dominated and restricted as these were. Through their work may be seen the customs, manners and tastes of their times. Embroidery, like other needlework — tapestry, quilting, smocking and patchwork — became a personal craft. It offered women a means of release for their longings, love, desire, not otherwise to be expressed, and for their aspirations, religious, philosophical, literary, poetic, all too rarely fulfilled.

Until the end of the fifteenth century embroidery was an art not only comparable to painting but superior to it, and its greatest competitor. Indeed, the history of embroidery does not complement the history of painting, it is an obligatory introduction and accompaniment to it. The most renowned painters devoted their talent almost exclusively to producing the sketches that embroiderers reproduced so magnificently. And if the technique of tapestry work, whether ordinary or highly wrought, French or foreign, is always the same, embroidery techniques vary infinitely.

Frequently embroideresses worked under harsh conditions, during days of danger and throughout nights of loneliness and fear. Here was the spirit of the feminine heart, hungering for love, beauty and peace, striving undaunted, keeping faith. Thus did embroidery, ultimately a social leveller, unite women of all races, nationalities, creeds and conditions.

1924, Madeleine Vionnet, motif for the famous 'Grecian horses' gown. Dark blue transparent bugles and gold beads incorporated into the 'Roman crêpe' made up especially for Madame Vionnet. (See p. 41 for detail.)

1942. Jules Berry as the Devil in Marcel Carné's 'Les Visiteurs du Soir'. Time: Middle Ages.

Civilizations advanced, women's hearts remained unchanged. Edward the Confessor's wife insisted on embroidering her husband's coronation mantle herself. A Finnish girl embroidered her fiancé's shirt. In Portugal a peasant girl embroidered a 'sweetheart handkerchief' for her betrothed. Social uses for embroidery evolved. A damsel in the Domesday Book was described as being offered land by a sheriff in return for teaching embroidery to his daughter. Guests came to Norwegian homes with gifts of bread which their hosts covered with embroidered cloths to convey the honour of the visit. Embroideresses, having proved their skill, were able to earn money exercising their craft.

Embroidery was not always the province of women. During the Middle Ages most professionals were men employing women. Their work was highly organized, and artistic in design and execution. In England many workshops specializing in embroidery for vestments were financed by merchants, and apprentices had to serve seven years before being admitted into the trade. The need for personal colours for identification in medieval military encounters led to the munificent heraldic embroidery seen on battlefields, and also at court functions.

In the dawn after the Dark Ages embroiderers took their inspiration, predominantly religious, from the arts: painting, frescoes, stained-glass windows, sculpture, engraving, woodwork, illumination. Painters such as Botticelli and Dürer provided designs. Elaborate embroidery reached truly glorious heights in medieval religious and secular garments, Tudor court dress, and in the court and churches of the Bourbons. A wealth of gold, silver, precious stones and enamels was embroidered by untold craftsmen on liturgical vestments — on mitres, chasubles, dalmatics, capes. Richly embroidered hangings vied with tapestries, altar frontals could scarcely be distinguished from paintings.

In Normandy the craft reached its apogee with the so-called Bayeux Tapestry of Queen Matilda. This remarkable undertaking, an embroidery over

Winter 1984-5. 'Monsieur' Yves Saint Laurent. Medieval inspiration. Detail of a bolero. Baroque coral motifs set in baroque arabesques of gold-plated strips and gold-thread braid turquoise faille.

seventy metres long narrating the story of the Norman conquest of England in 1066 by William the Conqueror through a series of scenes involving 530 characters, was executed by Saxon embroiderers between 1088 and 1092.

English embroidery represented a legacy equivalent in spirit to cathedrals. Embroiderers, designated in early statutes as 'chasuble-makers', existed as a recognized community from 1272. The thirteenth century in England was supreme for embroidery, marked by the advent of greater freedom in design, embroiderers turning to the manuscript illuminators for inspiration, in particular the East Anglian Schools. Exquisite samples of their art, *opus anglicanum*, are to be found in fourteenth-century inventories of the Vatican.

To woo the grace of God, monarchs all over Europe rivalled one another in the magnificence of gifts offered to their patron saints. They also showered presents on the mighty prelates whose protection they needed, exempting embroidery for religious uses from their sumptuary rules and regulations. Despite increased restrictions resulting from the Edict of 1629, Louis XIII ordered an embroidered ornament for the Church of the Holy Sepulchre in Jerusalem.

In France twelve articles governing embroidery had been published in 1292. Louis XI in 1471 decreed the brotherhood of embroiderers. They already shared with the gilders a patron saint, Clair, a Norman priest murdered between the seventh and ninth centuries. His name was not officially mentioned before 1648.

The fourteenth century marked the beginning of a major change in the dress of European women. Instead of Grecian-style draperies, garments — shorter than before and fitted — were now based on a stiff framework which descended from a point of support at the waist, like a cone with the apex removed. This concealed rather than enhanced the natural form, but richness of fabrics, furs and jewels, and embroidery, compensated for the loss. For almost six hundred years, except in France for the neo-classical Directoire (1795-99) and the decade of Napoleon's Empire that ensued, the dominant feature in feminine attire was trimmings.

The French court, particularly, used embroidery

1942. Arletty as the Devil's disciple in Marcel Carné's 'Les Visiteurs du Soir'. Time: Middle Ages.

1943, Elsa Schiaparelli uses silk thread and gold silk-thread bullion ('canetille') on a suede waistcoat to recall a page in a medieval book of spells. Seals of silk passementerie.

1954. Claudette Colbert as Madame de Montespan, Louis XIV's mistress, in Sacha Guitry's 'Si Versailles m'était Conté'.

to add glitter to its glory. Charles d'Orléans, Duke and poet, imprisoned for decades in the most stately homes of England during the Hundred Years War, ordered a garment with sleeves embroidered with the words and music of a popular song: the notes were represented by 960 pearls. François I collected Italian embroidery and commissioned Raphael to provide sketches.

Mary Queen of Scots, as Dauphine and later Queen of France, was trained in embroidery by an expert, her mother-in-law Catherine de Medicis, who reportedly stitched while the St Bartholomew's Day Massacre was being carried out according to her orders. Mary, influenced by French styles, embroidered throughout the nineteen years she was held captive in England, and even presented some samples of her work as gifts to her captor, Elizabeth I.

Henri IV, who housed his favourite artists in the Grande Galerie of the Louvre, assigned an entire apartment to a master embroiderer. This gentleman collaborated with a horticulturist in planning the King's first garden, planting it with the rarest of flowers to provide a new source of inspiration for embroidery. Other noblemen followed suit, and consequently many gardens were officially attributed to embroiderers.

For the baptism of one of her children, Marie de Medicis, Henri IV's second wife, had a gown embroidered with 32,000 pearls and 3,000 diamonds, so heavy that she did not wear it twice.

Religious sources of inspiration waned in the fifteenth century as paper became more widely available and printing presses were set up throughout Europe. Embroiderers — and weavers too — could now get new ideas for designs from the illustrations of flowers, animals, birds and insects to be found in herbals, bestiaries and books of emblems. They began to sketch their own inventions in paper copybooks, the forerunners of printed pattern books; the first was published in Augsburg in 1523. These did much to popularize embroidery in the years to come.

Embroidered pictures, particularly miniatures of monarchs, publicized the craft in the seventeeth century, while samplers facilitated the art of stitching and furnished a means for handing down designs. Initially a sampler, or exemplar, was a model for stitching. Then it came to be used to number household linen. As linens became more numerous they were embroidered with their owners' initials as a means of identification. In time little figures were added, and finally the sampler became an object of decoration, with embroideresses immortalizing houses, pets and mottoes. They expressed what was dear to their hearts. They translated their inner longings into verse. Bereaved sweethearts grieved over the urn of a betrothed felled in battle, maidens in love awaited their swains in enchanted gardens while perusing poesy. Other favourite subjects were scenes of battle by land or by sea, banners, and maps of the homeland and neighbouring countries.

France assumed her dominant world role in women's fashion when, in the seventeenth century, Louis XIV and his minister of finance, Colbert — fittingly the son of a draper — galvanized the French textile industry. 'Styles are to France,' Colbert would soon proudly declare, 'what the gold mines of Peru are to Spain.'

The embroidered furnishings in the Château de Versailles were especially sumptuous during the reign of the Sun King. The most fabled were to be

Winter 1983-4, Chanel. Louis XIV period. Karl Lagerfeld requests Boulle furniture marquetry designs as a theme. For a corsage, gold-plated strips on black sequins.

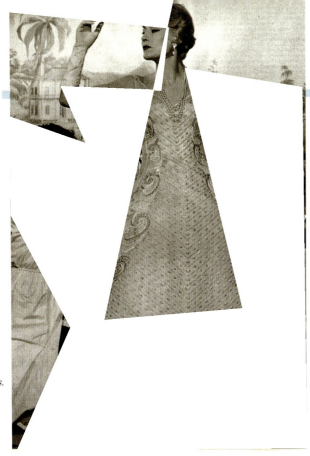

1958, Pierre Balmain. 'Infidèle', a version of 'Jolie Madame', a cream silk organza cocktail dress. The embroidery, inspired by eighteenth-century waistcoats, is of natural straw braid and natural pale-green silk thread.

1938. Norma Shearer as Marie-Antoinette in Adrian's 'free Hollywood adaptation' of the Louis XVI style.

found in the Throne Room; the walls were covered with a stupendous array of embroidery that resembled marble and had perspective. One item of the general inventory of the King's furniture reads: 'The bases and capitals of eighteen gold-embroidered grooved pilasters are decorated with a helmet of gold chenille embroidery on a silver ground constellated with pearls... A silk and embroidery vase from which rise realistic chenille-embroidered flowers covers the middle panel of each of the four doors...'

The French court took embroidery seriously. Louis XIV's first wife Maria-Theresa, his last mistress and second, morganatic wife Madame de Maintenon, and Maria Leczinska, Louis XV's wife, were all clever embroideresses, as were their daughters. They 'imported' orphans who showed promise as embroiderers from the convents they patronized, bringing them to live and work at Versailles. Embroidery was also recognized as a pastime at court, like cards and music.

At Louis XV's court Madame de Pompadour embroidered with all the finesse for which she was renowned, while her successor, Madame Du Barry, went personally to buy her trinkets and fans at the shop where she had once been employed as an embroideress, there to revel in the sight of her former employer bowing and scraping before her. The King boasted of his own skill in embroidering, and not a few of the officers in his armies were known to embroider when confined to barracks or out bivouacking.

In the mid-eighteenth century, the exquisite trimmings that the painters Watteau and Fragonard had conceived for the gowns in their canvasses inspired some young men working in notions shops to extend the range and quality of their wares. They called themselves *marchands de modes*, or style merchants, and in no time they covered the whole of Europe with their frills and furbelows — and embroideries. Women bought these *frivolités* in a frenzy. On the eve of the Revolution they accounted for over two-thirds of the price of a gown, and a successful *marchand de modes* assured the livelihood of ten thousand people.

All the many *marchands de modes* were dwarfed by Rose Bertin, the first dictator of fashion, who served Marie-Antoinette. Edmund Burke described the Queen as 'the most delightful vision I can remember ever having seen', and for John Adams she was 'an object too sublime and beautiful for my dull pen to describe... Her dress was everything that art and wealth could make it.' If Rose Bertin's prices had been lower, perhaps the history of France might have been different.

Towards the end of the reign of Louis XVI and Marie-Antoinette, the extravagances in dress were

1960, Pierre Balmain. Detail of a gown for Queen Sirikit of Thailand. Eighteenth-century Persian-inspired drawing style featuring gold thread and silk petals.

Mesdames being seen at the races.

all but eliminated, alas! too late to stave off the Revolution. Masculine attire abandoned all decorative effects. Napoleon saved embroidery as well as passementerie for men by ordering them for the uniforms of his glorious armies. Except for her coronation gown, even the prodigal Josephine — who spent more than half the price of the Louisiana Purchase on clothes in ten years — remained discreet about embroidery. For nearly a century, except for rare ceremonial and festive occasions, it was to be confined to lingerie and petticoats.

1907, Michonet. Roses in relief. Chiffons set in velvet, satin and gold and silver gauze, the whole a mixture of silk embroideries done in the darning-like running stitch ('au passé'). Typically turn-of-the-century.

That nineteenth century saw the end of monarchy and empire in France, and the corresponding decline of hereditary nobility. Hippolyte Leroy was the dictator of fashion who, rising above changes in regime, set the styles after the Revolution: Directoire, Consulate, First Empire and Bourbon Restoration. The enchanting Romantic mode devised by Mademoiselle Palmyre and Madame Victorine followed under the reign of Louis-Philippe, before giving way to the crinoline, or hoopskirt, which symbolized Napoleon III's Second Empire, aglitter with beauteous Empress Eugenie, newly ennobled aristocrats and the richly kept demimontaines immortalized by Marguerite Gauthier (Camille), all whirling to the strains of Offenbach and Johann Strauss. The splendour of the crinoline, dissimulating a basic lack of style, permitted the nouveaux riches to flash their wealth.

Meanwhile, with the invention of the cutting and fitting machines, mass-produced ready-to-wear was expanding; The embroidery machine, invented by Josué Heilmann of Mulhouse in 1834, initiated a process by which embroidery developed from an art, or fine craft, into an industry.

Money had been changing hands, and the hands were ever more numerous. The rise of the middle class signified that a bourgeois was no longer a small man fighting for his rights. He was a financier, a stockbroker, a businessman, a builder of railroads, an importer, a captain of new industries. He had money, piles of money, to invest. He bought and furnished fine houses, ordered coaches, dressed his servants in livery. He amassed works of art (which he probably did not look at) and precious books (which he surely did not read). He might not possess a title, but his riches were worth more than coats-of-arms, signet rings and banners.

1905, Michonet. Silk and cotton cord thistles, open-work stitch, or fagoting.

Obviously, this man of the world paid attention to his appearance. He sent his shirts to be laundered in London. Since embroidery and passementerie had gone out of fashion, he imitated Beau Brummel, whose influence had crossed the Channel and whose maxim was, 'If the common people look at you attentively, you are not well turned out.' As a result the wealthy bourgeois husband sent messages of status through his wife. He plied her with furs, jewels and gowns, accompanied her to the Opéra and the theatre, dined with her in smart restaurants, and showed her off at the races at Auteuil, Chantilly and Deauville.

The newly rich bourgeoisie would have nothing more to do with machine-made goods. Moreover, the ladies wanted gowns with more éclat than their dressmakers could devise from patterns in fashion gazettes. Their elegance had become a raison d'être. This was also true of Napoleon III; who wanted sumptuous attire for his Empress and the entire court. Anyway, ladies of every condition were wearying of hoopskirts, no matter how romantic it might be to waltz in them. The time was ripe for a new source of de luxe creativity in the world of fashion. It emerged in the form of haute couture.

Mesdames, encore.

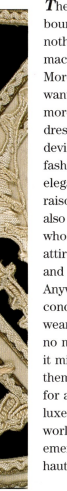

2 · THE · DAY · AND · AGE · OF · MESSRS · WORTH · AND · MICHONET

Charles Frederick Worth, an Englishman who emigrated to France in 1845, was the first couturier, or fashion designer. In the past a dressmaker had taken an order for a given article of clothing from customers who had a precise idea of what they wanted and had, usually, bought the corresponding fabric and adornment beforehand. Since the basic silhouette was the same for rich and for poor, all that differentiated the varying degrees of social status was the quality of workmanship, fabrics, trimmings and embroidery.

Worth transformed made-to-order dressmaking into haute couture. He foresaw and organized its immense development. He was the first to put a signature label on his clothes, first to present collections to clients invited to view mannequins on parade, first to use his wife and prominent ladies (such as Princess Metternich) to promote his offerings. No longer did the customer impose her tastes and desires on the dressmaker. Worth told her what she wanted to wear and what she was going to wear. In short, he dignified made-to-order dressmaking by creating snob appeal and commercialized it by duplicating originals when they were purchased by French and foreign buyers as well as by private customers.

Worth did not change the form of women's dress, based for almost six centuries on a fitted bodice and a stiff framework of skirt hiding the wearer's shape and given variety only through trimmings. If he took ladies out of hoopskirts, he put them instead into bustles, which, graceful as they appear in the Impressionist paintings and fashion sketches of the times, made women look — as

1880, Michonet. Beige and coral velvet incrustations embroidered with gold silk-thread bullion and wrinkled taffetas set in gold gauze roses and rococo ribbons.

1875, Michonet. Taffeta and handmade lace embellished by taffeta chiffons amidst leaves stitched with 'point de Beauvais'.

described by Paul Poiret twenty years later — like inverted S's towing barges.

Soon the Englishman could boast of dressing the courts of Europe as well as the finest bourgeois clientele. Not infrequently at Worth's, entire ateliers of thirty seamstresses worked all year for one customer. Other couturiers now sprang up to challenge him: Doucet, Redfern, Cheruit, Lanvin, Paquin and Callot Sœurs. There was no dictator of fashion, however. All these couturiers shared a general rather than an individual renown, for none distinguished himself by breaking with the convention of the old basic form, and all worked within the tradition of layering the women in garments. One could not distinguish the gowns, suits and coats of one couturier from another. A woman was not some one, she was some thing. From 1865 to 1914 there was no true style; the couturier merely produced his own version of the general look for each customer. (The exception to this was Poiret, the first designer to dictate precise lines.) A lady belonging to the beau monde had her own fitting room at her couturier's, where she spent three to four exhausting hours a day being encased in the originals cut, fitted and mounted just for her.

Embroidery as a mark of opulence as seen in haute couture began with Worth. He placed his trust in a brilliant young embroiderer named Michonet, who served him and his heirs, as well as other leading houses, for over sixty years. Michonet is intrinsic to the Lesage story.

Under Worth's impetus embroidery evolved so actively that forty embroidery houses mushroomed almost overnight. The history of hand embroidery from 1860 to 1914 can be described thus: Madame had a gown embroidered, just as she had her drawing room furnished. There was a close connection between her place of residence, overcharged, and her attire, overloaded. Madame dressed like her lampshades. For almost half a century she was a fancifully wrapped object in the spirit of the furnishings fashionable during the time of Napoleon III. She changed four or five times a day: for errands or fittings in the morning, for lunch, receiving for tea or being received, dinner or theatre, after-theatre dining. Embroidery was essential to dress from morning to night.

In a way embroidery as adornment anticipated today's accessories when it was, as often occurred, delivered in separate parts to the dressmaker, who added them as she fancied to clothes that were embroidered or not. Sometimes embroidery panels without any final form were supplied to her; she integrated them at will into a dress as a bodice front or a skirt panel. Michonet conceived of this method in the sense of the old composite Russian styles typical of Catherine the Great.

The open-work stitch, or fagoting *(ajouré)*, was widely employed. Before the spaces were indicated, grounds were inserted into a hand-guided machine, called a Cornely and greatly appreciated for its distinctive stitching, and encrusted with mother-of-pearl in the Napoleon III-Victorian style.

In another technical departure Michonet produced elements of passementerie (edging or trimming) and embroidery *au cousu* — that is, decorated with soutache, a braid which, in many forms, was sewn on to kraft to enable tracing the design before sewing the concordant parts together, after which the paper was removed.

Gelatine (ox gall, to be precise, obtained from the butchers in Les Halles) was incorporated into embroidery for purposes of relief. Magnificent motifs of this origin now appeared, as did the

1895, Michonet. Cut jet and mother-of-pearl beads, typical of a cape fibula.

1898, Michonet. Belt motif. Silver macrame (knitted bar work) and blown beads full of coloured wax.

rococo (rosette embroidered) ribbons finished with seeded fringing — a great embroidery accomplishment. It was not unusual to achieve even higher relief by placing bulging cord called *bigoudi*, also the word for a hair-curler, and soutache upright *(debout)*, actually on their sides, rather than flat.

Madame doted on shawls at all times of the day and night. These featured Chinese-type flowers embroidered with twist, and reflected Spanish inspiration in fringes and colours. With all the rest these vanished with the First World War, reappearing afterwards on grand pianos.

For day-time wear embroidery was often associated with passementerie, as worked into the long-skirted dresses and tailored costumes. Chenille was greatly used for the lower parts of sleeves and skirts and for pompoms, and was also mingled with encrustations of velvet and taffeta. Silk velvet was embroidered with it and with wrinkled *(chiffonné)* flowers, fine wool was overlaid with velvet embroidery very often featuring the inevitable flower motifs.

For the afternoon the *caracos*, boleros or long waistcoats sometimes attached to the gown, were frequently embroidered with soutache, gimp and macramé enhanced with touches of passementerie, completed by trimmings of velvet or silk ribbons, wrapped pampille and little jet motifs — all without any true unity. The mixing of techniques and parts was such that these outfits were a kind of samples card consisting of a jumble of unrelated elements integrated into the clothes helter-skelter, with black jet reigning supreme and closely associated with appliquéd velvet, lace inserts, flowers made of gold lamé gauze enveloping chiffon and satin, particularly the rose in every possible form, flower petals of wrinkled chiffon in various shades, sometimes handpainted, and leaves with veins simulated by the bulging *bigoudi*. The drawing style at the end of the nineteenth century was greatly influenced by the strained and complicated lines conceived by the German Friling for wallpaper.

It took between three and four hundred hours to do the embroidery for an afternoon gown. Buttons were also embroidered, a single one requiring from three to ten hours of work. Demimondaines, for obvious reasons, favoured afternoon and early evening at-home gowns of floss silk with floral embroidery and often painted chiffon. To dine, Madame wore a silk tulle gown, a shot silk gown with encrustations of Valenciennes lace and flower petals in relief or with embroidered flounces, or a long velvet or woollen jacket embroidered with soutache and tassels. For the theatre and gala occasions the good lady arrayed herself in a gown of lamé gauze embroidered with geometric motifs made of gelatine, a gown of tulle loaded with crêpe de Chine and silk floral embroidery on a beaded ground, a gown of satin or lamé embroidered in relief, or a gown of velvet or faille

1907, Michonet. On gold lamé, stylized flowers with wrinkled lamé hearts, gold thread and braid, gold-plated strips, gold sequins. A true embroidery 'sculpture' for theatre costuming.

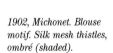

1902, Michonet. Blouse motif. Silk mesh thistles, ombré (shaded).

1912, Michonet. Silk embroidery uniting plain taffeta and a taffeta in relief printed with a silk cherry-tree branch.

with floral embroidery at times conceived in the spirit of baroque decorations.

Marcel Proust said of Odette de Crécy upon her first meeting with Swann in *'Remembrance of Things Past'* that she gave the 'impression of being made up of different pieces that had been badly fitted together...' Nothing irked Poiret more than knowing that women of the day — he called them 'decorated bundles' — thought of their bodies as shocking things to be made the best of, hidden and despised, and were grateful to their dressmakers for immuring them in monuments. And Jean Cocteau remarked after observing two 'corseted lionesses' lunching together: 'To undress one of these ladies was obviously a complicated enterprise that had to be planned well in advance, like moving house.'

How to determine the moment when a movement, a mode, a career is no longer at its apogee? Are there clues that will become discernible later and be interpreted? Undoubtedly the first generation couturiers went over the top when Worth's sons assigned practically their entire personnel for months to the execution of robes and gowns for the coronation of Edward VII in 1902. Coincidentally, and significantly, twenty-three-year old Paul Poiret, designing simple dresses ('fried potatoes') for this House of Worth, was about to strike out on his own. Still, his revolutionary designs would appeal at first only to the younger *élégantes*. The older generation would not renounce its styles — and its embroidery — until 1914, when circumstances would force it to do so.

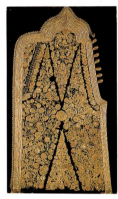

1897, Michonet. Moroccan inspiration. Gold silk thread and appliquéd felt on a brown velvet waistcoat front.

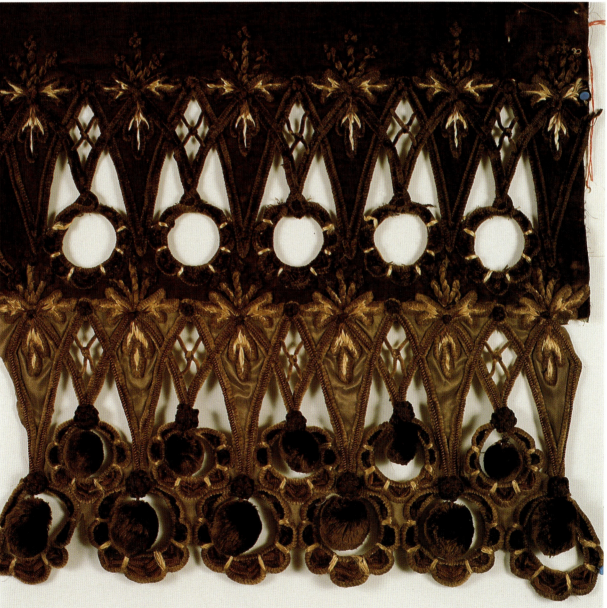

1875, Michonet. Brown velvet slash in the lower part of a cape, embroidered with chenille and silk pompoms in the open-work stitch, or fagoting ('ajouré').

1878, Michonet. Blouse front. Incrustations of black organza and blue taffeta embroidered with shaded rococo ribbons and chiffon roses, all enhanced by steel beads.

3 · ALBERT

Lesage is an old Norman name. After the Revolution, at the end of the eighteenth century, the family of landowners 'emigrated' from Normandy to Lorraine. They were to remain there only about seventy years, for, as a consequence of the Franco-Prussian War (1870-1), Lorraine fell to the Germans, who stripped the Lesages of their land. Whereupon they decided to settle in Paris.

At the beginning of the eighties Gustav and Adèle Lesage, Albert's parents, lived at the base of Montmartre on rue Fontaine near Pigalle and the Moulin Rouge. Adèle was a good wife, mother and housekeeper — and, like her husband, a devout Catholic. Gustav, a quiet, self-contained man with a deep sense of responsibility, was employed by Hachette as archivist. This meant spending six long days a week in cramped, dusty, ill-lit cellar rooms filled with bookshelves, laboriously classifying and cataloguing all the books and periodicals issued by this great publishing company.

Fortunately, Gustav had a passion which enabled him to dream and opened out vistas permitting him to escape from the confinement of his work and the routine of his home life. He loved to sketch, and he sketched everything — posters, advertisements, portraits. On Sundays, after Mass and the noon repast, come rain or come shine, he set off across the Seine for the bois de Saint Cloud, possibly the most elegant of all Parisian parks, and there he sketched near the sprightly castle, beside the fountains, along the wooded paths.

Albert, their son, was born in 1888. Of his studies there is little to report except that, unusual for a Frenchman, he was gifted in languages, received prizes for his Latin and German, and was excellent at spelling. Of significant importance, he inherited from his father the passion for sketching.

He had barely finished his secondary studies when he was called up for military service. This lasted for three years, and could only be deferred or reduced if a young man was pursuing higher studies, which Albert was not. Discharged in 1910, at twenty-two, he looked for work and found employment with one of the houses of the Commissionnaires de Commerce Extérieur. In former days a *commissionnaire* had been someone who ran errands. (*Faire les commissions* is still the expression in standard usage today.) At that time the *commissionaires* were 'brokers of foreign trade' — spies, scouts, advisers and agents who negotiated contracts of purchase and sale of all manner of goods and committed a client in his own name.

Before the First World War it was not common practice for American dress houses to send buyers over to Paris to view collections. Instead they engaged the services of these *commissionnaires*, who kept them informed, advised them what to buy and what not to buy, then acquired 'consignments' for them in accordance with their instructions. But only a privileged few American women in New York and Boston even knew about, much less could afford, Paris creations. And the

During the First World War, Albert Lesage dreams of women...

only means of communication — other than expensive and largely unintelligible transatlantic telephone calls — were letters or cables. Compared with the mad present-day rush, it was all very leisurely. Albert became involved in this area of clothes selling and started to learn something about fashion houses and styles through the toiles (muslin models) that his brokers bought and resold.

During his off-duty hours the young man, very sociable, sowed some wild oats with his friends. (A short-lived marriage warrants but a mention.) It was still an age of Renoir innocence. You could go boating and lunching above Paris at Nogent-on-the-Marne or below at Chatou-on-the-Seine. You went up to the top of Montmartre to hear Aristide

... in the Merseburg, Germany prison camp...

Bruant sing about the streets of Paris and *diseuse* Yvette Guilbert, in a yellow evening gown and black gloves, comment on vulgarity and vice. Or you attended the revues at the Néant, where drinks were served in skulls, and at the Chat Noir, dear to the *hydropathes*, a group of artists terrified of water except for external usage.

And what a spectacle was offered by the Champs-Elysées! Here were to be seen the tapestried limousines, equipped with costly furnishings and bouquets of flowers and driven by uniformed chauffeurs, in which lounged the *élégantes* of Paris in their Poiret harem-skirts, their eyes lined with kohl, an aigrette swaying on their turban or hairband. They were off on their rounds of shopping and fittings or on their way to tea dances in hotel ballrooms. Here in the arms of sultry gigolos they abandoned themselves to the raptures of the Brazilian matchiche, Argentine pericon, Venetian furlana, Cuban dansoon, and the American dances — Double Boston, One Step, Two Step, Turkey Trot, Lulu Fado and Very Mustard. At *bals musettes* Albert and his friends could also try their talents at the epidemic of lewdness condemned by the Kaiser, the Czar and the Archbishop of Paris: the tango. But they still liked to slide and twirl lasciviously to the strains of the Apache Dance.

Albert was open, personable and well-mannered. He had a glad eye for *les jeunes filles*, and these — more covertly, of course — were quick to flutter their eyelashes at him. And how pretty they were, the *midinettes* and shopgirls! Early in the evening they flitted out from their places of work like a flight of sparrows to join their waiting beaux. 'Paris', said Poiret, 'was an orchard in which you wanted to eat all the peaches.'

This paradise was not to last long. Early in August 1914 Germany declared war on France. Albert Lesage, twenty-six, was among the first to be called up. A corporal in the Infantry, he was wounded during the initial German offensive in the Meuse valley region of northeast France and sent to a prisoner-of-war camp at Merseburg, on the river Saale near Halle in East Germany, where he was one of the first to arrive. He would remain there over four years. Since he was fluent in German, he got on with the guards, whom he amused — along with his fellow-prisoners — by carving caricatures of them in wood. Being deprived of the company of women was Albert's greatest punishment during those interminable years of captivity. To occupy his time, he sketched and painted. To relieve his frustration, he began to draw women and design their clothes.

In the early months of 1919 Albert returned to civilian life in a country that had recorded dead or wounded four million men, largely its youth, and was contemplating bleakly its devastated provinces, ruined industries and imperilled finances. Without enthusiasm he returned to his job with the *commissionnaires*, hoping for a more engaging destiny. After only a few months this appeared in the form of a family friend, Simone Bouvet-de Lozier, who owned and operated an exclusive millinery shop on Fifth Avenue, New York. She had rushed to Paris in search of new post-war models and had engaged Albert's brokers to represent her interests. When she visited her friends the Lesages, she was interested to learn that Albert was working for the brokers and saddened by his dissatisfaction. When Albert told her he had prevented himself from going mad during his years of captivity by drawing, she asked him to show her some of his sketches and was impressed by those featuring women's clothes.

At present the brokers for whom Albert worked were handling consignments for Marshall Field and Company, the de luxe

... and whiles time away doing caricatures of fellow prisoners...

... as well sculpting wooden figures and...

department store in Chicago. Simone knew Mr Field, the president, very well. She selected some of Albert's sketches and took them back to New York with her. Several weeks later Albert received a telegram: he had been hired as the manager-designer of the women's made-to-order dressmaking department at Marshall Field's.

At the age of thirty-one, Albert embarked in June 1919 from Le Havre on a battered old steamer, *l'Espagne*. Since he travelled second class, he did not meet the first-class passengers. Among them were Count and Countess William de Wendt de Kerlor. Albert was to remain in the States three years. So was the Countess. Both were to be affected deeply by the American way and some fifteen years later would become collaborators — largely due to their mutual understanding of American attitudes and tastes acquired through the time spent in the United States. The Countess was to raise Lesage et Cie to pinnacles never before scaled by an embroiderer. Her name would then be Elsa Schiaparelli.

Upon arriving in Chicago, the Windy City, Albert was staggered by the same realization as Elsa in New York that the technological future, glimpsed in Europe only by artists and intellectuals, was here the present. They were assailed by the same startling sounds and images — cops' whistles, police-car and ambulance sirens, fire-engine bells; red fire hydrants, green letter-boxes, peppermint-stick barber's shop poles and life-size reproductions of Red Indians in front of tobacco shops; streets broad, parallel and sharply perpendicular; bridges long, light, open to the sunlight in a scaffold of voids; railway terminals that resembled temples of steel, illuminated advertizing signs, hundred-page newspapers.

In 1919 Chicago was a noisy, brawling and grossly materialistic baby giant, rapidly turning into one of the first commercial cities on the face of the globe, the greatest railway centre in the world. Imagine the effect of the skyscrapers on a newcomer from France: stark vertical lines, all steel structures, brick, concrete and gleaming glass. In Chicago they spread along Lake Michigan for some thirty miles — a thrilling sight, this 'Sky Line', when seen from a boat, even when the air, on leaden,

... posing as 'Monsieur Minet' (cat) for his friend Marty.

windless days, was permeated by the stench from the stockyards.

Like all American cities Chicago had its Downtown, the commercial business and entertainment centre on which everything converged. Downtown Chicago was unique in several ways. It was bounded by a square structure of elevated train lines, the 'El', inexplicably called 'the Loop'. Moreover, the buildings encompassed by the Loop were special. Chicago had been the cradle of modern architecture. From 1880 to 1910 a number of architects (William Le Barron Jenney, who invented the skyscraper, Louis H. Sullivan, and Messrs Burnham, Holabird, Roche and Adler) had conceived and built office buildings, department stores, hotels, theatres, housing units, warehouses, factories and schools in a system in which urban psychology was linked to a sculptural concept — known as the School of Chicago. The most characteristic were the buildings of the Loop, functional, utilitarian and relentlessly unimaginative, rectangular, compartmented, and of a verticalism dictated by the

... but his dreams of women recur.

Did Albert dream of Mata Hari? Had she only looked like Garbo, costumed by Adrian (1932)!

1919-22. Albert in Chicago...

need to ensure maximum output per square metre. In the centre of them, on august State Street, was located Marshall Field and Company. Here Albert was to spend nine hours a day, six days a week in a group of rooms overheated and airless in winter, rigorous as that was in Chicago, and ventilated only by inadequate ceiling fans during the torrid days of summer — a far cry from the clement maritime climate of the City of Light.

The Near North Side, just above Downtown, was a decent residential area (one called it a neighbourhood at the time) near the famous old Water Tower, a landmark that had escaped from the Great Fire. Here Mr Field had set aside lodgings for Albert on Walton Place in one of the three-storey, dark red brick apartment buildings typical of Chicago. Taking Dearborn Street or State Street and crossing the bridge over the Chicago River, the young man could, if he wished, walk to and from work. On days off he was only a few minutes away from elegant Lake Shore Drive, the vast beaches that lined Lake Michigan, Lincoln Park and the mid-city golf course. It was all quite unusual, to say the least, for an ex-broker's assistant who had lived most of his life in Montmartre and worked near the Opéra in Paris.

The general status of American women, so far in advance of the austere bourgeois-Catholic double standard under which Albert had grown up, also greatly impressed him. If true equality had not actually been achieved, universal suffrage had nevertheless just become law, household appliances were doing away with drudgery, divorce was easy in certain States, and fashions were freed. American women — who now played tennis and golf, went bicycling, roller and ice skating, drove motor-cars and wore corsetless garments — were enjoying a physical liberation illustrated by the movies. Middle-class girls were beginning to escape from old, staid patterns into the professions, the arts and business; the daughters of labourer immigrants could climb the social ladder through becoming stenographers and then secretaries.

But these were not Albert's customers. He was to deal with the so-called 'society matrons' whose fathers and husbands had made — and were increasing — their fortunes in public service companies, grain, delicatessen products, slaughterhouses, refrigerated meat, canned foods and the manufacture of farm machinery, train carriages, furniture and steel. Obviously, these ladies — like their nouveaux riches counterparts in France and the rest of Western Europe — had no true social background. Far more often than not the history of their families went back scarcely fifty years, they had rarely been to finishing school or had any higher education, were not well-travelled, and — like most people in the Middle West — knew very little, and cared less, about the outside world. A joke used to go the rounds: 'Have you seen the furniture in Mrs X's mansion?' 'No. What period is it?' 'Early Salvation Army'.

Such ladies duly attended concerts and operas in auditoriums built by their husbands, who also subsidized the resident and visiting symphony orchestras and singers. If they did not greatly appreciate the music, they consoled themselves with the thought that they were absorbing culture. They patronized exhibitions in museums, went to the theatre, contributed to hospitals and orphanages, all provided by their husbands' generosity. It they were simple and sincere about anything, and understood what they were doing, it was welfare work.

... working for Marshall Field and Co, State Street, in the Loop.

Selling made-to-order clothes in a department store was a good idea that did not click. In the beginning the matrons enjoyed the novelty of having designs prepared for them individually by 'Our French Gentleman', but actually what they asked of him was Chicago not Paris, and in time his Gallic charm cloyed. It was smarter to buy a Paquin ensemble (and label) at the Tailored Woman on the fashionable stretch of Michigan Avenue between the Wrigley (chewing gum) Building and the Drake Hotel than to display a Marshall Field label on a garment devised by an unknown.

In the beginning Albert was pleased by his new responsibilities and the authority these bestowed upon him. He had saleswomen, fitters, cutters and seamstresses to supervise, as well as administrative personnel to make appointments and keep the accounts. He was learning English; observing American customs — Lincoln's and Washington's birthdays, Moving Day (May 1), Tree Planting Day, Independence Day, Labor Day, Columbus Day, and Thanksgiving Day; going on picnics, wolfing popcorn and crackerjack at baseball and football games, dancing on Saturday nights to the rhythm of big bands in huge public ballrooms. But how he longed for a glass of wine in those Prohibition days, and how tired he grew of his dull, sexless, Puritan customers and of life in the anonymity of a department store. By the time Albert was thirty-four he had perfected his English, learned a great deal about business organization and its methods as the Americans practised them, and saved a tidy sum of dollars.

He felt that life, love and happiness should be pursued elsewhere.

And so the adventure ground to a halt. Albert, homesick, went back to France — where, ironically, his future would involve the daughters and granddaughters of the society matrons whom he had served at Marshall Field and Company in Chicago.

Some dreams never ever fade away...

4 · MARIE-LOUISE

When Mary Queen of Scots arrived in France at the age of fifteen to marry the Dauphin, soon to be crowned François II, notable among the members of her suite was a young couple by the name of Spencer (related to the ancestors of Winston Churchill and the Princess of Wales). During the few short months that she was Queen of France, Mary ennobled the Spencers as a mark of gratitude for their good and loyal services and bestowed upon them the Château de Motte and its accompanying estate de Railly in Burgundy. They Frenchified their name by changing it to Despense, and were thereafter known as Count and Countess de Despense-de Railly.

By the time the family had descended to Countess Berthe its fortunes had declined. Berthe was born in the château in about 1860 and lived there until she fell in love with a handsome young Parisian salesman, Paul Favot, whom she married. They rented a flat in Auteuil, a beautiful and placid residential suburb. Favot was attractive and charming, as befitted a salesman, but the word industrious did not apply to him. Fortunately, it did to Berthe. Artistic and extremely clever with her hands, she undertook dressmaking at home.

In 1895 the couple was blessed with a daughter whom they named Marie-Louise. As a little girl Marie-Louise was pretty, vivacious, intelligent and well-mannered; she was given a proper Catholic upbringing. By the time she reached secondary school, in 1909, she was showing an interest in painting, and Berthe, too busy to be able to express her own artistic inclinations, persuaded her husband to pay for lessons for their daughter. Her teacher was a professional painter whose studio was located nearby. He was very keen to teach his pupils to 'see' with greater acuity what they looked at. He took them out on painting picnics to the meadows, fields and woods of the lovely Ile-de-France countryside, as well as installing them in front of the great monuments of Paris. Perhaps partly through these field trips Marie-Louise became attracted to the Impressionists. Her teacher encouraged her to sketch, which she did well, and she preferred gouaches and aquarelles to oils. She was still too young to be aware of the contemporary explosions in the arts and thus to be influenced by them, but revolution was in the air, she was sensitive and quick, and she would soon scent the wind. Moreover, she heard through her teacher of the new young rebels, the Fauves, Cubists and Futurists, if only because he was so hostile to their innovations. Through growing familiarity with them she would become distinctly colour conscious.

1918, Marie-Louise.

Her mother, as a dressmaker, had by now noted Paul Poiret's impact on styles. It is unlikely that her conventional, suburban customers asked her to do a Poiret for them, but even acknowledging Poiret's existence meant recognizing his new Grecian lines and draperies, vivid hues and Oriental aspect, accompanied as these were by the bombs detonated by Isadora Duncan, Leon Bakst and Serge de Diaghilev's Ballets Russes.

At eighteen, in 1913, Marie-Louise received a diploma for her secondary studies. University was not out of the question, but it was too awe-inspiring and too lengthily expensive a proposition for her parents, and she was not, moreover, drawn intellectually to any of the academic subjects. The

· 34 ·

1922, Yo. Sketch of Michonet embroidery for a Vionnet gown.

decorative arts were another matter.

L'Ecole Nationale Supérieure des Arts Décoratifs was founded in 1766. Financed by the Ministry of Culture, it was located in the Latin Quarter near the Pantheon and the Sorbonne. The students were selected on the basis of applications and competitive examination.

*U*p to now the decorative arts had not been held in high popular esteem. If Marie-Louise came to be struck by them, it was because they were just then starting to come into their own. Delacroix had beaten the drum. After him all the great nineteenth-century French painters had acknowledged interior decoration as a valid creative activity, and Ingres had given impetus to the modern movement. In 1896 the initial Congrès des Arts Décoratifs had been held, with four hundred delegates proclaiming the unity of all the arts and 'the right of the Decorative Arts to exist... in the great federation of French art.' In 1901 these artists had founded the Société Française des Arts Décoratifs, and three years later they had inaugurated the annual Salon des Arts Décoratifs. Marie-Louise, attracted to this young movement, started attending the Salon. In 1912 she also went to the famous annual exhibition, 'Salon d'Automne', and was overwhelmed by the rooms assigned to Martine, Poiret's eighteen-month-old interior decoration school. The sketches deriving their inspiration from flowers, leaves and vegetables, the finished examples of curtains, drapes and wallpaper, all the revolutionary colours: Marie-Louise was enchanted. Moreover, Poiret's students, she did not fail to note, were girls, in their early teens to boot, and she even went up and spoke to a few of the 'Martines' who were present.

*H*er decision was made. The decorative arts it was. With her painting teacher, she drew up a portfolio of her gouaches and aquarelles, as well as some of her better sketches, and filled in an application form for the Ecole. To her delight and terror, she was authorized to take the examination — and to her wild joy she passed it.

For the next four years (1914-18) Marie-Louise Favot was to immerse herself in some of the most exciting non-academic studies offered anywhere in the world.

*T*here was no opportunity for the young men in

1924, Madeleine Vionnet, before the bias cut. Shaded (or ombré) chiffon embroidered with gold-thread arabesques enhanced by cut emerald rhinestones.

the school to tease this rare young lady student, for they were all called up for the war. Indeed, it was only the resolve of the French Government not to betray artistic traditions — on the contrary, to keep them alive — that enabled the school to remain open, even if, in winter, there was no heat. Considering electricity cuts and difficulties of public transport, Marie-Louise's attendance at the school, taking the Métro from distant Auteuil to the Latin Quarter and back every day, showed heroic determination.

*H*er father had been called up. Consequently, along with her studies she had to help her mother make dresses, and thus became proficient in fitting, cutting, sewing and stitching. (The Château de Motte was sold about that time, but Countess Berthe profited little from the sale.) Marie-Louise's graduation from the Ecole des Arts Décoratifs, at the age of twenty-three, coincided with the end of the war. So, what to do with her life? Which field suited her inclinations as well as her acquired knowledge and skills? Interior decoration? No. Photography? No. Fabrics? Upholstery? Household objects, glassware, dishware, lamp stands, vases? No and No. But... fashion? *Mais oui!* She would apply for a job in a fashion house. But which one?

*T*hrough the dressmaking with her mother Marie-

24 November 1920. St Catherine's Day party at Madeleine Vionnet's. Yo, just twenty-five, is the first 'Catherinette' standing on the left.

Louise had become acquainted with the features for which the various great couturiers were renowned. Obviously Poiret, now back from the war, attracted her most, but his reputation as a lady's man was disturbing. She applied to Madeleine Vionnet, Poiret's kindred spirit, and obtained an appointment. She gathered together her sketches and designs, her diploma, the recommendations from her professors. And off she went to 222 rue de Rivoli, where, across from the Tuileries Gardens, lay the house of Vionnet. The designer's secretary received her and took Madame her portfolio. Marie-Louise had waited in a little sitting-room only a short time when the secretary returned. She was not carrying the portfolio. 'Madame will receive you now.'

The woman who was to play such a significant role in Marie-Louise's professional life was, at forty-five, tall, buxom, with lively eyes, simple manners and a wide, high, untroubled forehead obviously treated with what Arletty called the finest beauty cream in the world, a clear conscience. Without a word she gestured to her young visitor to be seated opposite her. Marie-Louise saw her sketches and designs spread out on the desk. The couturier scrutinized her, still without speaking. Discomfited, Marie-Louise finally began to rise. 'Au revoir then, Madame.' 'Why are you leaving so quickly?' 'You haven't said anything. You can't like my work.' 'On the contrary, I do like it, very much. When can you start?' 'Tomorrow morning.' 'Good. I'll expect you.'

Marie-Louise's delicate features had a slightly Asiatic cast at a time when young women were being influenced by an Oriental vogue: Pierre Loti's exotic novels, Japanese engravings, Turkish rugs, *Madame Butterfly*, Poiret's Persian nights, the kimono-like styles for gowns and negligées, the Ballets Russes. There were several girls named Marie-Louise working for Vionnet, and our Marie-Louise wished to distinguish herself from them. She asked to be called Yo, and her work thus.

Madame Vionnet fell in with the Greek classicism which Poiret had renewed. Of the jobs she assigned to her new employee, one involved research in the museums. Marie-Louise colour-sketched ideas taken from Greek vases, friezes and decorative arts. These ideas were transformed by Madame Vionnet into projects for embroidery. (At that time embroiderers did not do collections which they presented to the couturiers. These gave them instructions.) Madeleine Vionnet never sketched. Like Poiret before her and Alix (later Grès) afterwards, she draped fabrics on a miniature wooden dummy, and on a customer once an order had been received. Upon conceiving a gown, she asked Marie-Louise to sketch on cotton canvas the place that an embroidery was to occupy.

M. Michonet, Vionnet's embroiderer, was ageing; he went less and less to his customers' workrooms. Consequently, Madame Vionnet asked Marie-Louise to follow up on her canvas sketches in Michonet's atelier, located on rue Feydeau, near the Opéra-Comique. Here Marie-Louise checked that the embroidery was being executed according to her employer's wishes. This was no mean responsibility, and a schooling of great value.

1920, Michonnet. Fashion is a butterfly, lovely, restless and ephemeral...

1918, Michonet. New art deco trend. Jet and gold micro-beads for a silk chiffon blouse.

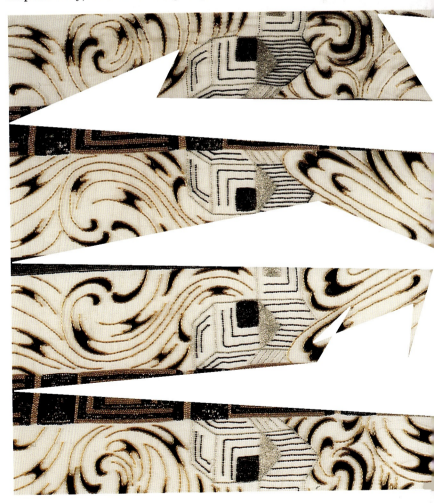

• 37 •

5 · FROM · MICHONET · TO · LESAGE

The Paris to which Albert returned from America was a city still struggling to recover from a devastating war. In 1922 *Les Années Folles* had begun. To shake off all the sorrow and sadness, Paris was turning for piquancy to the Ballets Russes, to Rolf de Maré's Swedish Ballet and the music of the young Six, chief of whom were Arthur Honegger, Francis Poulenc, Georges Auric and Darius Milhaud. Parisians were crowding into the Bœuf sur le Toit, where the swells hobnobbed with painters and plumbers and Jean Cocteau reigned supreme beside eighteen-year-old Raymond Radiguet. They were embracing, somewhat morbidly, the opium addicts, pomaded gigolos, homosexuals, and Russian dukes who drove taxis. They were writing automatically and, during sleep induced by hypnosis, exploring their nightmares.

This was not to be Albert's way of life. He was too solid, too mature and well motivated to be diverted from his objective: to settle down with a good job. (Almost immediately upon arrival he had another go at marriage, but it was doomed to be as short-lived as the first one.) After the experience he had acquired at Marshall Field's he wanted to continue in a managerial position, while also using his talents for designing. Duly, he returned to see his former employers, the *commissionnaires*, although he knew that they could not themselves offer him the scope of employment which he was seeking.

Albert soon observed that fashion, during his absence, had undergone significant changes. To start with, in the field of buying and selling, which was the business of his brokers, the tipping of the scales from France towards America was evident. Paul Poiret had been the first to foresee that Paris fashion would henceforward have to deal with the United States, rather than the reverse. His pioneer barnstorming across the country with his wife in 1913 had brought Paris to the attention of rich women in the hinterlands more immediately than before — as much because of his outrageously frank comments as his startling creations. Up to then, in Cleveland, Chicago and Denver, they had only seen foreign actresses on tour — Lily Langtry, Sarah Bernhardt, Eleonora Duse, Réjane — arrayed in ravishing Paris toilettes that were for them unthinkable. In 1916, as part of the vast propaganda programme designed to draw the United States into the war, the French Minister of Foreign Affairs had requested Poiret to create a special dress collection to be shown on the other side of the Atlantic at widely publicized shows. Of greater significance, the participation of the doughboys in the war had made the American masses more aware of France. After writing letters home from Paris, the Front and elsewhere, American soldiers had brought back French perfume, accessories and chocolates for their mothers, wives and sweethearts.

1925. Madame Albert Lesage.

With the anticipated spread of selling points for French clothes in the States, the owners of exclusive shops and department stores in America at the opening of the twenties were wanting to see for themselves, as it were, and they had started to send their own buyers over to Paris. These did not purchase directly from a couturier, as did private customers, but rather placed their orders with the *commissionnaires*, who saw to it they received the *répétitions*, duplicates of the originals, when the fashion houses had finished doing them. (The use of paper patterns did not become common until after the Second World War.)

Women in themselves, as Albert quickly remarked, had also greatly changed. The war had given them the role in life for which they had been rehearsing since the 1890s. While the men were at the Front, they had learned to be independent and had assumed new responsibilities, driving ambulances, nursing, running businesses for their fathers, husbands or brothers. After the Armistice they had seen no reason to relinquish these gains, and started defending their new right to a permanent place in what was threatening to become a man's world once again. They wanted to walk and move briskly, hop easily in and out of vehicles, and change clothes only once a day. Thus their dress had above all to be practical. So, while maintaining the long and slender pre-war Poiret silhouette, couturiers of the twenties — Lanvin, Vionnet, Patou, Chanel, Molyneux, Callot Sœurs, Jenny and Lelong — simplified fashions. They placed the accent on youth and freedom of movement, shortening skirts, which suited the spirit of the new age about to produce the bachelor girl, the flapper and the vamp.

These changes were not simply sociological. Financial considerations also underlay the modification of styles. Of the major industries in France, dressmaking had suffered most from the increased cost of labour caused by the war (before 1914 it had brought in eighty million francs annually in exports). Tailors demanded twenty-five percent rises in salary, seamstresses went on strike. A yard of velvet that formerly cost six to eight francs might now only be had for twenty-five or thirty. The price of silks, worsteds, woollen goods, linen and ribbons had risen to a similar degree. Since manufacturers did not dare to increase the price of finished products proportionately, their profits diminished. The high cost of cloth intensified research into the possibilities of replacement materials, whence the emergence of artificial fibres. In view of all this, there was little money left to invest in embroidery. Transmitting messages of opulence and social position was not the order of the troubled post-war day. Luckily, the situation was to change — spectacularly.

'Part of the enchantment of Paris in the twenties,' Scott Fitzgerald remarked, 'was that everything which happened there seemed to have something to do with art.' The first happening was the Colonial Exhibition (1922), which revealed Black African art to a wide public. At the same time Dada was giving way to Surrealism (André Breton was to publish the famous Manifesto in 1924). The New Realism glorifying the machine was about to assert itself, and the decorative arts to explode.

Only one factor in the twenties — an entirely new one — influenced fashion more than art: women's growing participation in sports. Rarely has the theory that the popular sportswear of today becomes the town and country wear of tomorrow been better illustrated.

Albert knew that his *commissionnaires* had their ears close to the ground of the shifting fashion scene and hoped that they might be aware of an opportunity for him. They were. Many of the houses that had sprung up almost half a century before, when embroidery had made its great come-back in the dress of the nouveaux riches ladies, had been forced to close during the war. About twenty were left, and in 1922 they were not overloaded with work. The head of the one that had started with Worth, M. Michonet, obviously an elderly man, wished to retire but was loath to shut down. His house, he reasoned, still represented a valid business proposition for someone wishing to take it over. It was small, thus without enormous overheads, and enjoyed an excellent reputation. Michonet had carefully classified samples of all his drawings and designs — both of embroidery and his associated speciality, passementerie — from the day he started: no mean heritage. Moreover, he and his salespeople had, with feathery penmanship, kept meticulous accounts, which were up to date and balanced to a centime.

Albert had heard of Michonet and was impressed. In working with Worth, the old man had made embroidery for the jackets, waistcoats and gowns of the ruling families of Europe, including some for Queen Alexandra, wife

1926, Madeleine Vionnet. Art deco trend. Stylized flowers in various shades of opaque brown bugles for a corsage.

of Edward VII. But since de luxe embroidery had ceased to be confined to kings and nobles and had swept into the mansions of the *grande bourgeoisie*, before the war he had also supplied Agnès, Lucile, Doeuillet, Drécoll, David Bechoff, Redfern, Revillon and Paquin — and, as early as July 1906, a modiste named Chanel, who did not officially go into business until two years later. Lanvin and Callot Sœurs had their own embroidery workrooms, but Michonet had also worked for them occasionally when they were overloaded. His ledgers closed at the end of July 1914 and were reopened in May 1919. To his former clients he now added Jenny, Doucet, Maggy Rouff, Lucien Lelong, Martial and Armand, and Jane Regny, but not young Jean Patou, who opened his house with his own embroideresses.

Michonet had, moreover, worked in the theatre. At the time leading actresses changed for each of the generally five acts of plays, if not their numerous scenes. Producers of operettas outdid one another in presenting dazzling costumes. For the stage embroidery had to be exaggerated, rendered even more spectacular, so that the motifs could be seen by the *Enfants du Paradis* in the peanut gallery as well as admired by the toffs in the stalls. Even for the times Michonet's contributions to the theatre were unusually... theatrical.

In the autumn of 1922 Albert made an appointment to see M. Michonet at the workrooms on rue Feydeau. He had been warned that the old man was difficult, but he could by now be firm himself. He knew where he wanted to go, could point to the American experience, and — at a moment when couturiers were not greatly promoting embroidery — had an ace up his sleeve: his bank account in dollars. The two men struck a deal. They agreed to a trial period of six months, whereupon, if all went well, they would enter into a partnership with a promise of sale within eighteen months.

One day, just before Albert was scheduled to take up his duties, Marie-Louise Favot came to rue Feydeau to attend to some matters for Madame Vionnet, who had recently moved her house to a mansion on Avenue Montaigne that would accommodate 1500 employees. 'I have just hired a prison guard,' Michonet informed her. A week later he introduced her to Albert. Electricity crackled at first glance. Soon afterwards they became engaged, and were married a few months later. Simone Bouvet-de Lozier, the family friend and New York milliner who had been instrumental in Albert's being hired by Marshall Field, crossed the Atlantic for the wedding.

Marie-Louise was not about to drop everything and stay at home preparing meals and raising children. She associated herself at once with her husband — and would remain active for over fifty years. In time she left Madame Vionnet's employment to work full-time at rue Feydeau, but Vionnet remained a Lesage exclusive, with 'Yo' coordinating between the two establishments.

Albert and Marie-Louise were not only a devoted couple, they were complementary in their work. Albert was an expert draughtsman and designer, Marie-Louise a colourist. Obviously, Marie-Louise was by now very knowledgeable about embroidery, particularly Michonet's. Helped by her, Albert soon familiarized himself with it, for Michonet's library contained many illustrated volumes hundreds of years old and his samples went as far back as the seventies. Michonet, like his fellows, had not used many colours; gold and silver predominated. During the two-year period of transition, the older man had an influence on the young couple: the Lesage samples show no break in Michonet's quality and ideas. Yet a change was soon to come, for the circumstances that were to direct the course of styles in women's clothes in the twenties now began to emerge.

1924, Madeleine Vionnet. Detail of the motif of the 'Grecian horses' gown. (See p. 17.)

1925, Paul Poiret. Corsage front motif of silver and dark gold bugles for the Arts Déco exhibition to which, in a swan song, he so greatly contributed.

6 · LA · GARÇONNE

The silent, steady revolution of French decorative artists continued apace until after the First World War, when it blossomed under the influence of the Bauhaus (1919-33). As the founder, Walter Gropius, declared in his Manifesto: 'Architects, sculptors, painters, we must all return to the crafts. An artist is a superior craftsman.'

Black jet had been the rage until 1914. During the war, it tragically became *de rigueur* for all women: not only bereaved mothers, wives, sisters, nieces and fiancées. Immediately after the war, anticipating the coming upheaval in dress, embroidery designs echoing the decorative arts began to appear, along with yards of cloth embroidered with paillettes and concave sequins. These anticipated the styles to come, characterized by embroidery that would lose relief, becoming flatter, being treated like a fabric, and depending more and more on motif drawing styles.

On to the scene in 1922 burst a young woman who was to give her newly emancipated sisters a great helping hand, at the same time setting a fashion destined to typify *Les Années Folles*. Her name was Monique Lerbier, and she came from a well-to-do, highly respected bourgeois family. At nineteen, she found herself surrounded by drug addicts, nymphomaniacs, lesbians, ageing Russian princesses paying for the favours of young men, and bankers and businessmen seeking prolonged youth and potency in Dr Voronoff's monkey hormones. Disgusted, she declared her independence and brazenly gave birth to an illegitimate child whom she proceeded to raise as a gesture against society.

Monique was the heroine of a novel entitled *La Garçonne* (bachelor girl) written by Victor Margueritte. The scandal was such that the book sold 750,000 copies in record time. The President of France struck the name of the author's father from the lists of the Legion of Honour. In indignation Anatole France wrote an open letter to the Government recalling that *Madame Bovary* and *Les Fleurs du Mal* had in their time been the object of like persecutions. Paris revelled in all the hullabaloo. At last it was coming alive again.

Within a year young women everywhere were following the lead of the *Garçonne*, flaunting conventions, treating men with contempt. To blazon their equality, they adopted a boyish look. They shaved the nape of their necks. The newspapers had a field-day. 'In Bordeaux short hair a cause for divorce.' 'Husband sequesters his wife because she cut her hair short.' 'Father kills his daughter rather than suffer the dishonour of seeing her with short hair.' The bachelor girls lipsticked a tiny bee-stung red mouth to match a handkerchief knotted around their necks. They banished all curves from their silhouettes, flattened their breasts and raised their skirts even higher. In a *robe-chemise*, or short straight dress, strongly influenced by the French decorative arts and the German Bauhaus tendency, they were from shoulder to rump a rectangle, from waist to knees a trapeze, longer on one side than the other. Little by little, in the same way that Gothic architecture passed from Rayonnant to Flamboyant, embroidery — beading mainly — was complicated by the addition of fringe, which at first was used to finish off a gown and ended up by covering it entirely. A velour felt cloche hid the hair, leaving only enough space over the forehead for a tiny spit-curl above the left eyebrow. The *Garçonnes* had become androgynous, hermaphroditic — but instead of striding manfully, as one might have expected, they minced, oh so demurely, middle fingers half-clenched and little finger crooked. Pursing their bee-stung lips, they batted their eyelashes a mile a minute. Once the full image was established, they had also become flappers and vamps.

The new embroidery, after the pre-war overloading of often dissociated elements, led to a major modification of the craft for haute couture. From time immemorial the embroideress has used a technique, *La Main* (hand), and has been called a *main-teuse*. Her embroidery needle differs from the sewing needle: it has a large elongated eye and a blunted point. The

1926-7, Jacques Doucet. A La Garçonne evening sheath edged entirely in silver bugles and bugle fringing.

1987, Lesage brooch. Les Années Folles style, from a Paul Colin drawing of Josephine Baker in 'Revue Nègre 1925'.

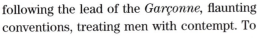

1926-7, Jenny. Lower part of a robe-chemise, short straight dress typical of Les Années Folles. Trompe-l'œil ribbon of bugles of different hues.

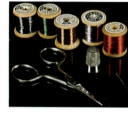

Ordinary needles for La Main.

Hook needles for Lunéville.

gave evidence of both techniques. The two groups never acknowledged one another, and had to be assigned to separate ateliers. They would not even mix for the traditional Saint Catherine celebration on 25 November when, according to custom,

design on the frame in front of her is right side up; she can see the piece progressing towards its final appearance. Embroidery houses now turned to *Lunéville*, a fairly recent and simple technique which rendered drawing more forceful.

*I*n 1867 a worker in Lunéville, a town near Nancy in northeastern France, had the idea of adding a little hook (a *crochet*) to the traditional embroidery needle. The new technique that developed represented a revolution in the activity. *Lunéville*, as it came to be called, had a great advantage over *La Main*: it was much faster. Time being money, it reduced the cost price of piece. *L*unévilleuses work on the reverse side of a fabric. They can not see the piece progressing, since only the stitching is visible to them. Nevertheless, they can work with almost everything used by the *mainteuses* — beads, sequins, silk thread, chenille, bulging cord ('*bigoudi*'), braid, gold and silver thread. But there are two serious drawbacks: they can not do rhinestones and metallic strips, and if one unit in a chain loosens, the others follow, like a run in a stocking.

*T*he *mainteuses*, proud of their artistry, refinement and traditions, looked down upon the newcomers with scorn, while the *lunévilleuses* considered their elders reactionary. With the reinvigorated production of hand embroidery before the end of the nineteenth century, however, both types of workers came to be found in the new fashion houses. But rare was an article that

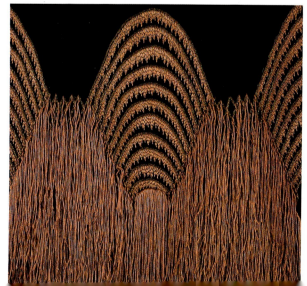

1926, Lucien Lelong. Silk braid embroidery and loose braid fringing to edge a black velvet gown.

unmarried girls of twenty-five or more devised the most fanciful of hats or headdresses for themselves and danced on the premises. The *lunévilleuses* came fully into their own when the

1927, Jean Patou. Sequin petals and shaded grey transparent sequins for 'Fugue', typically La Garçonne. *Model registration photograph of imported American mannequin.*

couturiers hired them in great numbers to cope with the beaded gowns ordered so furiously during the second half of *Les Années Folles*.

An event now took place which was to precipitate the course of these *Années Folles*. The French Government devalued the franc by 280 per cent. This occurred in 1924 just before Albert was due to change his dollars and, according to their agreement, buy out M. Michonet. What a start for Lesage et Cie! And what a joy ride Paris began taking! For the next five years the City of Light would live one perpetual 14 July celebration. There was not a berth on a steamer from North and South America to be had for months. Overnight sleepers from London, Berlin, Budapest, Vienna and the other capitals of Europe were booked solid, particularly the Orient Express. Hotels went so far as to provide bathtubs as extra beds. Apartments were at a premium. In Montparnasse you couldn't get a table at the Rotonde, Dôme or Coupole even if you were

1925, Jean Patou. 'Audacieuse', typically La Garçonne, *embroidered with stylized, fringed vine leaves of silver bugles. Model registration photograph of imported American mannequin.*

1925, Jean Patou. 'Clair de Lune', typically La Garçonne, *featuring trompe-l'œil ribbon of shaded blue 'clair de lune' (iridescent metallized) bugles. Model registration photograph of imported American mannequin.*

Ernest Hemingway, James Joyce or Henry Miller, unless you could go and sit with Foujita or Van Dongen. Americans came over for a fortnight in June just to eat French sand-grown asparagus and sip the latest cocktails concocted by that new social figure, the barman. The ravishing bachelor girls, flappers and vamps whirled off to Deauville, Cannes or Monte (Carlo) in sleek Hispano-Suizas fondling salukis dyed purple, vermilion or emerald green. To compete with the dazzling Dolly Sisters, in the *Revue Nègre* (1925) the new toast of the town, Josephine Baker, introduced the Charleston. From now on Paris danced. It charlestoned, fox-trotted, ragged, black bottomed and shimmied all over the place, on the pavements, going to and from the office, while lunching, taking tea, dining. Jazz bands played on street corners or at open houses. If a passerby heard music, he joined the party.

In such an atmosphere, women bought up clothes by the armfuls from the couturiers. Jean Patou, catering to the Americans like all his competitors,

1987, Lesage bag and belt. Art déco style.

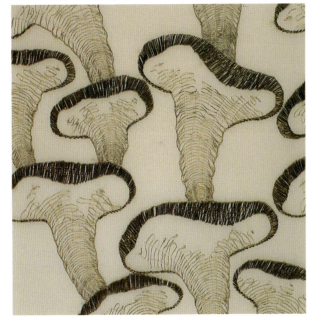

1926, Jacques Doucet. Bauhaus influence. Stylized gold- and grey-metal thread mushrooms.

even went so far as to bring several Yankee mannequins over to Paris to present his collections. During these, his 'guests' were seated at little tables where waiters plied them with champagne. He also invited husbands — or rich protectors — to have drinks at his bar while they waited for the ladies to finish with their fittings.

The *Garçonne* style not only mirrored women's increasing personal and political freedom, it carried the statement far and wide, since it could easily be adapted to mass production. From now until 1929 entire cargo ships were to transport the beaded and fringed Paris *robes-chemises* to the ends of the earth, where they were copied time out of mind. Simultaneously, newspaper fashion reporters began to flock to Paris in increasing numbers. A tendency to syndicate columns did not last long. Women in Seattle could want something different from their sisters in Chattanooga, Phoenix or Cincinnati. Local reporters also started crossing the Atlantic. To keep up, fashion magazines gave increasingly greater coverage to Paris : lengthier articles, additional illustrations. Fashion photography also developed. Whereas no leading society lady would ever have dreamed of allowing herself to be photographed in a suit, gown, coat or cape to which a couturier's name was added, she could, now that Paris fashion was becoming the smartest thing in the world, be inveigled into posing. As to the actresses and film stars — Corinne Griffith, Gloria Swanson, Ina Claire, Kay Francis, Constance Bennett — they not only turned French clothes into a publicity stunt, they also took to acquiring French titles through marriage to impecunious noblemen. French haute couture had come out of milady's closet.

Now came an event which set off the second current to influence styles in the twenties — and many aspects of French business and industry. In 1925 the Ministère des Beaux-Arts joined the Association des Artistes Décorateurs and the City of Paris to organize the Exposition des Arts Décoratifs, known as the Arts Déco. This exhibition, centred around the Eiffel Tower, represented the first concerted attempt by artist, engineer and artisan to combine beauty and industry with economical and social necessity. It was the most important decorative arts exhibition that had ever been mounted and confirmed the importance that the decorative arts had assumed in modern ways of living. Only art objects or substances treated in an artistic manner and bearing no trace of the past were admitted. The participants were convinced that reinforced concrete, lacquer, certain rare woods, smoked crystal, wrought iron and translucid enamels endowed modern life with new beauty. For Paul Poiret, who had so greatly encouraged the decorative arts and who installed three extraordinary barges on the Seine and a merry-go-round nearby, the exhibition was a swan song.

The Arts Déco exhibition was visited by sixteen million people and had a far-reaching effect on taste and styles. Over the following five years fashion was influenced by the architectural aspects of the Arts Déco. In embroidery this meant a highly stylized, often angular rendering of subjects, geometrical effects and abstractions. Coincidentally, it was at this very time that Madeleine Vionnet and Albert Lesage started to work together. Their collaboration was to have a great influence on the history of embroidery.

1926, Paul Poiret. For an evening sheath, stylized silk-thread bouquets with loose gimp stems, reminiscent of Poiret's pre-First World War art deco pioneering with 'Martine'.

7 · MADELEINE · VIONNET

Madeleine Vionnet was born in 1876 into a poor family in an obscure provincial French village. At twelve she was apprenticed to a local dressmaker and learned the rudiments of her trade the hard way. She saved her meagre wages and, when eighteen, set off for England with 300 francs and a tiny suitcase. To make some money while learning English, she accompanied inmates of a mental hospital on their walks. She also devised some dresses, and finally managed to find work with Kate Reilly, a London dress house. At twenty-five, in 1900, she returned to Paris, where she worked in the ateliers of Chez Vincent and then David Bechoff before being hired by Callot Sœurs as a workroom *première* (supervisor). The three Callot sisters were renowned for the Renaissance luxury of their embroideries. Young Madeleine worked particularly with Madame Gerber, the eldest of the three sisters, a great perfectionist.

Several years passed. Jacques Doucet, the Grand Gentleman of Fashion, was looking for an assistant. Paul Poiret had just opened his first little house, but he was having trouble, as Doucet knew, for his former employee and protégé had turned to him for help. Doucet approached Poiret about coming back to him, even as an associate, but Poiret was determined to win through on his own and regretfully turned him down. 'When I hired you, Paul,' said Doucet, 'it was to rejuvenate my house. Now, five years later, I need to rejuvenate it again. Do you know of any other excellent young person for me?' Indeed, Paul did, and thus it happened that in 1905 Madeleine Vionnet left Callot Sœurs to join Jacques Doucet.

With him, to her joy, she could at last add some designing to her supervision of workrooms. Not two years were to pass before she persuaded the Grand Gentleman to permit the mannequins to show her several numbers corsetless, following Poiret's lead, as well as barefoot in sandals. Doucet's staff, shocked and outraged, boycotted the newcomer's designs, just as the Worth saleswomen had outlawed Poiret's simple 'fried potatoes' only a few years before. Still, the young *élégantes* and actresses liked what Madeleine Vionnet had to offer, and in 1912 she whisked her clientele away from Doucet and set up shop across from the Tuileries gardens at 222 rue de Rivoli. Two years later, with the coming of war, she was not solidly enough established to withstand the consequent loss of customers, unpaid bills and restrictions, and was forced to close. Nevertheless, she went on designing her collections, and immediately after the Armistice, more determined than ever, re-opened her house and started hunting for new staff. Marie-Louise Favot was one of those to present herself.

Madeleine Vionnet was called 'the Euclid of Fashion' for the geometrical shapes which she applied to both functional and decorative devices. In this she was wholly compatible with the spirit of the decorative arts. Known too as 'the Architect of Fashion', she was the one designer in the middle and late twenties to oppose the trend of the *robe-chemise*. Her answer to this almost obligatory style was based on a technique which she launched in 1926, the bias cut.

She did not develop this technique overnight. Before Poiret, even lingerie had been structured and architectural; he created the need for undergarments which clung to the decorseted figure. Based on these, Vionnet introduced an entirely new mode. She had started by doing a lot of lingerie cut on the bias, a line at a 45-degree angle to the selvage, or edge of the fabric as woven. The idea occurred to her to adapt this cut to outer garments. As modelled on her half-size form, she could imagine the body not as a series of surfaces with backs and fronts, but in its three-dimensional aspect as a tube with a fabric that would cling naturally and beautifully when draped diagonally across it.

Imperturbably sculpting the forms of her lady,

1933. The Vionnet rose, made of bias-cut, shaded (ombré) chiffon embroidered with a silk-thread stitch.

1938. Madeleine Vionnet was renowned for her bias cut, 'Roman crêpe' and terra-cotta red, here united and embroidered with a crackle of coral beads and pronged rhinestones. Lesage drawing style inspired by Jean Dunand, famed for lacquered objects in the thirties.

Madeleine Vionnet issued the statement that feminine elegance was grace and restraint. Constantly she sought to perfect the flowing lines, balance and aerial appearance that were magical in her hands. To enhance the purity of the flow, she inclined towards soft fabrics, principally chiffon and crêpe de Chine. She favoured monochrome — off-white, ivory, cream, beige, pale green — and used few strong colours save the 'Vionnet red', a sun-drenched terracotta, deep green and, of course, black. She would not permit a dart to be seen and joined seams and yokes with the open-work stitch, or fagoting *(ajouré)*, to achieve greater fluidity. It was as if the alveoli of a beehive had been sewn together: a woman slipped her head through the top of a Vionnet gown and it dropped softly about her, occasionally fastened by hooks or pop-fasteners, never by a zip.

Obviously, fabrics cut on the bias did not fall in a way to which an embroiderer was accustomed, and yet embroidery for Madeleine Vionnet had to be in harmony with this cut to avoid disrupting the flow of the draperies and folds. 'Embroidery must look like a fabric incorporated into a model,' Albert Lesage said later. 'We embroiderers have to interpret according to the individual personality and vision of each couturier.'

Madeleine Vionnet taught him this. The originality of his collaboration with her was that, after the rather heavy-handed pioneering of Michonet and other embroiderers before the First World War, he perfected the adaptation of embroidery — light, light, light — to Vionnet's bias cut. Work done for Vionnet in the Lesage ateliers resembled lingerie rather than embroidery — as, in the end, did Vionnet's evening gowns. Compared with the heavy *Garçonne* beading and fringing, it was the attire of seraphims. As embroidered by Lesage, Madeleine Vionnet designed some of the most wondrous creations that Paris fashion has ever produced. They are still fresh and lovely when seen today.

Nonetheless, Albert had some tricky problems to face in working for Madame Vionnet. While planning an embroidery pattern, it has to be kept in mind that the two-dimensional fabric with its embroidery motif will assume a three-dimensional mass when it envelops the body. Embroidery has to be executed flat. Imagine embroidering a world globe; then imagine embroidering a world globe on the bias. To create effects of lightness, Albert searched for techniques associated with painting or vaporized colour on the reverse side of a fabric. He went so far as to use a logarithm table to calculate the design of a length of embroidery in relation to the fall of a gown. Using this table, he had recourse to a technique called smocking, whereby the embroidery was made by gathering cloth into regularly spaced tucks.

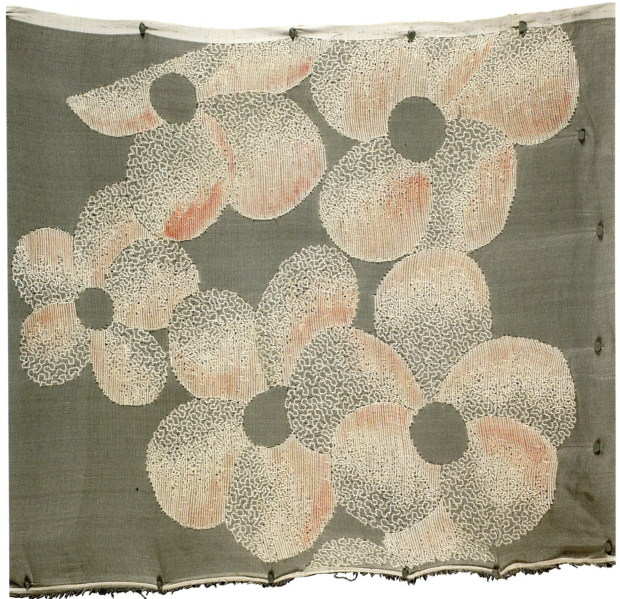

Winter 1932-3, Madeleine Vionnet. Sample underside showing the technique of passing from a strip to a vermicelli. Typically Lunéville. The beads are smaller than the head of a pin.

Madame Vionnet's cut necessitated inventing methods of embroidery that would retain the bias. The need to avoid embroidery stitches catching up the fabric and making it wrinkle resulted in the development of a new way of using vermicelli.

From the beginnings of embroidery, vermicelli — long, extremely filiform, serpentine lines — had been executed *du chic*, without drawing. That is, each embroideress was free to carry out the 'squeezing' *(serrage)* in her own way within the prescribed limits. The bias cut revolutionized the use of vermicelli. It could no longer curve but required angular treatment, which an embroideress was still free to improvise without a drawing being submitted to her.

Other unusual techniques also had to be devised for Vionnet. For silk embroidery Albert used a running stitch that resembled darning *(au passé)* and employed gimp — *ganse carré*, mat, *ganse Maurice*, shiny — to make

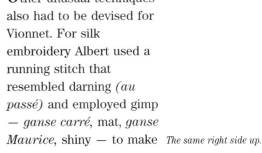

The same right side up.

1935, Madeleine Vionnet. Bias-cut evening gown of lunar crater-like white mat crepe overside, white satin underside, embroidered with gold thread and gold beads.

the fringes featured by Vionnet in her evening wear. Thematic with Madame Vionnet, as in the famous 'Gown with Horses', were Greek friezes with braid-like ribbons in trompe l'œil. Other themes involved flowers — the Vionnet rose was world famous — and polka dots of bugle beads treated *au carré*, in the direction of the weave, or *au passé* with the running darning stitch. Yet another method was the *biais de tissus enroulé*. Strips were taken from a fabric cut on the bias and embroidered in whorls, very often to form the heads of flowers, especially Vionnet roses.

Then there was the technique of ombré, or the shading of the colour of rhinestones, sequins, vermicelli and so on from light to dark on the gown. Usually, suppliers of embroidery materials did the dyeing as requested by a customer. For Madame Vionnet's bias cut Albert was obliged to do it himself. He had the back and the panels of a skirt dipped by hand, millimetre by millimetre, in a basin filled with dye, the upper part once, then the lower parts twice or three times to deepen the hue. Following these endeavours, Albert went on to devise methods of basin-dyeing to create ombré (used for georgette and crêpes), which remained unique within the House of Lesage, enabling a greater range of shades within one colour *(camaieu)* and a wider range of different colours.

During the five glorious *Années Folles*, Albert did over 1500 pieces of embroidery for Madame Vionnet. With the rising demands, he also took on Worth, Paquin, Jenny, Molyneux and young Lucien Lelong. In doing his beading he came to use several unusual techniques. 'Blown' beads had been devised by glass blowers; Albert had each bead pinched between thumb and index finger to lend variety of appearance. *'Sparterie'*, a resistant material derived from Spanish and Algerian esparto grass and looking like fine straw when employed for hats, he had softened by steam heating so that it could be shaped as desired. The beads, being hollow, were not too heavy, unlike so many others. One less successful innovation was the sequins made of beef gelatine (ox gall) bought from the butchers of Les Halles, which he superimposed on top of one another to produce a fish-scale effect. His wife and he were once awakened in the middle of the night by a

1936, Madeleine Vionnet. Ribbons of intertwined gold bugles on white bias-cut satin.

customer furious because her evening gown, greatly embroidered with these gelatine sequins, had melted in the heat of the Paris Opéra, leaving her drenched in consommé.

By now Lesage et Cie was flourishing to such an extent that Albert and Marie-Louise had to cope with the problems of mounting wages, increasing

Winter 1929-30, Madeleine Vionnet. Art deco style. Stylized gold tulle bats edged with gold bugles and covering chiffons of different colours.

Winter 1925-6, Madeleine Vionnet. Abstract art deco influence. Black marble-inspired drawing style. Transparent and jet beads for a tunic.

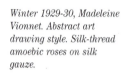

Winter 1929-30, Madeleine Vionnet. Abstract art drawing style. Silk-thread amoebic roses on silk gauze.

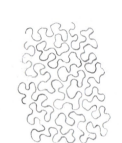

Ordinary vermicelli (up). Vionnet bias-cut vermicelli (down).

costs of materials, and the need to maintain quality but keep prices from soaring. The answer was self-evident: cut down on the hours required by a given article. As a result, they engaged the services of some *lunévilleuses*. The future looked bright.

*I*n those days fashion collections were prepared in a far less feverish way than they are now. Lesage received orders for embroidery months in advance. Albert and Marie-Louise thus had leisure time. Albert played bridge and chess, Marie-Louise painted. Together they listened to the radio, played the victrola, went to concerts, paid visits to friends in their new Hotchkiss. Of greater significance, they made a point of visiting museums and churches both in Paris and when on trips to Italy, Sicily, Egypt and Greece. This was a pleasure for them and, together with art exhibitions, also a means of renewing their general artistic inspiration and enlarging their ideas for embroidery design.

*I*n time they were blessed with three children: Jean-Louis and the twins, Christiane and François, whose godmother was Simone Bouvet-de Lozier, still running her millinery shop on Fifth Avenue in New York. So that they might raise their children far from the noise and bustle of Paris, they searched the environs of the capital for a suitable place to live. Outside the tiny village of Chaville they bought a property — house and grounds — located in the Bois du Fausses Reposes, formerly part of the royal domain of Versailles, from an engineer who had worked with Gustave Eiffel. It was not far from the Butard, a hunting lodge built for Louis XV by Gabriel, architect of the Petit Trianon, and restored in all the majesty and lustre of the *Grand Siècle* by Paul Poiret.

*S*ince the eighteenth century, the term employed to designate houses conceived in an extravagant architectural style was *folie* (folly). The Lesage acquisition was a *folie*. Built in 1880, it was of Spanish design in front, Norman at the back. As it had been the former owner's country house, it was rustic, like much of the furniture that Albert and Marie-Louise had bought with it. Surrounding the grounds were fields and farms (the last one of these disappeared only in the mid-seventies). The house had fifteen rooms, many equipped with huge fireplaces. Protecting it was a gigantic red cedar over a hundred years old.

*T*he garden had been designed to recall the former glories that were France. *A la française*, symmetrical, its straight and curved lines, perfected by Le Nôtre for Louis XIV, contrasted with the rustic simplicity of the rest. There was also a vegetable garden, and apple, pear, peach and cherry trees galore. At the far end of the garden a wall separated the property from a cloistered Carmelite convent. Here in the chapel the Lesage family attended Mass. At six in the morning, in addition to the birdsong, Chaville and its countryside could hear the bells chiming matins. It was charming, serene — and profoundly French. The red cedar, now two hundred years old, still stands guard there over the Lesage family.

1935, Madeleine Vionnet. Belt with trompe-l'œil ribbons of gold hand-painted bugles and rhinestones. Schiaparelli influence.

1937, Madeleine Vionnet. A black silk tulle evening dress embroidered with black sequins. Swallows of black and gun-metal grey cups and spangles. Worn by Baroness Eugène de Rothschild. Winter 1938.

Following pages: Winter 1984-5, Christian Dior (Marc Bohan). Recalling the art deco style of the twenties for a corsage, perforated spangles and silver bugles and micro-beads. Enlarged five times.

8 · EMPRESS · ELSA · OF · THE · THIRTIES

On 'Black Thursday', 14 October 1929, the New York Stock Exchange came crashing down, bringing in its wake to both sides of the Atlantic Ocean the greatest depression in the history of capitalism. During the next five years American tourists in Paris decreased by seventy-five per cent. Young people deserted the 'in' cafés of Montparnasse, while Montmartre was ancient history and Le Bœuf sur le Toit a sparsely patronized reminder of merriment that now seemed distasteful. All the night clubs closed. The streets were empty in early evening. The smart Plaza Athénée Hotel was so forsaken that the management invited people to stay: all such 'guests' had to do was tip the staff so that they would not leave.

1932. Marlene Dietrich gowned by Travis Banton as Josef von Sternberg's 'Blonde Venus'.

An unrelenting series of bugbears came to plague French exports. Luxury businesses were brought to the brink of ruin: not only had they lost the customers who came to France, but heated nationalism broke out in the respective customers' homelands. Customs barriers soared to hitherto unscaled heights, and quotas became prohibitive. It was not long before French industries were dying off, factories lay idle, and thousands were out of work.

Obviously, fashion was not spared. At the mid-season showings in December 1929 there was not one of the New York Seventh Avenue buyers, who, representing retailers, had been transforming haute couture from a group of small businesses catering to rich private clients into an international industry. Nor did any show up for the major summer collections shown in February 1930. During the ensuing years haute couture interests had to dip into millions of francs of accumulated profits in an effort to save the wages of 300,000 cutters, fitters and seamstresses, makers of passementerie, lace, gloves, bags, shoes, furs and buttons, not forgetting weavers, spinners, dyers, milliners and local dressmakers. All over the world hundreds of thousands of copyists trembled at the threatened collapse of the forty or fifty leading Paris dress houses.

Embroidery, and those who supplied materials for it, was also hard hit. Whereas Hollywood designers used hand embroidery until the Second World War more magnificently than ever, despite the Crash and ensuing Depression, who was mad enough to want to communicate messages of wealth and position in Paris fashion? Some anguished couturiers — Callot Sœurs, for example — tried to save the day with a desperate measure. They asked Albert to provide them with embroiderery to go with sportswear, which was still selling well, but deliberately kept lacklustre to fit in with the mood of the times. Adorning golfing togs with sequins, bugles and rhinestones proved at once to be a mésalliance. In no time a positive allergy to embroidery developed. 150,000 workers were laid off. The percentage was greater of course for machine operators, but 6,000 were to be without employment in Lunéville. The fashion houses went so far as to offer models to dressmakers for nothing, as gifts. Even Madame Vionnet, whose private clientele held fast, reduced embroidery to its simplest expression.

Lesage et Cie was no better off than any of its competitors, but a series of circumstances would provide it with a respite. The building on rue Feydeau had been sold to promoters planning to tear it down and build a new complex. One by one, the tenants had left the premises. Lesage et Cie was the only one remaining. Under the present conditions Albert was more prepared than before to accept an offer the promoters had made to encourage him to leave: 200,000 francs. Just as he was about to sign, a friend of his advised: 'Don't be foolish. Don't let them take advantage of you because times are hard. Hold out. Ask for a million and a half!' What

· 56 ·

 had he to lose? Albert held out — and pocketed a million francs, a fortune, a godsend, and a salvation. In 1931 Lesage et Cie moved to 13 rue de la Grange Batelière, east of the Opéra near the public auction house of Richelieu-Drouot. The name of the street derived from the thirteenth-century *Granchia Batiliaca*, designating the area of swamps and farmlands thereabouts. These were filled in during the seventeenth century and streets were laid. Henceforward a branch of the Seine flowed underneath, and would figure in *Phantom of the Opera*.

*T*he building, of off-white freestone with little balconies and wrought-iron balustrades, was typical of the turn of the century. The premises of Lesage et Cie and its reduced personnel were located in one of the two light and airy flats on the inner-courtyard side of the fifth floor below the maids' rooms in the attic under the eaves. As was common in Paris, such premises were basically residential quarters in which commerce might also be conducted. Whether or not the architects had thought of it (although, for the sake of individuality, being French they had refrained from designing two similar flats in any one building), the homey layout added a touch of humanity to working conditions. The previous tenant of the Lesage emporium had been a live-in dressmaker like Countess Berthe, Marie-Louise's mother. There was a little kitchen, a tiny bathroom, a fireplace here and there. From the windows facing north could be seen the roofs of Paris as well as Sacré-Cœur atop Montmartre hill, always a sight to spiritualize a day's travail, even when this was devoted to activity as quiet and beautiful as embroidery.

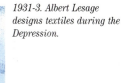

1931-3. Albert Lesage designs textiles during the Depression.

*T*o keep his business going while holding out on the strength of the unexpected windfall, Albert cast about for an area that was at least relatively untouched by the slump and would permit him to convert his talents. Oddly enough, the one he found most suitable was a rival of embroidery: printed fabrics. Because of houses like Bianchini (silks), for whom Raoul Dufy was designing, Rodier (woollens) and Bucol (formerly Colcombet, rayon and other man-made fibres), textiles were doing well. Albert therefore started to design prints derived from his embroidery motifs. His

Motif: itinerary for a Mediterranean cruise. Green, red and gold appliquéd suede on blue suede.

1934-5. Lesage et Cie embroiders belts for Madame Schiaparelli.

Gold-thread passementerie and semi-precious stones.

Abstract, appliquéd violet suede roses with gold hearts on white leather. Open-work stitch, or fagoting ('ajouré').

1935. Mae West is 'Goin' to Town' in a Travis Banton.

spirit of invention was, as usual, lively, his designs attractive, but ultimately he could not make room for himself in the already overcrowded sector with which, moreover, he was not associated. His earnings proved to be insufficient to cover expenses. Now to maintain even a skeleton staff of embroideresses, extreme measures had to be taken. The bookkeeper swept the floors and dusted, Marie-Louise handled the correspondence, Albert himself ran the errands. In 1929 there had been twenty embroidery houses, now only ten remained. Increasingly anxious, Albert came to fear that soon there would only be nine.

To add to the couple's woes, the health of their eldest child, Jean-Louis, seven years of age, now proved to be fragile. He could not be sent to school and had to remain at home in Chaville quietly taking lessons from a tutor.

In 1932 and 1933, when embroidery was not being used for clothes, the machine-made type had been turned to accessories, for what even that market was worth. In a final endeavour to stave off disaster, Albert did some accessories and even jewellery. He designed hand-embroidered belts, handbags, bracelets, necklaces and brooches. To produce them inexpensively, he resorted to stencilling. He cut out a design in paper or canvas and placed the resulting stencil on a fabric. This absorbed the ink that he applied to the stencil. The design was then embroidered by his workers in whatever colour or colours he designated. The effort never took off, but this did not mean that the idea of accessories and jewellery made of hand embroidery was not original or the designs unappealing, only that the moment was inopportune. Indeed, half a century later his son and successor, François, would recall his father's attempts and renew them brilliantly in a secondary activity.

Early in 1934 Albert was just about to announce to Marie-Louise his decision to close when he received a telephone call. 'Lesage?' 'Yes.' 'Elsa Schiaparelli. I want embroidered belts. Bring samples. I expect you in half an hour.' Happy days were here again! Within twelve months Lesage et Cie would be swept up into a five-year whirlwind such as no other embroiderer had ever known.

French couture in that year, 1934, still showed a two-billion franc deficit. Elsa Schiaparelli, for one, was not concerned. On New Year's Day 1935 she moved from 4 rue de la Paix to a 98-room mansion at 21 Place Vendôme. By then she knew that her customers were ready for fun and games in glamorous yet startling clothes — and able to pay whatever she asked for them.

Unlike Poiret, who revolutionized fashion before the First World War, and Vionnet, whose star of refined femininity and grace scintillated most brightly during the second half of *Les Années Folles*, the Empress of the Thirties was neither French nor to fashion born. Curiously, both these facts contributed greatly to the impact that she had on Paris haute couture. She spent her childhood and adolescence in Rome before the war in a family of Neopolitan aristocrats and well-to-do Piedmontese

Hand-painted butterflies set in gold silk-thread bullion on silver leather.

intellectuals. The post-war years found her living and working to provide for her infant daughter and herself in New York — at the same time, as already mentioned, that Albert Lesage was in Chicago. She crashed on to the Paris fashion scene at the end of the twenties, aged almost forty and with practically no preparation.

*E*lsa Schiaparelli's comet-like rise was extraordinary, silhouetted as it was against the Depression. The explanation was nevertheless simple: in anticipating what women were going to want by way of new styles and in accentuating youthfulness and freedom of movement, she attracted all the private customers away from her competitors. Practically single-handed she established the throwaway elegance American women were to adopt. In her own behaviour as well as in her designs, she reflected the New Woman's determination to be assertive and independent.

*B*y the end of *Les Années Folles* women had grown weary of the bachelor girl-flapper-vamp with her scooped and hollow silhouette, angular shoulders, flattened breasts, low waistline. They now frowned at the black that Patou and Chanel had imposed in reaction to Poiret's colours. Still, haute couture could do no less than reflect the atmosphere of the economic crisis and remain demure and subdued — and dull. Nonetheless, wealthy women became impatient with the practicality that had become so much the order of the depressed days. Recalling the madness of the mid-twenties, they yearned to dress excitingly again, be jolted and swooped up into some fun and games. Elsa Schiaparelli felt the same way.

*B*y the beginning of the thirties the reshaping of the feminine silhouette had been completed. Through diet, exercise and modern underclothes, women's bodies had slimmed down, though remaining curvaceous. Clothes, as presently cut close to the body, would reveal physical deficiencies, but now — according to the Schiaparelli creed — they would protect the New Woman from counterattacks by the male of the species, whose alleged superiority and often real domination she was challenging and whose territory she increasingly invaded. In the battle of the sexes Schiaparelli's clothes reflected an entire

1936, Elsa Schiaparelli. Waistcoat. A l'Italienne, wrought-iron motif in gold silk-thread bullion ('canetille') and ceramic flowers also used for the 'Shocking' perfume bottle stopper.

social revolution: defensive by day and aggressively seductive by night. The time had come, Elsa felt, to be shocking, and the word became her theme. 'Be yourself, be daring,' she insisted. 'Above all, have fun doing it.' To broadcast the message, she designed chic, witty, often surprising, sometimes outrageous attire.

*A*t the end of 1933 Schiaparelli had, through her increasing sales to American outlets, judged the effects of Mr Roosevelt's New Deal to be encouraging and sensed the general upward trend that business was to reflect everywhere. Still, despite her success, she had used passementerie to obtain the spectacular, built-up effects of her

1937. Elsa Schiaparelli. From a Jean Cocteau drawing. For a blue silk jersey evening coat, roses raised ('soulevés') to lend depth and strength to relief. Typical of the Schiaparelli-Lesage collaboration. The rest of the embroidery is of gold silk-thread bullion.

1938, Elsa Schiaparelli, Astrology (or Zodiac) Collection. Waistcoat embroidered with gold-and silver-plated strips, micro-beads and glass.

Winter 1938-9, Elsa Schiaparelli. Egyptian inspiration. Necklace with drops of coral and jade beads. Open-work stitch, or fagoting ('ajouré').

Skyscraper Silhouette rather than embroidery, associated with boom times. Thus her phone call to Lesage could be seen as confirmation of her conviction that a new period was approaching.

Obviously, she had not contacted Albert out of sheer impulse. She was a member of the Chambre Syndicale de la Couture Parisienne. During meetings over the past few months and years, the couturiers had of course reviewed the situation in their profession and discussed ways and means of saving the various sectors of the imperiled industry. In due course they had discussed the position of Lesage et Cie, and it had deeply concerned them. After all, Albert had worked exclusively for Madame Vionnet, the member of the Chambre whom Elsa most deeply respected; also for Jacques Worth, the current president, and Lucien Lelong, the future president, besides many others. They were all fully aware of Albert's efforts to save his business, but only Schiaparelli was presently in a position to place any orders.

Prudently, she began with a trial run, the embroidered belts. Then, satisfied, she added necklaces, yokes, trompe-l'œil collars. In these first efforts the typical Schiaparelli elements, highly coloured and baroque, to be developed so fruitfully later, could already be glimpsed. Shortly, pleased with Albert's work but also trusting in her instinct as to the renewal of business, she started embroidering her jackets, suits, coats, gowns and boleros. And the capes!

When beginning to work with Albert, Elsa had not known that he and she had crossed the Atlantic on the same ship fifteen years before and that they had spent the same formative years in the States. Nevertheless, she quickly realized that their mutual understanding of tough American pragmatism, perfected organizational methods and free-and-easy manners, as well as Albert's instant grasp of her wants, could lead to a much closer and far more profitable collaboration.

Many of the great artists of the period worked with Elsa Schiaparelli: Dali, Cocteau, Vertès, Van Dongen, Giacometti and Christian Bérard. Perhaps the most significant aspect of her genius, however, was her ability to find and employ the unsung heroes — the furriers, dyers, and designers and manufacturers of jewellery, trimmings and accessories, as well as the workroom tailors, *premières* and seamstresses — without whom French fashion could never have achieved or maintained its unique position in the world.

Elsa Schiaparelli did not treat her collaborators as just so many mere suppliers, as did most of her competitors. They were not servants to her, but colleagues. She never kept Albert cooling his heels in a back room; she requested him to come up the main stairs rather than use the service stairs as was the custom in other houses.

In this France of Jean Renoir, Marcel Pagnol, Raimu, Fernandel, Tino Rossi, Jean Gabin and Viviane Romance, Paris fashion, as led by Elsa Schiaparelli, swept everyone up in a swashbuckling whirlwind of nostalgia and romance. For five years, termed by Winston Churchill 'the long, dismal, drawling tides of drift

1937, Elsa Schiaparelli, Music Collection. Butterflies of metallized spangles and gold- and silver-plated strips. For this technique dating from medieval times, Albert used a special horizontal-eyed needle which he kept secret.

1937. The Schiaparelli Lady listening to the music. Her corsage is embroidered with sculptured baroque flowers of gold-plated strips set in bits of ruby mirrors.

1937, Elsa Schiaparelli, Music Collection. Motifs of silver beads, rhinestones and blue and pink plastic beetle wings.

and surrender, wrong measurements and feeble impulses', Paris, catapulting towards what was to be its blackest time since the Revolution, was more scintillating and frivolous than ever. The world of elegance and refinement whirled giddily on the edge of the rumbling volcano in a succession of brilliant parties and lavish balls.

Undoubtedly no fashion designer has ever mirrored contemporary history and moods more spectacularly than did Elsa Schiaparelli at this time. Nor had haute couture ever known such excitement, and to this Lesage et Cie was an essential element.

By now Schiaparelli was inaugurating her famous theme collections. To interpret these themes in embroidery, she progressively involved Albert — in 1934 for the Cone Silhouette and Stormy Weather or Typhoon Silhouette (corresponding to American streamlining) and in February 1936 for the lovely, pacifying Celestial Silhouette.

The renewed interest in embroidery initiated by Elsa Schiaparelli denoted the end of the dire years following the Depression. This revival originated in the Roman-born designer's religious inspirations. Slowly, in a reaction to the beading of the twenties, she returned to the use of embroidery materials employed centuries before — paillettes from medieval times — and asked for designs recalling stained-glass windows and liturgical ornamentation of the sixteenth century. Nor did she overlook military adornment. As with all the great Schiaparelli embroidery to come, the early designs were often fanciful, amusing and very decorative, highly sculptured, with deep relief *(bourré)*, as in ancient liturgy whether Copt, Roman Catholic or Greek Orthodox. This type of work required the services of *mainteuses;* there was practically no need of *lunévilleuses* chez Schiaparelli.

Albert introduced materials into his embroidery that were equally imaginative: Murano-blown glass for little flowers; imitations of hard minerals — lapis lazuli, jade, turquoise matrix with a little black filament; glass stones and beach pebbles, cabochons and so on. He crushed gelatine beads to lend them the appearance of hammered coins and combined chenille with of all things grand, mink.

At Schiaparelli's behest, Albert brought back into fashion bullion *(canetille)*, a spiral-twisted metal thread, and then employed metal to reflect its new uses as demonstrated by the Arts Déco exhibition that had wrought such an impact on her and led to her introducing into fashion many of the new substances of the modern industrial world — plastics, latex, cellophane, rayon crêpe, tulle and knits.

Schiaparelli favoured the use of gold in all its forms: gilded wood treated like metal, semi-precious or artificial stones set in gold embroidery like jewels, embroidery recalling the gold chiselling of Benvenuto Cellini. Albert developed the use of *laminette*. Hereby hangs a tale. In ancient times gold thread was used in sewing. Since gold was too pliable for the threads to serve in embroidering, it occurred to embroiderers in the Middle Ages to envelop cotton thread in a metallic thread of gold, silver or tinted silver which they called *laminette*. This procedure lent it the solidity required for them to use it, as did weavers. Around the turn of the century embroiderers, including Michonet, often flattened the thread between the two copper rollers of a mill to lend it greater brilliance.

*T*o enhance relief and lend it an even greater play of light through shadow, Albert improved the use of metal-plated strips *(lames*, not to be confused with lamé), which could look like ribbons. These were either smooth *(lisses)*, hammered *(martelées)* with various motifs, zebra-textured *(zébrées)* or wrapped *(guipées)*. The latter was enveloped in an iridescent silk of a colour different from its own, taken from the remains of spools used in weaving. Albert rendered the silk even more iridescent by rubbing on it a fish-scale powder fixed with varnish. Schiaparelli employed these strips particularly on fuchsia and turquoise taffeta, itself iridescent.

*B*y 1936 Schiaparelli, whose style was more or less tailored, had imposed her embroidery ideas on Paris fashion to such an extent that even Madeleine Vionnet, who still favoured a very loose-fitting style, fell under the influence, along with the other couturiers. That year Lesage embroidered the stylized flowers of which Vionnet was still so fond with the metal-plated strips typical of her Italian competitor.

*U*ltimately, the great difference between the two designers was that Vionnet considered that embroidery should be integrated into her clothes, whereas Schiaparelli conceived garments that would enhance their embroidery, most spectacularly her magnificent Roi Soleil capes. Albert provided Vionnet with subdued designs which were stylized, geometric and flat. Schiaparelli's fanciful designs were related to the themes that she wished to depict, and generally necessitated deep, strong relief *(bourré)*, as illustrated by the raised embroidery *(soulevée)* employed to execute prickly medical herbs and

1937, Elsa Schiaparelli. Music Collection. Gold-plated strips and gold silk-thread bullion in relief.

1936, Lucien Lelong. Decolletage of minute, fancy sequin flowers with mesh hearts of perforated metal strips. Schiaparelli influence.

1935, Madeleine Vionnet. 'Roman crêpe' gown fringed with square braid.

plants. A fine possibility of illustrating this type of relief was provided for her by Jean Cocteau, who drew an urn formed by two heads in ambiguously pursed-lip profiles and a woman's head with flowing hair. Deep relief was also to be found in the execution of the surrealist drawings that Salvador Dali provided for 'City of Drawers' and 'Venus de Milo of the Drawers', which served as the basis for Schiaparelli's Desk Suit (December 1936). This featured a vertical series of true and false pockets embroidered to look like drawers, with buttons for knobs.

No one couturier has ever done more to promote embroidery than Elsa Schiaparelli, doubtlessly because she could trust so implicitly in the inventiveness, artistry and technical perfection of Albert Lesage. Now she no longer issued instructions to him, but simply announced themes for which he conceived and designed the embroidery, using materials more or less specific to these themes and presenting the finished samples to her. Schiaparelli rejected very few. Indeed, she even extended the motifs to her prints, buttons and accessories.

'**L**esage! Elsa Schiaparelli! Music!' Here in February 1937 were butterflies, singing birds and buzzing bees, violins, drums and mandolins, sheet music, lyrics... The two conspirators had worked out this Music Collection by mingling several techniques. For tamborines, the bells were made of gold-plated strips, the rest of the design executed in silk. The staffs and scales were devised with tulle flounces embroidered with musical notes of 'beetle wings' or gold cabochons.

New industrial techniques made it possible to change a look by mixing unexpected substances, such as gilded leather used to sculpture reliefs. Following collections reflected Schiaparelli's fondness for applications of felt, even after the war. Made of rabbit hair, it had the advantage of not being woven and thus did not unravel; she used it for designs of a crab, a mushroom, a butterfly, a bird nest (pocket) and birds with bodies of multicoloured sequins, beads and silk ending in an avalanche of real feathers. For a collection featuring Fra Angelico, Albert employed gold *laminette* and silk to produce the effect of hand painting. In folkloric reminiscences, such as bright blossoms suspended in pots from the wrought-iron balconies of eighteenth-century Italian houses, he approached authenticity through the use of little embroidered flowers in spun glass, which Schiaparelli also used for her 'Shocking' perfume bottle stopper.

Other designers were now going in for themes too, but no one could compete with Schiaparelli. In 1938 came her apogee: four spectacular shows in the one year. 'Lesage! Circus!' Mayhem at 21

Winter 1938-9, Elsa Schiaparelli. Fra Angelico inspiration for a bolero. A flying angel of gold silk-thread bullion ('canetille') and gold bugles.

Place Vendôme in February. The most riotous and swaggering fashion show that Paris had ever seen. Performing horses, elephants, acrobats: corresponding embroidery designs delicately represented them in silk embroidery standing out against a background of gimp. The Ringmaster, the Skeleton Man, the Fat Lady, clowns, equestriennes wearing tutus constellated with sequins in the form of stars. Confetti, balloons, razzmatazz... One of the most spectacular effects was achieved on

Winter 1938-9, Elsa Schiaparelli. Pagan (or Forest) Collection. Decolletage of thistles of long bugles in relief and leaves of silver braid. Open-work stitch, or fagoting ('ajouré').

1937, Elsa Schiaparelli. Jean Cocteau drawing. Detail of the interpretation in embroidery on grey linen. Hair: intermingled gold bugles and 'bumble bee' cord (gold-thread wrapped cotton), like the eyebrow. Face: silk thread. Eye: a cat's eye stone.

dresses adorned with garlands embroidered with little mirrors in the form of Chinese lanterns.

*F*or April: 'Lesage! Pagan Collection!' For this, also referred to as the Forest Collection, angels in voluminous white embroidered shirts flew out of the Botticelli paintings that Albert had studied, while Venus after Venus came gliding along in lushly embroidered capes covering simple clinging gowns embroidered with delicate flowers. For the leaves, Albert combined scintillating lamé with *laminette*, more mat, to produce an effect of

• 65 •

supple relief. He created the impression of the transparency of the painter's chiffon veils by treating elements of relief with a very light touch.

*T*he Astrology (also known as the Cosmic or Zodiac) Collection in August was a particular triumph for Albert's embroidery. He stunned spectators with the theme of Phoebus Apollo, emblem of Elsa's 'Shocking' perfume bottle designed by Dali, and with the extraordinary embroidery based on the fountain of Neptune at Versailles depicting the god being drawn on his chariot by four horses.

*I*n October Harlequin, Columbine, Pierrot, comediennes and wandering troupers tripped out to present the Commedia dell'arte Collection. This featured patchwork overlaid with pieces of felt, faille and satin intermingled to give the impression of fabrics, like the lozenges embroidered *au passé* (the darning-like running stitch), in order to create a Harlequin style which Elsa extended to many garments and accessories.

*T*his was the last thematic show. In March 1938 Hitler had invaded and occupied Austria, in May he had annexed the Sudeten German part of Czechoslovakia. In Munich in September Chamberlain and Daladier had sold out cravenly to the mad Führer, supported by Mussolini. Surely, Elsa reasoned late in 1938, she would not have time to market another great collection. How right she was! Hitler gobbled up all of Czechoslovakia in March 1939, Mussolini followed suit in Albania. The implacable goose-step advance was on.

*D*uring the five great years up to the war, Schiaparelli had employed Lesage et Cie exclusively for her embroidery. But Lesage had also been supplying former customers who had returned with the upward swing in business and the necessity of trying to keep pace with Schiaparelli: Vionnet, Worth, Drécoll, Jenny, Lelong and young Robert Piguet. Moreover, Cristóbal Balenciaga had arrived in Paris. He had been an enthusiastic customer of Schiaparelli when in Spain, buying from her many of the models that he sold in his shops there. Some of her designs included Lesage embroidery, which he greatly admired, and it seemed only natural to him, on launching his house in 1937, to secure the services of Lesage et Cie for himself.

1938. Queen Farida of Egypt gowned for the coronation of her husband, King Farouk. A night-blue satin train embroidered with Albert Lesage-designed symbols of the Nile River in bulging gold-thread cord ('bigoudi') and gold silk thread.

*I*n 1927, the Lesage books had shown a turnover of 800,000 francs. For 1937, it was 1,551,539 francs. Albert and Marie-Louise were beginning to feel that their embroidery, which had become known outside France greatly thanks to Schiaparelli duplicates, might well be now exported directly. Albert, already very American-minded, duly contemplated the United States.

1938, Lucien Lelong. Schiaparelli influence. For a bolero, raging waves embroidered with mat silk and shaded blue- and shaded green-plated strips. Examples of 'camaieu', ombré - or shading - within the range of one colour.

1938, Elsa Schiaparelli. Circus Collection. Grey silk-thread dancing elephants and performing acrobats on a background of vermicelli stitched à la Cornely (machine). Chinese lanterns of tiny cut mirror.

1942, Elsa Schiaparelli. During the Occupation, an appliquéd black satin Parisian fiacre (for a coat pocket). Driver and whip: silk thread. Lanterns: gold-plated strips and ruby glass. Wheels: gold-thread. Suspension: fuschia gimp. In the window, sweethearts kissing openly to defy the Nazis in the name of love.

1938, Elsa Schiaparelli. Circus Collection. A 'stage curtain' of gold silk thread stitched à la Cornely (machine) opens the black velvet bolero to reveal trained horses embroidered with gold silk-thread bullion ('canetille') and silk. Chinese lanterns of gold-plated strips and ruby mirrors.

1938, Elsa Schiaparelli. Circus Collection. Silk and Shocking pink lamé acrobats performing under silver micro-bead spotlights on a blue bugle ground.

1952, Elsa Schiaparelli. Detail of her famous frock coat. Autumn-coloured chestnuts of rhinestones and real mink and leaves of chenille and silk-wrapped and hammered metal strips. One of François Lesage's most striking early models.

9 · THE · LIGHTS · DIM

The resplendent SS *Normandie* sailed from Le Havre for New York on 28 August 1939. Among the two thousand passengers was fifty-one-year-old Albert Lesage, returning to the States for the first time since his crossing on the *l'Espagne* twenty years before.

Earlier in the year he had signed a contract that was history-making for French fashion: the first between a French and an American hand-embroidery company. The deal called for Albert, under a Lesage franchise, to design collections in Paris as adapted to the American tastes that he now knew so well through his work with Elsa Schiaparelli, then take the designs to New York and have them executed there under his supervision for Mr Toussaint, his American partner.

The *Normandie* had been at sea three days when, on the morning of 1 September, the wireless operator received a chilling communiqué that the Captain at once transmitted to the breakfasting passengers: at 5.45 a.m. Adolf Hitler, without troubling to declare war, had ordered his army to bomb Poland. As the liner continued to ply her way to New York, all the stunned passengers could do was await further news. 2 September: Britain and France mobilized. 3 September: war declared on Germany. 4 September: to their terror, the voyagers learned that a British liner had been sunk by German U-boats. By the time the Statue of Liberty came into view they had been apprised of the first German air raids on Britain. Albert remained in New York only long enough to honour his contract. (Because of the war it was forcibly discontinued, and soon after Mr. Toussaint died.) Albert obtained a booking on an imminent departure of the grandiose *Queen Elizabeth*, launched only the year before, and managed to regain France without any incidents in late September. What changes in a month! Paris was arrayed in battledress: sandbags blanketed precious statues and monuments, gigantic anchored balloons billowed over the Tuileries, a State-issued gas mask in a tin can dangled from the shoulder of every French citizen and schoolchild (foreigners had to buy one), and orphans were being evacuated to the countryside with name tags around their necks. Sugar, tobacco,

1940, Worth. Flowers in relief made of 'cups' (concave sequins) enclosing small sequins and coloured beads. Stems of gold-plated strips and gold silk thread.

coffee and petrol were rationed — and hoarded. The black market flourished.

*T*he importance to France of the dressmaking industry — second only to metallurgy — as a continued source of income and morale was widely recognized. A few houses closed. Madame Vionnet felt that at her age she could not face what was undoubtedly coming; she had survived one war but that had been twenty years ago. Chanel, too, closed down, and skipped off to Switzerland. (To tell the truth, she had been wanting to throw in the sponge ever since, three years before, her employees, in the context of the strikes encouraged by the Front Populaire, had had the effrontery to picket the premises, but she had gone on if only not to bow to her arch enemy, Schiaparelli.) Mainbocher, an American citizen, had returned to the States. 'Captain' Molyneux had gone back to England to serve in the army. But the others were carrying on, despite the difficulties caused by the mobilization of the men.

*E*very summer for the long school holidays the Lesage family had gone with Marie-Louise's parents, Paul and Countess Berthe, to the extinct volcanic mountains of Auvergne in the Massif Central. Here they rented a house in Mont-Dore, a quiet and unspoiled spa high in the superb Dordogne Valley. Mont-Dore had been appreciated for the curative effects of its hot springs since the Romans. It was excellent for the health of Jean-Louis, still extremely fragile, and it offered all kinds of distractions and sports activities to youngsters accompanying their elders without any of the pretentious, artificial chic of Deauville, Biarritz, Cannes or Monte Carlo.

*I*n July of 1939 the Lesages and the Favots had repaired to Mont-Dore as usual. With Albert en route for the States on the *Normandie*, the declaration of war surprised Marie-Louise and the others there before their scheduled return to Paris. Marie-Louise decided that, under the circumstances, it would be prudent for all of them to stay put, far from the menaced capital. She found a tutor for Jean-Louis, who was then fifteen, and enrolled the ten-year-old twins, Christiane and François, in school for the winter. Albert, upon joining them after his return to France, agreed with her and spent the following months tending to business in Paris at 'rue Grange' (as they referred to the embroidery house in rue de la Grange Batelière) and going down to see them as often as he could manage to do so. Meanwhile, with the German offensive expected at any moment, he had induced his mother Adèle, widowed for a good many years, to close the apartment in rue Fontaine at the base of Montmartre and move out to Chaville.

*A*utumn went, the Germans did not attack, and everyone became accustomed to the *drôle de guerre,* or phoney war, which continued throughout what Winston Churchill called 'the winter of illusion'. Led by Lucien Lelong, now head of the Chambre Syndicale de la Couture Parisienne, the Paris couturiers joined forces to keep unemployment from hitting their sector and to show that French morale was still high. In the bleak February of 1940 they announced as usual

September 1939. Albert Lesage in New York to work with his American partner, Mr Toussaint.

ten days of elaborate, dazzling collections of new summer clothes. To demonstrate their solidarity, leading American reporters and buyers, laden with food parcels for friends, crowded on to the *George Washington* to cross the submarine-infested Atlantic to Genoa, struggled through complicated customs formalities, mined areas and bitter snow and ice up to Paris, where they checked without complaint into unheated hotels. The effort was successful and highly publicized. But the Americans were not to return to Paris for six years.

*I*n spring 1940, the quiet deepened ominously. Suddenly in April, Hitler pounced on Denmark and Norway and in May struck down Luxemburg and neutral Holland and trampled over Belgium. His stukas and panzer divisions outflanked the 'impregnable' Maginot Line and hurtled towards Paris. Within one week France was lost. During the early days of June, exceptionally hot to add to the horror, the northern French joined their shattered neighbours streaming south in a tragic exodus and the Parisians then also took wild flight.

*W*hat remained of fashion had been idle for months already, but Lucien Lelong, determined to hold the profession together come what may, united with a few designers in making for Biarritz with the hope of presenting a semblance of the winter collections in August. Crammed into cars and vans, the little group braved the heat, dust, thirst and indescribable disorder of armies, government officials and refugees fleeing under incessant enemy strafing of the teeming roads.

*T*he day the German advance was announced Albert had closed Lesage et Cie, entrusted Chaville — greatly shuttered up — to his mother, packed his sales manager, M. Christian (who had been with the house for over thirty years), Olga, a *première*, and embroidery materials and supplies into his Hudson Terraplane and joined the hordes of refugees on the stifling road to Mont-Dore. Within a few days the Third French Republic, in profound humiliation, capitulated to the Third German Reich. The Nazi Occupation of France began with the division of the country into two zones, north and south, occupied and free. Thereupon, over the following autumn and winter, the Germans pillaged the hapless land, commandeering her industries, grabbing up her raw materials and food and energy supplies.

*O*ver these nine months Albert remained in Mont-Dore, which was in the Free Zone, with his family and token team, chafing with fury and frustration, but nevertheless obstinately preparing with Marie-Louise new sketches and samples. Life, they felt convinced, would go on.

*M*eanwhile, Jean-Louis's health had been causing the family increasing anxiety. With the continued disappearance of doctors, nurses and medical supplies, the Lesages decided to move Paul, Countess Berthe and the children to a house in Thonon-les-Bains, in the Upper Savoy Alps just on the southern side of Lake Geneva close to the

1940. Elsa Schiaparelli, during the 'drôle de guerre' (phoney war), predicts: 'The Nazis will throttle France!' as Lesage embroiders a Shocking pink satin padlock (pocket) with gold silk thread, gold-plated strips and bulging gold silk thread cord, all in relief.

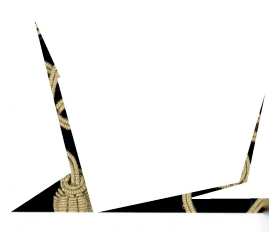

1944, Lucien Lelong. For a black wool suit, trompe-l'œil flax-thread tassels, a subdued adornment typical of the Occupation.

border of Switzerland, where at nearby Montana they arranged to place Jean-Louis in a sanatorium.
*I*n March 1941, refusing to accept the idea of continuing to live on dwindling capital, Albert took M. Christian and Olga and left the Free Zone via Vierzon, one of the few crossing points left by the Germans on the line of demarcation, and, entering the Occupied Zone, returned to Paris. Scarcely a motorcar was to be seen on the streets of the capital. The pigeons had disappeared, for no one had an extra crust of bread to feed them. And how not to lose weight oneself on a diet of rutabagas, herbs, ersatz flour, coffee, oil and mustard?
*H*ardily, Albert reopened Lesage et Cie, hired a couple of embroideresses and started canvassing for business. The fashion houses had started up again too, and Albert obtained orders at once from Elsa Schiaparelli, who had not yet felt sufficiently threatened to leave for the States, and from Lelong, Piguet, Jacques Fath and Balenciaga. He had stock left over from the days of Michonet and from his great years in *Les Années Folles* and then again in the late thirties, but he still had to face enormous problems. Since everything was rationed, tickets

1942, Cristóbal Balenciaga. Spanish religious inspiration. In relief on black wool, baroque votive flowers of coloured rhinestones set in simple and hammered gold-plated strips. The petals could be opened and closed.

for fabrics were hard to come by. Real silk had to be replaced by rayon, when that could be obtained. Even thread was difficult to find, and he had to slip a louis d'or to a manufacturer of gold thread if he hoped to receive any. Sequins were out of the question: there were no oxen available to provide the gall from which to make the gelatine.

*I*t became excessively difficult to get hold of any kind of materials. The providing of braids and passementerie to embroiderers and other makers of adornment had traditionally been in the hands of Jews. At present most of their houses were shut down: they had either fled or been deported.

*A*t the beginning of the Occupation the couturiers had leftover stock, but however sparing they were they soon used this up. Trafficking in ration tickets and black market with the complicity of their customers did not solve their problems for long either. There was very little chiffon, taffeta, satin or even rayon, while velvet was hoarded like gold, and soon there was none to be had at all. Since the Nazis had seized textiles and raw materials, Albert exercised his ingenuity by adapting embroidery to natural substances: animal and vegetable fibres, straw from cereal grasses, raffia from palm trees, flax from herbs. He even had pieces done with the jute used for potato sacks. Since yarn for embroidery came to be lacking, he resorted to cord, even string. Somehow, for a while there was wool — but of what quality! Nevertheless, customers clamoured for it: here was the only opulence in embroidery during the period. Wool took dyes, of course, but no chemicals for dyeing remained. Colour was obtained through fibre rather than glass or metallic beading, and shading (ombré) was out of the question except for combining two close hues. Finally, almost everything in this dreary, drab, ugly, evil period of history was black, with a return — especially in the bordering of suits and pockets — to the pre-First World War era for the use of jet and passementerie and with the imitation and stylizing

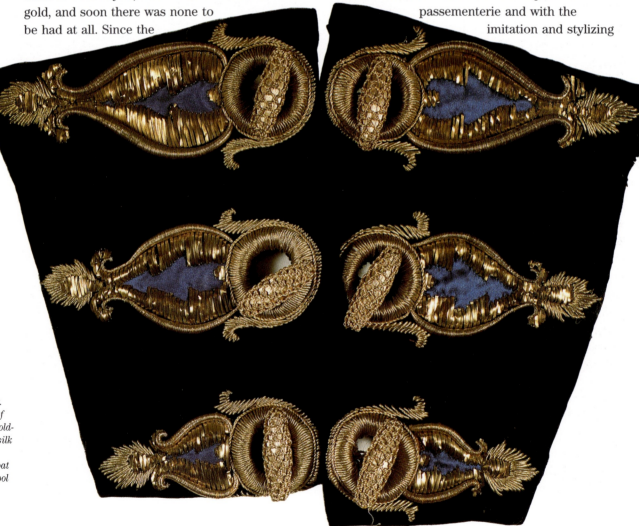

1943, Marcelle Dormoy. Detail. Brandenburgs of appliquéd blue satin, gold-plated strips and gold silk thread, and gold passementerie duffel-coat pegs to close a black wool jacket.

of brandenburgs. Oddly enough, the Nazis left milliners largely unmolested, and the Parisienne made a stab at relieving the gloom by adopting the most extravagant of hats.

*O*n his return to Paris, Albert lived in the apartment-office-atelier on rue Grange. Once every fortnight or so he bicycled out to Chaville to look after his mother Adèle. For fifteen months he did not see Marie-Louise, his children and his in-laws. When they were reunited at last, it was under tragic circumstances. In June 1942 he learned from his wife that Jean-Louis, aged seventeen, had died in the sanatorium in Montana of tuberculosis complicated by meningitis. Travelling by train, he crossed into the Free Zone via Vierzon and joined his grieving family. After a fortnight he was obliged to return to Paris, but he had neglected to obtain a laissez-passer. As the train approached Vierzon, he requested the conductor and engineer to slow it down long enough for him to leap off. He was not very young any more and he had put on flesh. In jumping he injured a leg and also impaired his heart — this would trouble him from then on — but managed to sneak across the line of demarcation without being arrested and take another train. Shortly afterwards, the Allies invaded North Africa and the Germans occupied the whole of France. For over two years, until after Paris had been liberated, Albert would not see his wife, in-laws or children again.

*P*aris fashion was high on the list of French activities the Nazis intended to take over, along with the French textile sector revolving around it. They announced at once that haute couture was to disappear. The fashion houses would be absorbed by a German organization with head offices in Berlin. The professional schools were to be disbanded and set up in Berlin and Vienna to train young German talent. The couturiers would also be transferred to these cities. So would their workshops and the people employed in them, to supply the skilled labour lacking in Germany.

*L*ucien Lelong, President of the Chambre Syndicale, stood up to them, arguing, remonstrating, and somehow managing to obtain respite after respite. The occupants banned the showing of collections abroad, increasingly rationed materials and textiles, made it practically impossible for fashion magazines to be printed. Yet Paris fashion houses stayed alive, and the French clothing business, with 30,000 companies depending on it, survived. How, with only 100 tons of material officially allotted each year, did they maintain 97 per cent of their labour force?

*T*here are several answers. The wives of officers of the German High Command in France ordered in abundance. Many of the German officers had French mistresses with expensive tastes. The

1941, Marcelle Dormoy. Black cord and black passementerie for black wool pockets. Typically Occupation.

wives of well-remunerated French collaborators, as well as wealthy Frenchwomen in general, continued to buy, and so did personalities in the public eye, especially film and stage stars. Then, in 1943, a new phenomenon appeared: the BOFs. These were the owners of bakeries, dairies, and butcher and sausage shops who collaborated with the Nazis and sold to their French compatriots on the black market, trafficking in *Beurre, Œufs* and *Fromage* (butter, eggs and cheese). The BOFs could not, in time of war, spend the tremendous sums gained from their profiteering on de luxe cars, holidays in glittering resorts and spas, or world cruises. Consequently, while the BOF men bought up modern paintings for astronomical prices and gorged themselves in wildly priced restaurants, the BOF ladies showed off in expensive clothes, furs, jewellery and scents.

The ingenuity of Paris designers was perhaps never so striking as during the Occupation, when shortages of materials became desperate. Embroidery was not to be outdone. Since balls, dances, receptions and cocktail parties were *verboten* (except for the Nazis), Lesage et Cie did little that was brilliant and sumptuous. This did not mean that it had ceased to produce, only that its activity, like that of the fashion houses, was greatly curtailed. Embroidery was no less a means of communicating messages of wealth and position than before, and why should the ladies in view — whoever they might happen to be — refrain from parading themselves? Jacques Fath had started out in 1939 in minute lodgings with five workers and two mannequins. The war-profiteer ladies and nouveaux riches came flocking to this gifted, ill-starred young Endymion in such droves that not five years later he was able to set himself up in an elegant mansion. Chez Paquin, Antonio del Castillo, who had been a junior designer with Chanel before the war and joined Piguet briefly at the start of the hostilities, was the talk of smart Paris, designing for women to dress as if oblivious of contemporary events.

Relentlessly, the Nazis intensified their efforts to destroy Paris fashion in the interests of German National Socialist styles. They planned to remove employees and reassign them to war-priority jobs. When M. Lelong did not fail to remonstrate with them, they closed Grès and Balenciaga to set an example. In May 1944 they announced that German citizens who were no longer physically able to contribute to the war effort at home would be brought to Paris to replace the skilled employees in fashion. M. Lelong reacted at once, but they now retaliated by informing him that they were fed up with his resistance and then simply ordered all the houses to shut down within eight weeks — that is, by mid-July. Only one month before that, on 6 June 1944, Allied forces stormed across the Channel towards the Normandy coast.

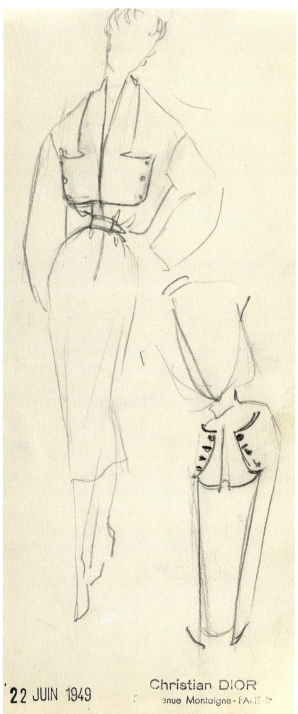

The *New Look*.

10 · A · NEW · DAWN

After the horrors and privations of the Occupation and the savage pursuit and punishment of collaborators by members of the Resistance, nothing could ever be the same again in France, physically and spiritually seared like all the other countries brought to heel by the Nazis. With the end of the war not only were customs altered, traditions discarded and standards questioned, but the very foundations of civilization shaken. Moral apathy was universal. France and the rest of Europe, exhausted by Hitler's evil, instead of being restored by a sense of peace were now paralysed by the fear of nuclear annihilation and the stalemate of cold war.

In Paris, art, as always, anticipated the changes. Artists, as well as writers, philosophers and economists, were more acutely aware of their day and age than they had ever been. They set out on a search for new directions in which to find fulfilment. The prewar names had achieved the status of monuments, but their audiences had been small and elite. The postwar artist was to find himself so influenced by the mass media that he would be forced to bend his creativity towards it and himself become a commercial product. So, in their own way, would the couturiers — and this accounts for everything that was to happen in fashion from then on, with the possible exceptions of Grès and Balenciaga.

One vital imperative of the French post-Liberation reconstruction programme was the recovery of foreign markets, and the export companies immediately set out to prove that the country, though bloodless, had lost none of its creative powers and versatility. Paris fashion inevitably remained a major export item. Unfortunately, in 1945 there was little activity in the field. It may be harsh to say that none of the prewar luminaries was showing any leadership. How could they with the continued restrictions? Only sixty models might be shown at a collection. It was forbidden to line a coat with wool, fur was inexistent, no dress could be composed of more than three yards of fabric. And how to produce smart clothes with the poor quality of such fabric? Obviously, textile manufacturers would renew their activity after having been plundered by the Nazis, but this would not be accomplished overnight.

Another vital imperative, with the entire world looking to Paris for fashion excitement again, was the desire of the Parisiennes for something new. They were weary of the styles of the Occupation — box shoulders, flat hips, over-short skirts, over-long jackets, cork wedgies and turbans like towering storks' nests. They did not want to be practical and realistic any longer. After the dreary years of utility, they wanted to forget everyday problems. Furthermore, both the authorities and business interests, in their attempts to recapture foreign markets, firmly believed that the magnificence and glitter for which Paris was known and the traditional high quality of French products had to be emphasized anew. While the British were stoically putting up with continued austerity, French life again veered to frivolity and illusion, and fashionable women, who at the outbreak of the hostilites had feared to lose irrevocably what was left to them of youth, now breathed freely again: they were not, after all, too old. They wanted to feel young and beautiful again in their clothes, to recover unforced femininity and to attract tenderness and care after all the ugliness and brutality.

The market for embroidery remained depressed, and Albert did not believe that present conditions would enable it to flourish again in the short term, even though Madame Schiaparelli was back. As he had done during the thirties, he now sought to extend his activities. An opportunity arose in the person of Jean Barioz, a Lyons silk manufacturer whose affairs were not going well. Barioz knew

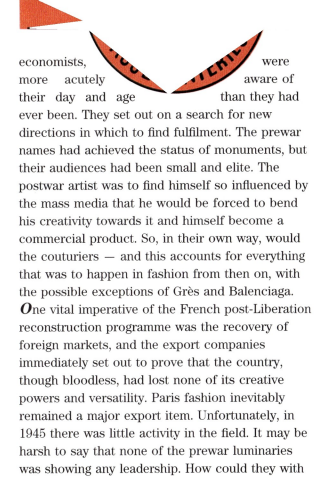

1945. The Lesage et Cie label, a key opening the doors to Paris fashion as well as to a new haute couture textiles department in association with Mr Jean Barioz of Lyons.

· 77 ·

that Albert had easy entry into the fashion houses and asked him to act as an agent for him. Albert was all the more happy to agree because Barioz was President of the Lyons Chambre Syndicale des Tissus, which, during this time of continued restrictions, could offer him priorities in supplies of fabrics. While representing Barioz for silk, he provided couturiers and lesser dress designers with such other fabrics as the Lyons manufacturers could send to him. He also, as artistic and technical adviser, counselled the Lyons manufacturers — having first consulted the couturiers as to what fabrics and textiles they might well push or develop: rhodia, an acetate, the first artificial fibre, and other synthetics. All this worked out excellently. As the country started to come alive again, Albert made a lot of money while slowly recovering his embroidery clientele. Significantly, when choosing a new label he adopted a key — opening the doors to Paris fashion. It was coloured Schiaparelli Shocking pink, and he added the word *tissus* (fabrics) to *broderie* (embroidery) and *passementerie*.

1938, Cristóbal Balenciaga. Folkloric Spanish inspiration. A linen bolero embroidered with silk-thread flowers.

1949, Cristóbal Balenciaga. Corsage embroidered with pampille 'dingle-dangles' of real pearls and crystal. One of the last Albert Lesage models.

There are two basic forms between which fashion has alternated ever since clothes took shape: the furled umbrella and the overturned tulip. What happened after the Second World War was that the tulip took over from the umbrella that had been imposed by Poiret at the begining of the century. In fact, the new look that women were longing for in 1945 — younger, more romantic, softer — had been in the air for some time.

At this point Cristóbal Balenciaga has to be brought into the story. With Poiret remaining as the great originator, the Spanish-born master of cut and fit shared the throne of fashion with Vionnet for creativity and purity of construction, before bequeathing it to *Monsieur* Yves Saint Laurent. In Balenciaga's designs, severe, intense, dramatic, the influence of postwar couture had its beginnings, for, never having served an apprenticeship, the Spaniard owed nothing to anyone.

Balenciaga gave intimations of a new look as early as 1937 when inaugurating his Paris house. Next, American *Vogue* for 15 July 1939 noted that 'Schiaparelli amplifies the hip theme'. That year the vague new look began taking veritable shape in the couturiers' imaginations: the bust was being emphasized, the waist tightened, hips were rounded and skirts flared over stiffened petticoats. Immediately after the Liberation in May 1945 *Vogue* queried: 'What's the new look in Paris?'

With this new look, embroidery began to make its comeback, but because of the tiny waists it had to be refined. The bold Schiaparelli-type of design that had dominated since 1935 gave way to two currents that now emerged: Lesage, to whom Balmain turned; Rebé, employed by Dior.

Pierre Balmain opened his house in 1945. As a junior designer, he hired Irish-born John Cavanagh, who had been with him at Molyneux before the war, had recently refused to join Elsa Schiaparelli in favour of Balmain, and would open his own house on Curzon Street in London in the early fifties. Balmain was soon also to hire Erik Mortensen, a Dane who became his assistant and later succeeded him.

At the Ecole des Beaux-Arts Pierre Balmain had

studied to be an architect. Often he surrounded his drawings and models with sketches of women's clothes — first as a pastime, then as a preliminary to becoming a couturier. At the sight of his sketches Molyneux hired him for his Studio. When 'The Captain' had to depart upon the declaration of war, Balmain joined Lelong, who had also hired young Christian Dior. 'Clothing,' Balmain held, 'is the architecture of movement.' Always remaining sensitive to the beauty of architecture, he sometimes drew vertical, horizontal and cross sections around his fashion sketches. No wonder that, from the outset, he ordered most of his embroidery from Madame Vionnet's former supplier.

'*A* leaf', Albert maintained, echoing for embroidery Balmain's conception of dress, 'must always have movement and balance.' Duly, he adapted the classical eighteenth-century spirit to the new imperatives, but with an accent on the style of drawing. One of the reasons for his success with Balmain was that the couturier, an extremely cultivated man, was keen on the eighteenth-century volute (scroll-shaped) form.

Behind every famous great man, the saying goes, is to be found a woman. Be that as it may, behind Christian Dior was Raymonde Zehnacker. As Lucien Lelong's assistant, she introduced Dior into that house, perceived his genius and was instrumental in securing the backing of Marcel Boussac, the textiles magnate, that led her protégé and herself as his assistant to Avenue Montaigne. With his first collection on 12 February 1947, forty-two-year-old Dior was tumultuously proclaimed the creator of *the* New Look. In truth, what he himself had called the Corolla Line — calves hidden, waists pulled in tight and breasts uplifted — was but an inspired continuation of the rounded line that had been seen since the first post-Liberation collections: no revolution, rather an innovative use of themes that had been crystallizing for seasons past, interrupted by war, and that now — on Lucky, Bettina, Victoire and Alla — seemed fresh and inviting. Paris was back on the world map.

Rebé, to whom Dior turned for embroidery, had a different conception to that of Lesage. His wife was a milliner and she induced him to incorporate

The *New Look*.

1947, Jacques Fath's New Look, featuring...

... a purple velvet corsage edged in mink and embroidered with arabesques of gold-plated strips and gold silk-thread bullion ('canetille').

complications from hatmaking into his designs. This did not mean that Rebé was lacking in finesse — without it he would not have enjoyed such a long-standing success with the greatest couturiers — just that he went in for superimpositions that became too intricate for the developing styles.

The success of the February 1947 New Look summer collection was repeated in August with the 1947-8 winter collection. During the following October, M. Boussac, the textiles magnate, called a meeting with Dior, Jacques Rouët, the brilliant young managing director, Raymonde Zehnacker and the other executives. 'Shall we remain a small house like Balenciaga? Or take advantage of our good fortune, trust it to last, spread our wings and become international?' Today the answer seems simple. Then it took courage and daring to vote for the latter. At all events, they decided to exploit the Dior label as widely as possible. Early the following year they laid the foundations for Dior-Perfumes and Dior-Prêt-à-Porter-New York and then gave a great impetus to fashion licensing agreements. Under such deals, a couturier lends his name to a manufacturer, exercises quality control and collects a royalty on the finished product, a principle Paul Poiret tried to establish as early as 1922, in vain.

One day not long after the historical decision Dior said to M. Rouët, 'Jacques, in my collections I have the girls wear American stockings. We pay for them in dollars. Why not use our own name?' We are still in 1948 and French stocking manufacturers had not yet altogether recovered from the Occupation, but soon Dior stockings were being manufactured in France and sold under the Dior label abroad. Jacques Rouët could not claim to having been responsible for the first French haute couture licensing deal, for prior to the war Elsa Schiaparelli, with her usual farsighted business flare, had licensed her stockings, the only accessory ever to have borne the name of a couturier. Rouët, however, could stake a claim to fame for popularizing the practice of licensing.

An American specializing in silk prints presented himself. 'Ninety per cent of ties for men are bought by women. I'll provide the fabrics. Stern-Merritt will manufacture. All you have to do is provide the Dior designs — and the name.' The

1948, Pierre Balmain's New Look. Black soutache braid and jet embroidery on grey flannel.

subsequent second licensing was the first to authorize a couturier's label to be sewn on to ties. Many rivals quickly followed suit. By the mid-eighties thirty different 'names' would have issued licences for ties, sold in shops patronized by women seeking gifts for men. Dior next issued licences for bags and men's shirts, and by 1951 for gloves, scarves, hats, knitwear, costume jewellery, glasses, sportswear winter and summer, pyjamas, as well as lingerie, bras and girdles. By 1954 the house had no competitor left for these articles.

In 1947 Dior had employed eighty persons. The turnover, translated into francs of today, was 1,300,000 francs or $300,000. In 1968 the turnover had mounted to 180,000,000 francs, $50 million. By 1983, with Jacques Rouët still in charge, now of a staff of a thousand, the turnover was 4,065,074,000 francs, or $534 million, 21.60 per cent up from 1982. These figures do not include the perfumes.

Ultimately, the contribution of Christian Dior to French fashion was his adaptation of its creativity to articles other than dress. Through capitalizing on his name under the management of one of the most remarkable unsung heroes in the contemporary French business world, Jacques Rouët, he enabled the specific worldwide fame of couturier clothes to expand into new fields by licensing accessories and beauty products whose success derived from couture prestige.

PART·TWO·LESAGE, FRANÇOIS

Summer 1986, Chanel (Karl Lagerfeld). A Vasili Kandinski drawing interpreted on organza entirely embroidered with sequins and bugles and edged (right) with rhinestones and crystals in an imitation of a Cartier necklace. Specially requested by Mr Lagerfeld.

11 · BIDUL

It is rare for twins to be born on different days, but the fact remains that François Lesage appeared on the scene at 23.40 on 31 March 1929 and his sister Christiane at 0.20 on 1 April: the family liked to claim it was an April Fool's joke. Albert, now forty-two, and Marie-Louise, thirty-four, were overjoyed. They had long been wanting to present Jean-Louis, almost five, with a brother or sister. And here were both for the price of one. To 'François' they added the names Paul Gustav, those of his grandfathers, and requested Simone Bouvet-de Lozier to be his godmother. The lady who had played such a significant role in Albert's life, and would repeat it in her godson's, came over expressly from New York for the christening.

The twins were two years old when it became apparent that Jean-Louis would not be able to lead a normal active life. Yet happily, through the compassionate and intelligent guidance of his tutor, he found fun and adventure in literature. He particulary loved poetry and wrote poems from an early age. François, also from infancy, proved to have inherited his parents' gifts for drawing and painting. As a tiny child, he sketched scenes from imagination. In a few years he began drawing what he saw: still lifes and portraits of his parents, brother, sister and grandparents, the garden and the surrounding countryside. By the time he was eight he was doing aquarelles, and soon he attempted oils, supervised by his mother, who taught him how to mix his paints and sharpened his eye for colour.

Marie-Louise, a devout Catholic, was as strict with her sons and daughter as with herself in regard to respect and honesty. At seven years of age François served as an altar boy during the masses celebrated in the chapel of the Carmelite convent on the other side of the garden wall. It became his responsibility to present the cruet to the officiating priest. One Sunday he spilled a bit of oil. The following day, to pay for it, he put a five-centime coin in a collecting box. (His mother's injunctions did not, however, prevent him, when he was a few years older, from climbing atop the garden wall of an evening with the gardener's son to spy on the nuns as they undressed in their cells.)

Marie-Louise did not buy toys for her children. Feeling that they could never become educated enough, she gave them books, mostly illustrated art histories, and tirelessly conducted them to museums — nearby Versailles was obviously high on the list — and to churches in Paris and wherever they happened to travel, even when going somewhere in the country to lunch with friends. Patiently, she pointed out in detail what they saw and instructed them how to look more keenly at composition and hues.

It must not be gathered from this that the Lesages were cold and rigid people — on the contrary, they were warm and fun-loving. They called each other by affectionate names: Albert was

1931. Bidul and his co-peanut, Titane.

'Papatoche' or 'Patoto', Marie-Louise, an amusing woman who even sometimes recounted off-colour stories, was 'Mamanpetite', and her mother, Countess Berthe, 'Mémée' (Granny). They nicknamed François 'Bidul', or thingamajig, and Christiane 'Titane'. When she wrote to her twin, Titane signed herself 'Your co-peanut for life'. The Lesages were outgoing, unaffected and modest. They could not have been petty had they tried. The brilliant, ephemeral tumult of the lives of the *monstres sacrés* of fashion is not be found in this chronicle, rather a calm, fraternal constancy that takes its source in dignity, tact and fidelity.

Art instruction was given to students at an early

age in French schools. To complement it, when François was nine his parents sent him to take lessons from an artist in Versailles. Here, from reproductions of drawings — by Leonardo or Michelangelo, say — and of sculpture he learned to mould plaster casts. On Thursdays, the day which schoolchildren then had off in France, he drove to Paris with his father, who dropped him on rue Fontaine to see his grandmother Lesage, Adèle. After lunching with her, he would walk down to rue Grange. Ceremoniously, he went from atelier to atelier greeting everyone individually like the little gentleman he was, stopped to observe the embroideresses at work, took a look at what the draughtsmen were doing, then spread out his materials on whatever long table happened to be available and sketched. As little by little he became conditioned to the specific activity, the draughtsmen guided his drawing and encouraged him to design for embroidery, starting with decorative patterns associated with the plane geometry he was learning in school. From time to time Olga, the *première*, would take one of his drawings and have a sample done from it. Generally the motif was flowers. When his parents went off somewhere, he sent his mother bouquets by covering the blank spaces in his letters with sketches of roses or geraniums. He was ten when his future for six years was determined by the *drôle de guerre* and the Occupation.

When the family moved from Mont-Dore to Thonon-les-Bains, François did watercolours of the chapels and villas to be found here and there on the Lake Geneva shores. A frank and loyal youngster who easily made friends everywhere, he also enjoyed skiing, went swimming, and liked to fish because he enjoyed listening to the silence in the beautiful natural surroundings.

In the sanatorium in Montana, Jean-Louis suffered cruelly from being separated from his family, no matter how often Marie-Louise and his grandparents managed to cross the frontier to visit him. Happily, M. Lapeyre, an elderly and well-known Swiss painter, also a patient there, befriended him, offering a measure of protection and reassurance beyond the professional care and interest of the doctors and nurses. Still, the old man's presence could scarcely make up for that of the family. In the autumn of 1941 Marie-Louise arranged for François, now twelve, to go to Montana to keep his brother company. He remained there, lodged in a private house, all winter and the following spring. Naturally, Jean-Louis presented him to M. Lapeyre, who was impressed by his artistic inclinations and undertook, with Jean-Louis in increasingly semi-comatose attendance, to give him lessons in painting, especially the technique of oils.

Had François been nothing but blithe and carefree, which he was not (what adolescent during the Occupation could be?), the life of a sanatorium and the sight of his brother daily growing more and more feeble would have sobered him. As it was, the experience deepened the basic steadiness and gravity of his character.

When Jean-Louis died, Albert and Marie-Louise transferred their love for him to the two other children, particularly to François, now the only son. They became almost obsessive about the children's health: for a 'oui' or a 'non' they kept them home from school. François profited from this extra, and oh how welcome! leisure time to do charcoal drawings — remarkable — of all the prophets on the ceiling of the Sistine Chapel as reproduced in a book on Michelangelo that his mother had given him.

Bidul and Titane were sixteen when, in the summer of 1945, they returned at last from Thonon-les-Bains to Chaville. In September François enrolled anew in St Jean de Béthune, the private school in Versailles that he had attended before the war. In his free time, both winter and summer, he painted out of doors in the lovely Ile-de-France environs of Chaville and Versailles. As he was good-looking, personable, well-mannered and full of beans, he pleased both boys and girls — and their parents — and developed close friendships, some to last a lifetime.

On his free Thursdays and during the Christmas and Easter holidays he went to rue Grange. With the revival of business, Albert had hired more embroideresses. Some had worked for him before the Occupation and, with many houses remaining closed, were only too delighted to return. In all, the staff now numbered twenty-five. François began to draw designs for the embroidery and worked with the embroideresses to produce samples. Soon he was accompanying his father to see the Lesage customers, and thus became acquainted with Madame Schiaparelli, Rochas, Heim, Fath, Balenciaga, Griffe and Balmain. All of them appreciated this knowledgeable and attractive youth, so mature for his years.

During a short school holiday in the spring of 1946, to start making up for the trips prohibited during the Occupation by the Nazis, Albert and Marie-Louise took the twins to Bruges. Here François had his first close-up glimpse of Flemish primitives. During the following summer, the parents offered their children a trip to Italy — Venice, Florence, Rome. Now François discovered the Italian Renaissance in depth, and was particularly impressed by Botticelli. The following year (1947) during the Easter holidays, when he had just turned eighteen, his parents went down to the Riviera for a few days leaving him in charge of Lesage et Cie. Perhaps it was a deliberate trial period. At all events, a Roman customer arrived one morning to order some embroidery. What could the house offer her? Inspired by the Italian Renaissance paintings he had seen the previous summer, François did his first commercial design for her: he took his inspiration from Botticelli's *Venus on the Half-Shell*. In the trade a 'sample' is an embroidery done for presentation; when sold and adapted to a garment, it is a 'model' — and registered as such. This was François's first model.

The following June 1947 he obtained his baccalaureate and started to work full time at rue Grange. At once he took an interest in the development of the business, studying the accounts and analysing prices with the bookkeeper. He took to accompanying the salesmen when they visited the various fashion houses to present the Barioz silk collections to the couturiers, and he went down to Lyons with his parents to observe them dealing with the manufacturers of fabrics and textiles.

By the summer of 1948 François had shown such an artistic and creative touch, had proved to possess such technical aptitude and was so well-liked by customers that Albert and Marie-Louise, envisaging the future of the company in the middle and long term, felt it would be an excellent idea to send him to the United States and familiarise him first-hand with American ways, means and tastes. Albert had not forgotten his experiences in Chicago twenty years before, nor failed to measure the effect that they had had on his career. Always fresh in his mind too was the abortive hands-across-the-sea contract that he had obtained and begun to honour in 1939.

There were multiple other justifications and motives for such a trip. Undertaken by the young son of a supplier, it would impress Lesage customers — couturiers were not yet flitting back and forth to the States. (If Albert had considered renewing American contacts himself, at sixty he knew he was not the man he used to be — perhaps he even sensed he was pressed for time. And both he and his wife were sure they could rely on their son, despite his youth.) Obviously, the trip would widen François's horizons and enable him to gauge the possibilities of opening a Lesage embroidery branch over there somewhere and unearthing a possible distributor of French textiles into the bargain.

Inevitably, one major problem conditioned the trip: the cost. While Albert could deduct a reasonable amount from his income tax as overhead expenses for prospecting, a goodly sum would still remain for traveling and a six-month stay. Two businessmen came to his assistance. The first was his brother-in-law, Louis Favot. Together they owned, and Louis ran, a slide rule

1942. Père et fils in Thonon-les-Bains.

manufacturing company, 'Graphoplex'. Why shouldn't François, representing them, do a market study in the States to gauge the possibilities of selling French slide rules, though in metres, to stores dealing in drawing materials?

The second businessman was a diamond merchant. At the time of the Liberation three years before, the Lesages had opened their house in Thonon-les-Bains to an injured member of the Resistance, a Belgian, who had not forgotten their care and kindness. His brother-in-law, Edouard Sirakian, had a diamond cutting and setting business in Antwerp. He bought almost exclusively from de Beers in South Africa, and was busy promoting his company's export trade. M. Sirakian often came to Paris, where he had a branch office. One day he dropped in to Lesage et Cie to give Albert and Marie-Louise news of his ever grateful brother-in-law, together with some gifts. When he learned that François might soon be leaving for the States, he had an idea: why should not the young man represent him over there and, through canvassing prospective customers, take orders — for a percentage of the sales price? The deal was concluded, and M. Sirakian proceeded to send $10,000 worth of sample diamonds to his New York agent with instructions to turn them over to François Lesage when he presented himself at the office.

Another matter had to be cleared up. It was all very well for François to go to New York, but New York was not the United States. There were other cities that offered possibilities, but what guideline, what itinerary, to adopt? Simone Bouvet-de Lozier, François's godmother, was the determining factor in this. She had given up her New York shop and moved to Los Angeles to be near her children, and there she was managing a branch for the fashion designer Don Loper. She had been urging her friends to come and visit. If François's ultimate destination was Los Angeles, Albert and Marie-Louise reasoned, he would have to cross the entire country. Through Lesage customers and Sirakian agents stopping places could be arranged here and there. This would be excellent for his thorough introduction into American business circles and families, for the judging of eventual embroidery outlets, and for possible sales of slide rules and diamonds.

One last detail remained to be worked out. It was a major one. Recently a Paris-to-Lisbon plane had crashed into a mountain. Taking off from Copenhagen airport after a stop, an Amsterdam-to-Stockholm Dakota had exploded, burning alive Prince Gustave-Adolph of Sweden and the great American opera singer and film star, Grace Moore. In the disappearance of a Yankee Clipper out of Lisbon for New York, Marcel Cerdan, the French boxing idol beloved of Edith Piaf, had also perished. Consequently, the very thought of air travel terrified Albert and Marie-Louise. François was not to fly, period. But autumn had come, the ships were booked solid. Still, some way had to be found for him to leave before winter set in.

1943. François's charcoal drawing of the prophet Ezekiel, from the Sistine Chapel ceiling.

12 · A · BABE · IN · TOYLAND

The Liberty Ship *Myriam*, out of Hampton Roads, was an old collier flying a Honduras flag and manned by a Greek crew. Since Le Havre had not yet been rebuilt and was over-congested, the *Myriam*, being flat, had mounted the Seine River to Rouen to unload its cargo of coal. It was scheduled to return empty to the States on 9 November 1948. Through the French Line Albert managed to secure nineteen-year-old François a passage on it. There were eleven other passengers, including two nuns and several Americans.

1948, Paris. François, nineteen years of age.

The crossing was to take nine days, but they ran into trouble. First they were pounded by storms which lasted nearly a fortnight and attained such violence that the passengers had to be strapped to their berths and went without sleep for almost three days. At one point the cargo-less *Myriam* listed to 37 degrees in the raging seas — 'a boogie-woogie dance', François later reported home. During a lull, the captain turned her round and continued backwards: the flat boat held the sea better that way. When at last the storms subsided, greatly thanks no doubt to the nuns' incessant praying, the radio operator received some disturbing news : a dock strike had been declared in the States, and with ships piling up outside ports many of these were unavailable. The Captain negotiated night and day. Finally, after seventeen days at sea, the *Myriam* put in to Baltimore on 26 November. The passengers and crew were obliged to wait eight hours before disembarking, and that entailed descending a rope ladder and then leaping into a motorboat.

François had studied his map of the eastern states and perceived that Philadelphia was on the railway route to New York. The City of Brotherly Love was not unknown to this young Frenchman. The Declaration of Independence, which owed so much to Montesquieu and Rousseau, had been signed there; Benjamin Franklin, representing the newly constituted Congress there, had been the first US Ambassador to France; before returning to France after the British had been defeated, General Rochambeau, head of the Louis XVI's expeditionary forces, and Lafayette had been publicly thanked by the President of Congress there and, along with their descendants, made honorary citizens of the new United States. However, if François alighted from the train in Philadelphia for a twenty-four hour stop, it was not only to take a look at the Liberty Bell; he wanted to get some idea of the slide-rule market in a large American city. He registered at the St James Hotel. After studying the telephone book with the help of the desk clerk, he came to the conclusion that only Brown and Earle, general agents in Pennsylvania for a national firm, could be of interest to him. 'With the thermometer rising slightly' (as he described his apprehensive state in a letter to his parents), he presented himself — and impressed the managers to such an extent that they requested him to ask his uncle Louis Favot to send them prices for fabrication in plastics.

And so to New York, where he was welcomed by Lily Daché, a renowned milliner, and Countess Mara, a friend of Elsa Schiaparelli, whose clothes and accessories she featured in her exclusive shop. The window of his Times Square hotel room faced an enormous neon-lighted face of a man enjoying a Camel — day and night smoke came puffing out of his mouth.

A large pile of letters was awaiting François. Papatoche addressed him not as Bidul but as Donald Duck and Popeye because of the ocean voyage. Marie-Louise and he had written every day, his father's letters in particular being almost overwhelmingly loving: François would sadly understand why soon. Notes were added by 'Mémée' and his co-peanut Titane. At once he adopted the habit of sending everyone at home gifts of chocolates, rice, cigarettes and nylon stockings and of writing long descriptions in such a scrawl that the entire family lamented they could not read a word, whereupon he took to laboriously typing his letters, which for all the errors were scarcely more legible.

*N*aturally Marie-Louise, as became a mother, worried about him being so far away for so long. Constantly, she enjoined him to dress warmly so as not to catch cold, to get enough rest so as not to lose weight, to eat plenty of steaks almost raw and eschew American canned and just-add-water food in favour of fresh fruit and vegetables. Happily, she knew he would be cherished by his second mother-cum-godmother, Simone. 'Dear God,' wrote Marie-Louise, 'how wonderful it is to love one another. I still see our lovely darling Jean-Louis saying that to me a week before his great departure. Well, let us not give in to sorrow. He is always with us, and he is watching over you, be sure of that!'

*T*he New York Agency of the Antwerp Diamond Merchants Bank was located at 607 Fifth Avenue. The manager may have been startled when a nineteen-year-old Frenchman speaking imperfect English turned up and asked for 11.35 carats of polished diamonds, but he had indeed received instructions about M. Lesage from Edouard Sirakian. In letters he was holding M. Sirakian listed the names and addresses of some fifty prospective clients for François to visit in Detroit, Chicago, Saint Louis, Denver and San Francisco. And off the young man set from the bank with the diamonds tucked into a little pouch attached to his belt by a chain.

*W*estward ho! In Cleveland he took orders for $1260 worth of diamonds but soon realized that the moment to sell was ill chosen: in early December prospective buyers had already stocked up for Christmas and were loath to commit themselves further. As a result, François gave Detroit a miss and went on to Chicago, where he booked into the Stevens, the largest hotel in the world, on Michigan Avenue across from Grant Park and the lake. The stores to be visited were all located in the nearby Loop, on Washington, Madison, State and Clark Streets. But even dropping the name of the Marshall Field family, which received him, did little good, and after visiting the scenes of his father's life there, he set out for St Louis. Here he succeeded in taking orders in two shops, one on Locust Street, the other on Olive Street. Denver and the Rocky Mountains might have impressed him more had he not spent so much time in Upper Savoy and Switzerland, but he was nevertheless pleased to receive letters of intent (depending on Christmas sales) from three jewellers on 16th Street. The next stop was Salt Lake City. Having visited the Mormon Temple, he sent a wire to Simone Bouvet-de Lozier announcing the time of his arrival.

*H*is godmother was waiting for him when his train pulled into the Los Angeles station. It was a joyous reunion, but he was sorry to perceive that she was not very well and to learn that she had stopped working. Simone lived in Lafayette Park, in the Wilshire Apartments, 671 South Coronado

1949, Los Angeles.
François with a roommate.

1949, Hollywood. François, carrying samples, about to pay a visit to a film studio designer.

Street. When they arrived, François found that she had opened his trunk with a key he had sent under separate cover, and there in his room were all his suits pressed and neatly hung up in a closet and his linen arranged in a chest of drawers.

There was in Los Angeles and Hollywood a large and active French community. Simone, one of the leaders, introduced him into it. The French Consul, Alexandre de Manzlarly, received him, as did Charles Boyer, who had set up a foundation for the perpetuation of French culture in the States. All of them supported a French-language newspaper, *Les Echos de l'Ouest*, which was distributed throughout the country. Welcoming Simone Bouvet-de Lozier's young Parisian godson, the editors requested him to write an article about Paris fashion from the point of view of his family's profession. He certainly did:

*I*nstead of revealing to you what the woman of 1949 is going to look like, which is still up to the gods in their heavens, I am going to introduce you, rather, to an unknown personage who collaborates with them both to offer women ever newer and more beautiful adornment and present an ever more magnificent showcase for their charms.

Obviously, he meant the unsung hero hidden in the back room, the embroiderer.

*W*hen you leaf through the history of costume, are you not leafing through the history of embroidery? How mournful would be the Middle Ages without its colourful notes, how boring the sixteenth and seventeenth centuries without the opulence of the gowns and costumes...

As a chronicler of the times declared: 'The second king of France is the embroiderer.'

Certainly, embroidery is not essential to fashion, he went on to say, but fashion does not really pass muster without it.

*I*f the embroiderer does not emerge from the shadows, it is because he rarely has any direct contact with the customers... His ways of working are little known. The effects are recognized, but the hand that devises them remains concealed...

Embroidering was not, as many people thought, merely placing rich materials here and there.

*I*t is creating with rigour, suggesting while appearing to follow, possessing instinctive and measured foresight. It is not yet altogether an art, but it is no longer just a craft...

This article did much to establish him in the eyes of the French community for himself, rather than just as Simone's godson and guest. In particular, it pleased the affluent group in smart Pasadena, which plagued Simone with invitations for him.

His social graces apart, it was obvious that François had to improve his English. Every Saturday night he attended NBC radio shows opened to audiences. After visiting the campus of the University of Southern California (so far removed from the funereal, prison-like Sorbonne), in January 1949 he signed up at Hollywood University for twice-weekly night classes for foreigners and at Los Angeles City College as a free auditor. This enabled him to meet some young people. As he was the only Frenchman (he claimed that he was twenty-five so as to reassure anyone inclined to recoil before a minor), he was chased by everything that could hop, skip or jump.

He did not, however, forget the motives for his trip. The potentialities of centimetre slide rules proved to be discouraging, but he kept pursuing leads and even succeeded in interesting some scientists at the august Pasadena Institute of Technology. He took the beautiful train trip up to San Francisco in order to display his diamonds to some twenty jewellers located mainly on Market and Post Streets, and obtained a few, but only a few, orders. He had counted on Christmas being over but had failed to realize that the jewellers were in the middle of January stocktaking.

American embroidery gave him pause. Upon visiting the largest Los Angeles firm ('Everything

Lesage et Cie atelier. Spools of silk thread...

here is the largest, biggest, most modern...') he was surprised to observe that collections were not prepared beforehand; the embroiderer waited until a customer explained what he wanted, then did some sketches. Moreover, 'Their conception of *rich* embroidery is most amusing.'

Meanwhile he was doing everything he could to help Simone in the house, but it became evident to both of them that her health did not permit him to continue to stay with her. Simone found him a room for $5.25 a week in an apartment at 412 Norwich Drive, West Hollywood, leased by the son of an old friend of hers and shared by two other young Americans.

In no time he was showing such initiative and enterprise in business that Simone considered setting up a 'corner of Paris' featuring Lesage embroideries in a department store. When such a venture proved to be too risky, she thought he might well explore the possibilities of selling to the motion picture companies. Duly, she sent him to Columbia Studios to see Jean-Louis, the French-born designer famous for Rita Hayworth's strapless evening gown in *Gilda*. At the time the major companies were undergoing a transition because of the impact of television. They were getting rid of their stables of stars and cutting back in every field of production. With foresight, Jean-Louis had gone into private designing. The idea of Parisian-imported embroidery appealed to him, and he asked François to show him samples. The young man wrote off to Albert for some and, on returning to see Jean-Louis, met a few of his private customers, Marlene Dietrich, Lauren Bacall and Lana Turner.

Heartened by the designer's positive reactions, François asked Simone to obtain admittance for him to other studios — MGM, Warner Brothers, Paramount, 20th Century-Fox — and was received by Adrian, Irene, Orry-Kelly and wonderful Edith Head. During his visits, he met Myrna Loy, Claudette Colbert, Gene Tierney, Olivia de Havilland and Jennifer Jones. Still, despite the unanimous interest, serious calculations forced him to conclude that it would not be profitable to import embroidery into the States from Paris because of customs duties. Was the enterprise to end there? No. Why not set up an atelier on the spot and work from the samples that Albert could continue to send him? He had met a young Cuban embroideress, Elsa Diaz, who was supervising several of her own workers. He drew up a proposition that she accepted. For ten per cent of sales, he would provide the samples, go to see customers and buy materials upon receiving an order, while she would pay the rent and the embroideresses. Where to open shop? They found a wooden house on Sunset Boulevard that they decorated with posters of Paris and regions of France provided by the local French Chamber of Commerce.

The inaugural drinks party of 'Lesage-Sunset Boulevard' was attended by the French Consul, Charles Boyer, Jean-Louis, the editors and staff of *Les Echos de l'Ouest*, all of Simone's smart friends from Pasadena, and a goodly number of young people from Hollywood University and City College.

From the very start business went well. François — now dubbed 'the Frenchman with stuffs out of this world' — sold to dressmakers, designers and the wardrobe departments of the various studios. In no time Elsa Diaz and he were keeping ten embroideresses busy, and François was plaguing his father for more and more samples. In fact, scheduled to return home in May, he obtained his parents' authorization to prolong his stay in the interests of developing Lesage-Sunset Boulevard. Moreover, he now had medium-term plans. For one thing, several studios were planning costume epics, and his expectations were high. 'This business may soon be most profitable,' he wrote home. 'It is possible that this year earnings will

... and metal thread.

1949, Hollywood. Jean-Louis sends instructions to François for the embroidery of a gown.

At once François left Elsa Diaz in charge of Lesage-Sunset Boulevard with Simone looking after his interests, such as they could continue to be. The four-day train trip to New York seemed endless. Passenger ships were booked solid for the summer months, and he became frantic. Yet his troubles were not over. When he reported to the Antwerp Diamond Merchants Bank to turn over his accounts and give back the diamonds, the manager informed him that as a result of internal trouble at de Beers in South Africa, all the orders he had taken were cancelled.

Finally, he obtained a berth on an American troop transport ship returning undesirable aliens to their countries. After a stop in Cork, he reached Le Havre late in June. Uncle Louis was waiting for him when he cleared customs — and told him not to ask any questions. In near silence they drove straight to Chaville, with a halt only for a *café-crème* and croissants. As they approached the house, Uncle Louis stopped the car and turned to face his nephew. 'François, you have been the head of your family for a fortnight.'

only cover expenses, but with the next collection… it may very well work most satisfactorily.'

His hopes and enthousiasm were soon dashed. At the end of May both Simone and he received a similar letter from Uncle Louis. Marie-Louise's brother informed them that his nephew's presence at home had become imperative and urgent: Albert was suffering from heart trouble and had been ordered to take a long period of absolute rest. At that, he had recently had several 'warnings', but Marie-Louise and he, minimizing the situation, had refused to let their son know. 'Their love for him has blinded them a little to the present circumstances.' François, Uncle Louis nevertheless stressed, was not to be unduly alarmed and did not have to make a mad dash for home. Above all, he was not to take a plane: his parents' morbid fear of air travel might have a pernicious effect on Albert's state.

1949. Sample sent by Albert in Paris to his son in Hollywood for Jean-Louis. Flowers of silk-thread wrapped metal strips with sequin hearts and blown glass cabochons on a brown velvet ground covered with 'lophophore'-coloured peacock feathers and edged with bugles and sequins.

13 · LESSONS · IN · FASHION

With the success of the New Look, the couturiers became cock-a-hoop. They made it hard to obtain a seat for a showing, presented every afternoon for six weeks. (Today video transmits repeats of the parade.) They pulled out all stops, able now, with the end of restrictions, to present two hundred models per show and revelled in their growing international renown. Newspapers and magazines vaunted haute couture the world over as never before. Radio and express air post made it possible for reporters to send drawings and articles home overnight and thus meet earlier deadlines. French fashion was a force no woman could, or wanted to, resist. And if she wasn't able to buy in Paris, she was damned well going to look as if she could.

1953, Cristóbal Balenciaga. For a frock of Chantilly lace on silk taffeta, re-embroidered marquesses and marchionesses in rococo ribbon and silk thread with a soupçon of grey beads. One of François's earliest prides.

*F*everish with regained freedom and the New Look, the City of Light, ablaze anew, recovered its *joie de vivre*. Montmartre and Montparnasse dredged up all the folklore they could muster. Ballet companies were founded by rich patrons of the arts. Painters and sculptors came rushing back. Art galleries sprang up like mushrooms. Foreigners fought over Paris flats and Riviera villas. The prewar British and American residents wrested back their homes, which had been requisitioned by the Germans, and reorganized their little colonies. The French were hospitable to GIs who came over to study at the Sorbonne and the Beaux-Arts on the Bill of Rights, and some leading social figures gathered a coterie of fledgling writers, painters and musicians around them.

*T*hese leaders of society greatly added to the postwar glitter. They gave balls conceived like works of art for which the couturiers provided the stunning costumes. Then the couturiers too wracked their imaginations — and added to their overhead expenses — to give balls. The Chilean Marquis de Cuevas, snugly married to a granddaughter of John D. Rockefeller, gave magnificent parties both in Monte Carlo and in his Quai Voltaire apartment in Paris to publicize his ballets. The Comte de Beaumont, noted for his prewar parties, gave the Bal des Rois: Christian Dior came as a lion, king of animals. Christian Bérard gave a fancy dress affair, 'Panache', that was memorable for the glorious costumes, and the Bal des Oiseaux, an enchantment of feathered masks. Elsa Schiaparelli had a vividly coloured helium-filled balloon anchored in her garden for the Montgolfier party. Jacques Fath, having wanted to be an actor in his youth, loved dressing up. He gave some of the most lavish parties of the postwar period in his beautiful seventeenth-century castle near Paris. Each one had a theme: the square dance, Hollywood 1925, Brazil.

*W*ith the expanding international fame of individual couturiers the world over, a new social attitude towards them evolved. Gone were the days when a Madame de Rothschild could order Poiret, whom she considered to be just another one of her suppliers, to send his collection to her home for presentation. Now it became smart for a leading social figure to have at her dinner-party table a name couturier, milliner or hairdresser upon whom she

1952, Elsa Schiaparelli. Ocean theme. Scattered on a felt jacket, a crab of silk-thread wrapped metal strips, mat silk-thread and coloured rhinestones.

1954, Pierre Balmain. 'Jolie Madame' enters the Paris fashion scene. Embroidery of organdy flowers and white silk thread.

bestowed her patronage, and she was pleased in return to accept invitations to their receptions, which became more and more numerous and ostentatious as they tried to outdo one another in grabbing the limelight.

The day was to dawn when couturiers, following the lead of Lelong and Schiaparelli, would hire princesses and countesses to add a touch of class to their publicity. On the other hand, in their autocratic spheres they modified little their high-handed manner of keeping those who worked for them, the unsung heroes, in the shadows. Rare was the couturier self-assured, and big and generous, enough to feel that in acknowledging their help he was in no way diminishing his personal glory. In 1987 the programmes of the collections specified the suppliers of stockings and panty-hose, and the hairdressers, but never once the embroiderer. Be that as it may, you are holding in your hands proof that voices have at last been raised to sing the praise of one hitherto unsung hero.

By 1950 the postwar euphoria had subsided. Paris had calmed down; life was becoming more serious. For the majority of French people the anguish and vindictiveness of the Occupation had begun to slip into the past. They had accustomed themselves to the nuclear threat and the cold war: anyway, caught between the two Super Powers, what control did they have over either of them? Although the war in Indochina was present in the minds of all, it affected events in France little. The Reconstruction Programme supported by the Marshall Plan, which provided 45 million dollars' worth of aid for Europe, heralded developments which were soon to become familiar: a staggering materialization of new ways and means of living hinging around the decrease in distances, the increase in speed and the growing domination of science and technology. The Paris of 'Parlez-moi d'Amour' had become, like the Faubourg St Germain of Marcel Proust, a bucolic souvenir.

The shock of his father's death was only one of the many blows that François would receive upon resuming his life and work in Paris. Leaving Le Havre and driving across Normandy with his uncle, he at once found that, after the States, everything

A grand 'Monsieur' pays the first tribute to an unsung hero. 'For my dear Mr Lesage, who has throughout the years lent me his marvelous talent, also his precious assistance and his constant friendship - with my admiration and warmest affection...'

1952, Elsa Schiaparelli. A Chinese porcelain vase of 'cups' (concave sequins), spangles and gold silk-thread cord for a pocket.

1954, Jacques Fath. On white satin, branches of broom. Wrinkled organza, gold thread and silk-thread cord, silver blown-glass 'olivettes'. Colette Lesage drawing.

looked miniature — the houses, the trees, the fields, the roads, the motorcars. From Brobdingnag Gulliver had been propelled to Lilliput.

The difference between American and French mentalities also struck him. Generally speaking, Americans invested in youth, banking on the thrust it would bring to business activities. Moreover, in his field of hand embroidery American craftsmen, long removed by the war from the inspiration of French fashion, had extended a hearty welcome to this young colleague fresh from Paris. In contrast, the French tended to trust only middle-aged persons with, say, twenty-five years of experience. Several well-entrenched embroiderers were still active on the marketplace; Lesage et Cie's chief competitor, Rebé, was over forty years older than François. All of them would certainly take advantage of Albert's passing to try to grab his customers away from his presumably helpless widow and callow offspring. Happily, Marie-Louise proved to be dynamic and resourceful, and François gifted both as a designer and a businessman.

At rue Grange François was greeted warmly. He was, after all, the son and heir of a man whom the employees had loved and admired and, moreover, with his mother, the key to their future. Above and beyond that, many had known him as a little boy, all of them had observed his father training him when he had joined the company after receiving his baccalaureate, and, most important, they both liked and trusted him.

Still, Marie-Louise and he had to face his drawbacks. Though precocious, he had never designed a collection — in Los Angeles he had worked on the basis of samples sent by Albert. And no matter how knowledgeable he might be about the history of embroidery, he possessed no fashion culture. Visiting the couturiers with his father had not taught him much about their individual styles of designing and tastes in embroidery (Madame Schiaparelli was perhaps the exception). In Los Angeles and Hollywood he may have been a little prince who had written an article on French creativity and set up an embroidery business on Sunset Boulevard. But in Paris he was a mere twenty-year-old taking over his Papa's business with his *Maman* and capable only of lugging the suitcases when she went to

Winter 1950-1, Christian Dior. Silk-thread cord branches of chenille mimosas for a short white organdy frock.

display samples to their customers. This was brought home forcibly to him when one day he went by himself to see Jacques Fath, who was doing very well with the racy, youthful designs that pleased society women and had hit the headlines with his wedding dress and trousseau for Rita Hayworth's marriage to Prince Aly Khan. Fath always haggled over prices, and did not fail to do so upon this occasion. 'My mother,' said François, 'told me to tell you *that* was the price, to be taken or left.' Fath grew angry. 'I ought to slap your face!' François gazed at him sadly. 'You wouldn't have spoken like that to my father, Monsieur.' 'No,' replied Fath, 'and even less to

1950, Jacques Griffe. Schiaparelli influence. A surrealistic coffin with a loose handle to open a black wool suit pocket. Bulging silk-thread cord ('bigoudi'), steel 'nails' (beads) and wooden balls wrapped in steel thread.

your mother. Sorry.' And continued to haggle.

For several other customers, however, the young man had earned respect because of his trip to the States. This attitude was particularly true of Elsa Schiaparelli, who, now that her star was declining, had become more difficult than ever. Yet never was she cross with François, she even liked him. She could not bear stupid people — most for her were — and she found François intelligent as well as fine mannered, forthright (like herself) and attractive. For his part, he was amused by her shocking remarks and her accent in both English and French, and when he laughed so did she.

Marie-Louise, for all her beauty, elegance and charm, could be very authoritative and most realistic. She knew how to make her employees toe the line, and she kept a strict eye on the ledgers. In substituting for her husband until François was ready to replace both him and herself, she knew she was facing vicious competition. In 1940 Lesage had lost Vionnet. Schiaparelli still did four sumptuous collections a year, but how long could she continue? And the unpaid bills were mounting. Furthermore, in concentrating on the profitable transactions with Jean Barioz and the other Lyons manufacturers, Albert and she had not really kept promoting their embroidery interests, and the market remained depressed. They had added Jacques Heim, Maggy Rouff, Jean Déssès and Carven to their list of customers, but were troubled as well as saddened by the disappearance of many of the old guard: Lelong, Piguet, Callot, Agnès Drécoll, Marcelle Dormoy, Jeanne Lafaurie, Rochas and Marcelle Chaumont, who had designed for Madeleine Vionnet and opened her own house when her former employer closed. Also about to vanish from the scene were Worth, Germaine Lecomte, Mad Carpentier and Henry à la Pensée. Fortunately, Lanvin had closed its last embroidery atelier and turned to Lesage, while Nina Ricci occasionally placed orders. Louis Féraud and Guy Laroche were on the ascendant, but they did not require the services of Lesage. Dior might not be ordering as much from Rebé as before, but the old man was ready to go to almost criminal lengths to prevent the slightest business from being entrusted to Lesage. (Still, it was not long before Dior did turn to Lesage precisely because of the new youthful spirit emanating from François.) Rebé intrigued to lure away Fath, who nevertheless remained faithful — he had come to appreciate François greatly. But Rebé did not even try to influence Balenciaga, with whom Albert had begun to work during the Occupation: the Spaniard was intractable. As to Pierre Balmain, he simply loathed Rebé. To the old man's claim, 'I am the last embroiderer,' he retorted, 'No, just the utter end.'

In the article that he had written in Los Angeles for *Les Échos de l'Ouest* François had stated: 'The prime quality of the embroiderer resides in his intuition, for he has to sense the orientation of a fashion to come, preparing, as it were, the layette of an infant yet to be born. He has both to

1950, Robert Piguet. On brown velvet, vine leaves of gold lamé chiffons set in iridescent sequins and sprinkled with turquoise and garnet beads. Typical 'La Main' technique. One of the most striking samples in François's first collection. (See page 171).

Winter 1951-2, Marcelle Chaumont. For a black velvet corsage, baroque arabesques of real enamel cabochons with applications of wrinkled gold lamé and iridescent rhinestones.

anticipate a couturier's idea and follow it. In this duality, which may seem strange to you, is to be found the true embroiderer.' This was a judgement of some maturity, undoubtedly based on what he had heard from his father and mother, for to him it was only theoretical: he had yet to learn from experience and practice.

First, what were the basic essentials of his work as an embroiderer? A sample was not conceived as an isolated article; it had to be regarded as an element of a garment. An embroidery collection was not 'a kettle of minestrone', as François himself put it, full of this and that. Nor was an embroiderer 'a dog chasing helter-skelter after rabbits, pheasants, partridges and ducks at one and the same time.' Moreover, the individual designing characteristics and tastes of each customer had to be taken into consideration in order to be able to suggest to him where to place a piece of embroidery without seeming to impose the idea on him.

Second, how was he to learn about fashion? There was only one way: through fashion. He had never seen a show. Marie-Louise now took him along with her to all of them, and continued to do so year in and year out. Like the painter who had taught her as a young girl to 'see' what she was looking at, she now instructed her son how to scrutinize lines, cut, fit, forms, fabrics, colours. Lugging the suitcases for her, collection after collection, when she went to show their samples to the couturiers — who still considered them suppliers, had them use the service stairs and kept them waiting interminably in a stockroom — he observed the customers at close range, and through their collaboration with his mother he slowly came to grasp with her help the differences in their approaches.

At the outset mother and son took stock of the prevailing circumstances. In those early fifties young girls were still eager to look like Mummy. Balls and garden parties, tea dances and gala days at the races continued to be all the rage, and every débutante still longed at her coming-out party to descend the curving staircase of a lovely colonial mansion à la *Gone with the Wind* arrayed

1952, Jacques Fath. Bustier of white feathers protected by an invisible silk net sprinkled with rhinestones and transparent sequins. The skirt is of white silk satin.

1953, Jacques Fath. Branches of mimosa interpreted in twisted horsehair braid with tiny mother-of-pearl glass hand-painted in pink. For a long brown tulle evening gown.

Winter 1951-2, Jean Dessès. Detail of a huge white tulle gown embroidered with horsehair honesty as well as with silk-thread wrapped strips and rhinestones.

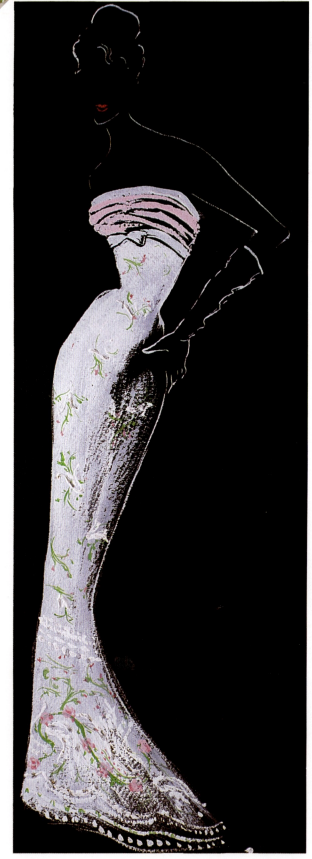

Summer 1956, Pierre Balmain. 'Capodimonte', a white satin evening sheath embroidered with eighteenth-century scrolls of bulging mat white silk-thread cord ('bigoudi'), tiny appliquéd silk petals and blown glass beads. Colette Lesage drawing.

in a ravishing Paris gown.

In general, however, young chicks no longer needed plumage to attract or resist, as the case might be, the male of the species. They had affirmed their equality sufficiently now to scorn the use of ruses and were determined to continue the fight head on. Dress expressed the uncertainties of the times, and by 1950, after only three years, the New Look was old hat. No Messiah of fashion was needed any more, and none would emerge, only magicians of style.

'**T**he Napoleon of Fashion', Christian Dior, had obviously not anticipated the roaring success of the first New Look collection, for only a year later, in February 1948, he brought out his Zigzag Line and a year after that his Trompe l'Œil Line. Soon, to maintain interest and spur sales, he launched new lines — stunning, beautiful, glamorous as they were — with bewildering rapidity: Vertical and Oblique Collections, 1950; Oval, Princess and *Longue* (Long) Lines, 1951; Sinuous (or Open Tulip) and Profile Lines, 1952; Cupola and *Vivante* (Lively) Lines, 1953; Lily-of-the-Valley Line, 1954. Then he let out the old New Look waist for a four-year era of looser fitting shapes: H-Line, autumn 1954; A-Line, spring 1955; A-Line inverted to Y-Line, autumn 1955; Arrow and *Aimant* (Magnet) Lines, 1956; *Libre* (Free) Collection officially announcing the freer forms; and *Fuseau* or Spindle Line, 1957. Here Dior suddenly died, and the culmination of all his dizzy-making changes came with the first collection, Trapeze, in February 1958, signed by his twenty-one-year-old assistant, Yves Saint Laurent, and rapturously received.

When Dior called in the Lesages, they had difficulty understanding one another because of Rebé's influence on the designer. Little by little, however, Dior was won over to François's youthful enthusiasm for stylized ornamentation and embroideries that were less showy than those he was accustomed to from the flashier older embroiderer. After a while, Marie-Louise felt she could (and should) leave François to deal with Dior alone. On summer fashion the two men collaborated most happily. The dresses were lighter and more to François's taste than the winter ones, for which Dior still wanted Rebé's superimpositions. A slowdown in haute couture occurred towards 1953, but Dior, already changing lines several times a year, opened up a vast new world market for the Lesage-embroidered summer dresses (to Rebé's fury) by publicizing them as worn by rich customers such as the Duchess of Windsor and the Begum Aga Khan on the Riviera. Yet ironically, when all is said and done, Dior perhaps learned more from François than François from Dior.

*J*acques Fath's star was not of the same magnitude as Dior's, but in the early fifties it nevertheless shone very brightly indeeed. Embroidery for embroidery's sake was not Fath's glass of champagne. He conceived of a piece functionally. From the moment an idea for a motif streaked into his mind, he took into account the placing of the sample on the garment for which he already intended it. This way of working made François also plan ahead with him the steps of an embroidery original.

*F*ath's mischievous, sexy and flirtatious clothes brought young women flocking, and he also managed to give older women a youthful appearance. He urged for younger colours at a time when brown and black were still *de rigueur*. He could not sew, did not know how to cut. In front of a mirror he would whirl huge swatches of woollen fabrics, silks and velvets about himself or wind the fabric around his lithe body. For him François had to learn to adapt embroidery to swirling movement. Fath could afford to be unusual. One summer he combined blue velvet and white organdy with the addition of 'seasoning', embroidered gold dots strewn here and there. For a costume to be worn by his wife Genevieve at one of his glorious balls he had François secure fresh asparagus between two nylon nets scattered with rhinestones. The

1953, Jean Déssès. Opaque bugles and iridescent blown glass 'soap bubbles' embroidering a tulle petal gown.

1958, Pierre Balmain. Detail. 'Paris', an evening gown of white organza sprinkled with silk roses, the petals secured by tiny silk thread.

1950, Jacques Fath. 'Fern'. On tulle, glass beads in pink 'camaieu' (shading within the range of a single colour).

• 99 •

Summer 1952, Hubert de Givenchy. Bustier of white piqué encrusted with blue faille and embroidered with pampille 'dingle-dangles' and transparent blue bugles.

Winter 1953-4, Hubert de Givenchy. Motif of real ermine tails, bulging silk-thread cord ('bigoudi'), rhinestones and silver silk-thread bullion ('canetille') mounted like a jewel on a black velvet gown.

gown had to be sprayed with water at regular intervals to keep the delicate foliage fresh. This seeming insanity was intended to publicize in advance the fern theme to be featured in the couturier's 1950 summer collection.

With Fath François learned a trick, 'contradictions', of which Madame Schiaparelli was a past-mistress: transform errors into surprises — a sleeve sewn on backwards, a skirt being removed above the head and stuck at the breasts, a gown put on back to front. His shortlived pinnacle, from 1952 to 1954, was marked by enlarged forms — what were then called bodices (now properly, bustiers, the French word) featuring strapless bras, two-piece blouses and skirts. He featured this style, as enhanced by his typical raciness and freshness and modelled by Bettina and Lucky, in his final, winter, collection shown in August 1954. It was to lead to the explosion of Brigitte Bardot in her bustier dress with red flounces in Roger Vadim's *Et Dieu Créa la Femme* (1956).

In collaborating with Jean Déssès, François learned a great deal about classical sculpture. For his Greek and Egyptian clientele Déssès, a Greek from Alexandria, made draperies designed on ancient Greek and Roman lines. His clothes recalled those of Madame Grès, formerly known as Alix, but, as Marie-Louise pointed out to her son, they were sexier than hers. With Déssès François also deepened his knowledge of the grand uses of ombré for embroidery, sometimes intended to match shaded fur coats, and the utilisation of glass soap bubbles.

Jacques Griffe represented a follow-up to Madeleine Vionnet, whom François knew only through his parents. Griffe draped, sometimes cut on the bias and closely related fabrics to the body, sprinkling embroidery lightly all over a gown.

François was to work little with Pierre Cardin, who had opened his house after gaining experience as a cutter at Paquin, Schiaparelli and Dior. However, the embroiderer followed with interest the couturier's experiments in new techniques until in 1957 Cardin was recognized by the wide feminine public for his architectural dressmaking. Two years later Cardin proved his genius in business by bringing out a *prêt-à-porter* line. No big fashion name had ever put a label on ready-to-wear, and the Chambre Syndicale de la Haute Couture struck him from their lists.

On returning from the States after the war, Elsa Schiaparelli had resumed her use of themes, for which she once again depended on Albert Lesage. After his death, she saw no reason not to continue her policy with Marie-Louise, a good personal customer, and François, who had been accustomed to her ways since he was a young boy. This put the idea of developing themes for embroidery collections into his mind. With her he also became involved in the search for unusual, unexpected and amusing effects and objects.

In contrast to Schiaparelli's shocking colours, Pierre Balmain favoured quiet eighteenth-century tones — gold and cream, beige or tan and mother-of-pearl, blue and beige, pink and grey, pale green and pale yellow. For Balmain a dress was no longer to be merely decorative and functional but to become again in its own right an object of beauty, grace and delicacy. If his daytime frocks were very simple, the evening dresses and ball gowns — 'Oriane', 'Paris', 'Coromondel', 'Zaire', 'Versailles' — were royally embroidered.

Balmain's designs incorporated not only the baroque arabesques but many other eighteenth-century motifs. In embroidery this finally led François to his designs for *'Jolie Madame'*. In 1954 Jacques Fath died, Schiaparelli closed and Chanel

Summer 1952, Pierre Balmain. 'Zaire', so named after the heroine of a Voltaire tragedy. A short white silk satin evening gown embroidered with rococo ribbons and blown beads over shaded (ombré) hammered silver spangles. Colette Lesage drawing.

Perfumes hauled their septuagenarian originator out of reclusion. The same year Balmain sent Praline out on his runway to present *'Jolie Madame'*, destined to last five ravishing years. Prophetically, that year too Balmain executed the coat design that had won the annual top prize offered by the International Wool Secretariat. It had been submitted by a brilliant young newcomer, Hamburg-born Karl Lagerfeld, whom Balmain then hired.

Cristóbal Balenciaga did not concern himself with young — or rather, unmarried — women. His designing was rooted in an age-old, patrician Catholic society composed of a privileged few. His monumental, architectural structures were more important than the bodies which they enveloped. A collection was characterized by several themes and marked by a use of elements specific to them but treated in various original ways. Here again François's inventive spirit was fired with the idea of developing basic themes in his embroidery collections. Reminiscent of Schiaparelli's theatricality, Balenciaga's dramatic quality attracted François. True to his origins, the

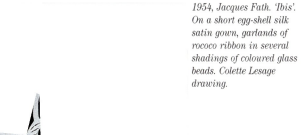

1954, Jacques Fath. 'Ibis'. On a short egg-shell silk satin gown, garlands of rococo ribbon in several shadings of coloured glass beads. Colette Lesage drawing.

1952, Elsa Schiaparelli. Détail. A watermelon of green felt, Shocking pink organza and jet seeds — motif for the skirt of a short evening gown.

Spaniard loved black — red and black, pink and black, black on black, contrasting colours on a black ground, black jet, black pampilles. He applied them with particular success to his boleros and tight velvet jackets recalling a matador's suit. Through him François learned how to use Chantilly lace in embroidery and apply it to satin, to do baroque edgings, and to design pieces that resembled Cordoba leather. Also through Balenciaga he became aware of the new uses of plastic, notably mixing black strips with black chenille, and for him introduced rhodoid into haute couture. Preceded by rhodia, an early artificial fibre made of acetate, rhodoid was a thermoplastic with a cellulose acetate base, analogous to celluloid. François followed up with rhodoid motifs of cabochons, triangles in relief and *pastilles* (pellets) enclosed by a chiffon made of cigalene, a crinkled nylon gauze which soon became all the rage.

1951. Elsa Schiaparelli models a Shocking pink velvet beret embroidered with hammered gold-plated strips, iridescent glass 'soap bubbles' and pampille 'dingle-dangles'.

Balenciaga considered Hubert de Givenchy to be his heir. This young man had opened his house in 1952 and called in Marie-Louise from the moment he started preparing his first collection. He had become familiar with Albert when working for Lelong, Piguet and Fath, and had met François when, just after Albert's death, he was Madame Schiaparelli's assistant and designing for her famous boutique. Only naturally, at the beginning of his career Givenchy was influenced by the Italian designer's style and personality, and François followed his development as he removed himself from that influence in favour of Balenciaga's.

From 1953 onwards François introduced new uses of materials: rococo ribbons, straw paillettes, hammered sequins, exquisite silk flower petals obtained from the renowned Judith Barbier. As various couturiers ordered them, a certain unity in their creations developed along with François' themes.

At once floral motifs could be seen reflected concurrently in the work of two designers. Balenciaga did a lace representing a *toile de Jouy* with human figures embroidered in rococo ribbon and embellished by little jewels and concave sequins. The embroidery for 'Jolie Madame' proceeded from the same technique, but in the eighteenth-century waistcoat design dear to Balmain's heart.

Jacques Fath was the couturier who most quickly came to trust François for themes. For Fath's bustier dresses the young embroiderer conceived motifs that would be in keeping with the upper part of the bustier and, instead of producing mere samples without any finishing touches, suggested their positioning as completed pieces, an initiative which delighted the couturier.

François's somewhat stylized

Winter 1954-5, Pierre Balmain. 'Oriane', an evening sheath in two hues of egg-shell satin and appliquéd brown taffeta embroidered with gold silk thread, brown chenille and real mother-of-pearl 'snails'.

• 102 •

Winter 1955-6, Pierre Balmain. 'Coromandel', so-named to recall eighteenth century Chinese lacquered panels. An egg-shell silk satin corsage embroidered with gold silk thread, machine-diapered chenille, bulging silk-thread cord ('bigoudi') and rhinestones. Typical of Mr Balmain's taste for the baroque. Colette Lesage drawing.

Summer 1956, Pierre Balmain. 'Jolie Madame'. For a pale pink silk organza corsage, embroidery inspired by eighteenth-century waistcoat motifs: shaded rococo ribbons, wrinkled taffeta leaves and, here and there, a touch of glass beads to catch the light.

method of drawing motifs also found approval with Fath, who adopted it for his short skirts. This was François's first real contribution to a couturier's way of working.

François early discovered that Fath was a great lover of bushes and trees and mirrored the pleasure that the couturier derived from branches and leaves through the presentation of motifs in horsehair braid for his summer collection in 1953. The year before, he had already supplied the same material to Jean Déssès in the form of shells.

François enjoyed Fath's penchant for fresh floral embroidery motifs for the summer and these were also adopted by Dior and by Balmain, who for that season even gave up his decorative designs in favour of them. With Balmain the flower theme reached a kind of peak in the 1958 summer collection with the world-famous 'Paris' and its rose. On the other hand, for the winter François kept in mind Balmain's undiminished liking for Louis XIV and Louis XV motifs.

At the end of the fifties the apprenticeship period was over. ('It is never over,' claims François.) Thenceforward the further François would go, the more he would stress style of drawing and colouring and shading of motifs rather than rely on the effects to be obtained by his materials. Herein he was following the precepts of his parents and perfecting what was soon to become the Lesage touch.

Winter 1959-60, Cristóbal Balenciaga gowns Princess Grace of Monaco in a bolero of black tulle and appliquéd turquoise chiffon grape-vine leaves embroidered with chenille, silk thread and transparent pink blown beads.

Summer 1950, Cristóbal Balenciaga. Detail. Stylized flowers of silk-thread, wrapped and hammeved metal strips and fancy plastic motifs to embroider a black satin evening gown. An early appearance of plastic in Paris fashion and another one of the most striking examples in François's first collection. (See p. 146).

14 · YOUTH · WILL · OUT : THE · SIXTIES

A demographic evolution in the Western World that had risen upon the heels of the Second World War accounted for an upheaval at the beginning of the sixties that was to have a great effect on fashion: the baby-boom. Compared with the period between the two wars, births had doubled.

Generally speaking, the youngsters had easy access to money and its amenities, more and more were enrolling in universities, possessed far greater knowledge of the ways of the world than their parents at their age, rejected Marlon for Jimmy and Elvis and took to soft drugs.

The youth movement originated in the United States. Here the adolescents had scarcely been affected by the war or by the nuclear threat of the cold war, which, to all intents and purposes, ended when in late 1962 Khrushchev backed down before President Kennedy's plans to invade Cuba.

Exhibitionism and violence are two sides of the same medallion. The former aims to cause a scandal, the latter to injure. Exhibitionism set the tone for the styles to reach a paroxysm in the sixties. The period was one of creative anarchy. The 'youth-quake' (Diana Vreeland's expression) would — in dress — result in two groups: the freak and the glamorous lady.

Various influences led to the great changes in clothing. At the dawn of the sixties, first, all over the world expensive traditional costumes began to give way to occidental-type dress, whence a huge new, and much less costly, market for mass production. Second, many young people adopted these costumes in the Western hemisphere to manifest their solidarity with the Third World. Third, communications were constantly being improved and expanded: colourfully illustrated magazines, motion pictures, television. Finally, ready-to-wear was being greatly improved.

For the first time in history young people asserted themselves as a class apart, with their own manners and tastes. Naturally, they expressed these in dress, arraying themselves in clothes meant to illustrate their burgeoning strength, what they were interested in, and the roles in society that they intended to assume.

Duly, they put on any garment they could find, especially antique. Never, in Paris, had such crowds streamed to the Flea Market. Adding

1956, Hubert de Givenchy. Audrey Hepburn in a bustier embroidered with transparent chalk-white beads.

daring to defiance, they resorted to body paint, masses of jewellery and elaborate hairdos incorporating wigs and hairpieces. The Beat Generation in American universities adopted the accoutrement of the lowliest classes: jeans, tieless shirts, leather jackets. They were followed first by the non-violent, community-minded, LSD-addicted hippies, who rejected all urban influence, and then by the charming marijuana-smoking flower children, all for love, beauty and peace and ready to go to any lengths to avoid becoming involved in the Vietnam war.

Emulators quickly took up the crusade in Europe, but with a basic difference: the beatniks on motorcycles wearing helmets and decorated jackets over jersey T-shirts came mainly from the lower classes but were not rebelling against society, merely flouting convention in order to prove their own identity and assert their right to be considered as equals of other, more 'accepted' groups of their own age. Paris haute couture was to take inspiration from the street, particularly through *Monsieur* Yves Saint Laurent.

A new attitude on the part of clothes-conscious

women also influenced the change. During the past few years the rich, frivolous débutante, thinking only of the gowns she would wear to balls, dances and parties, had matured. She had become a married jet-setter taking into account — as Elsa Schiaparelli had foreseen — the weight allowance on her luggage and reasoning that each season the same dresses would be suitable in New York and London as well as in Paris. Since it was no longer smart to be idly rich, this newly responsible woman offered her services to non-profit-making enterprises. She could no longer put up with unending hours of fitting clothes and would not pay the astronomical prices that rising labour and fabric costs were forcing Paris designers to demand. Moreover, younger women had long begun to withdraw from French fashion through bewilderment with Dior's twice-yearly changes of lines; and, as the sixties progressed, they found inappropriate the elegant haute couture look embodied by Balenciaga, Givenchy, Cardin, Lanvin, Ricci, Patou, Laroche and Balmain.

1963, Hubert de Givenchy. Audrey Hepburn wearing a silk shantung organza corsage edged with an embroidered jumble of mother-of-pearls and crystals as well as motifs of small plastic rings to fill in the background.

All of a sudden, early in the sixties, mothers who still bought Paris or Paris-inspired clothes scrutinized their daughters, then examined themselves in a long mirror. What a shock! They looked over-fastidious, even a bit precious. In a historical turnabout, they now wanted to look like their offspring. After all, had not Marlene Dietrich added twenty years to a woman's desirability by pointing out that she was a grandmother? And what about all those 'maturing' former Hollywood stars who, thanks to face-lifting, were making a comeback on television looking as they had in the thirties and forties?

The desire of older women to recapture the sweet bird of youth through clothes gave rise to a conflict that influenced further the already shifting scene. On the one hand, the sloppy youth-inspired styles were not compatible with the high-quality fabrics and finish of French couturier made-to-order garments. On the other hand, for women with money and fine taste used to well-cut and well-fitted garments in excellent fabrics ready-to-wear was unacceptable, even if reproduced by the couturiers in their boutiques.

There was yet another influence. Women were questioning the hitherto basic suppositions about their place in society more strongly than ever before. Though troubled as to what new standards would emerge from the changing conditions, they did not lose confidence in their age-old charm and femininity. Because of the chic life-style that they and their well-groomed gentlemen maintained, they came to be known as the 'beautiful people'. The top models of the time were Veruschka, Marisa Berenson, Twiggy and Jean Shrimpton. The Sixties Lady was embodied by Jacqueline Kennedy: thick bouffant hairdo, bateau necklines, sleeveless narrow-skirted dresses, shoes with square toes and heels reduced from the preceding stiletto heights, lovely evening dresses often from Paris. Mrs Kennedy was young, pretty, modish and intelligent. She lived through historical moments as no modern women in the public eye had ever done, with courage, dignity and elegance. In standing her ground, she had a profound effect on women zealous of their independence and conscious of what they were wearing. So did the lovely Audrey Hepburn, who influenced an entire generation dressed entrancingly in both her films and in real life by Hubert de Givenchy.

Lesage et Cie. Packets of beads.

In 1962, four years after Charles de Gaulle had been restored to power, the French and Algerians put an end to their prolonged war. Metropolitan France had not perhaps been directly affected too much by the tumult, but fashion had kept a low profile in regard to embroidery, mirror of opulence and glory. That year, in response to the need for a youthful renewal, a new race of young ready-to-wear designers surged forth. Their movement was based on a desire to compete with the couturiers' 'Boutique Collections' (and associated de luxe articles), a watered down adaptation of their big twice-yearly collections, and the *prêt-à-porter* they had been developing since Cardin's revolutionary

Winter 1959-60, Pierre Balmain. The famous Balmain Thai rose, entirely embroidered: opaque glass turquoises and garnets, gold braid and gold-plated strips - all in relief.

introduction of it into Paris fashion. These ready-to-wear newcomers came to be known as *stylistes* in contrast to the *modélistes*, the junior designers in the couturiers' studios. Emmanuele Khanh (a former Balenciaga mannequin), Gérard Pipart (later to be grabbed up by Nina Ricci as senior designer without any haute couture experience), Daniel Hechter, Chantal Thomass, Marie-Martine, Cacharel, Celine, Dorothée Bis, Elie and particularly Sonia Rykiel and Karl Lagerfeld — these *stylistes* tramped about the streets looking for inspiration. They came roaring on to the scene with bowlers, culotte skirts, T-shirts, knickerbockers and battle jackets, opening boutiques as fast as they could, preferably in the environs of St Germain-des-Prés.

It would take the couturiers about five years to recover from the shock of the *stylistes*, add some piquancy to their own *prêt-à-porter* through well-made clothes based on sportswear and the separates idea as well as through a revitalized adaptation of their haute couture lines, and assert anew their competitiveness.

With the advent of the sixties, François Lesage began increasingly to impose himself on haute couture. His designs were now less scholarly, freer, more imaginative and flexible. Nevertheless, his style of well-balanced, high quality drawing remained basic to his concepts. In his words:

> The art of traditional embroidery consists of employing the same techniques and the same classical materials for the various styles of drawing.
> The very essence of embroidery for haute couture is to associate techniques and materials that we are not used to seeing combined.
> That is the secret of creating.
> New textiles cannot be developed by weaving wool on silk looms, or silk on wool looms.
> Embroidery is renewed by introducing all kinds of elements that are not predestined for embroidery. Feathers, furs, shells, leather, wool meshes, rock crystals: they can all be integrated now. Our sequins, instead of being positioned one by one, can be pushed into place in packets. To obtain reliefs, bugle beads can be arranged so as to lend depth...
> What matters is creating a new and always unexpected effect and carrying it out perfectly.
> Unlike a machine, the hand knows no limits.
> While keeping in mind the great French traditions,

Winter 1960-1, Cristóbal Balenciaga. Gardens of chenille roses adorn: left, a suit jacket; right, a frock in black satin shantung organza.

Winter 1961-2. Cristóbal Balenciaga announces the 'official' arrival of plastic embroidery in Paris fashion. For a pink faille evening coat, hand-cut plastic sheets and pink rhinestones, stitching of pink silk thread and pink chenille.

Summer 1961, Cristóbal Balenciaga. François Lesage recalls an eighteenth-century brocade drawing style for flower motifs of silk thread and real straw chenille, dyed. On yellow faille.

François now introduced new interpretations of drawing styles. They were often lighter than his previous work, largely thanks to the use of silk, particularly for the summer, with echoes of painted wallpaper and sophisticated country scenes, applications of chiffon on tulle, cotton organdy embroidered with point lace and mat gold, new fabrics such as the organza satin shantung favoured by Balenciaga, an effect of weaving through a play of materials, the mingling of silk thread with straw or cellophane chenille, delicate arabesques giving the impression that François had designed them with a fine gold- or silver-tipped brush.

*I*n the early years of the sixties, marked by the start of Balenciaga's absolutism as supported by Givenchy, couturiers were still designing the New Look, close-fitting bustiers and crinoline-like skirts. But a revival of the Empire line, looser with the waist higher, was setting in, as was the use of the new 'spring' fabrics, which were... springy.

*T*he showings of winter models in August 1961 denoted a shift in François's ideas : he now sometimes played down the drawing styles and placed a heavier accent on materials. He filled in backgrounds with bugle beads (called 'bugles') and into them incorporated floral motifs to create 'chain' effects, for example. He began positioning his materials on tulle or crêpe so as to produce a likeness of an opaque print. When Balenciaga requested him to combine plastics with other materials for evening wear, he felt encouraged in his belief that he could increasingly produce different and exciting effects by using his materials in new ways — gelatine; true straw annexed by Balmain, sometimes in the form of rings; rhodoid which, following Balenciaga's lead, Givenchy employed to imitate Venetian blinds; beetle wings; cabochons in mosaics (Givenchy); cellophane braid and sequins (Balenciaga); the

Summer 1961, Cristóbal Balenciaga. Stylized branches and floral motifs of mat silk thread, dyed cut guipure and rhinestones for a long evening gown in shantung organza satin.

addition of feathers encased in protective tulle. The colour of the moment was 'lophophore', a word having no relation to its usual meaning, an iridescent or gleaming combination of blue and green not altogether turquoise.

It was obvious now that embroidery could no longer be a simple adornment. It had to be integrated into a garment, somewhat as it had for Madeleine Vionnet, but subject to a new imperative: the fabric was stiff.

With the short passage of years, Balenciaga remained faithful to his tulles embroidered to recall the capes of Spanish madonnas. Chez Balmain '*Jolie Madame*', which had gone out of vogue in 1959 after five years in its original shape, traded some of its opulence for a less ostentatious, more refined luxury. Givenchy had a passion for the unusual, especially the Balenciaga-inspired boleros that could be worn over an embroidered gown and the enormous stoles over a bolero that replaced the ubiquitous and boring mink coat. It was all extremely sumptuous.

At the time Lesage et Cie's principal customers were Balenciaga, Givenchy and Balmain, now and then Lanvin, very occasionally Madame Grès and '*Monsieur*' Yves Saint Laurent rising. Towards 1964 Dior joined the ranks more and more. Rebé was now very old and about to retire in 1966. François's star was not only on the ascendant, it was seering the firmament. Boldly, he renewed Michonet's theatricality but in a less complicated manner and always mindful of the need both to maintain quality and to respect his customers' individual tastes. New effects sprang from backgrounds filled in with fanciful sequins, little

Winter 1967-8, Grès. Two-coloured suede cut out with stamped flowers of tiny gold-plated strips and topaz and turquoise beads.

Winter 1960-1, Pierre Balmain. A corsage of brown faille with blue chiffon applications adorned with silk-thread stitching and tiny topaz mirrors.

flowers, clover leaves, stars, plastic squares, cabochons, Scottish plaids, and plastic feathers.

Nevertheless, it has to be said that the sixties, with certain exceptions, were not wildly exciting years in French haute couture — nor, thus, in embroidery. With fashion's indubitable decline, fewer departures were to be noted. Forcibly, the old guard was practically extinct. Grès continued imperturbably to design her exquisite Grecian robes, and dear old Chanel was still pottering about, but Jean Déssès had gone and Jacques Heim was soon to follow him. In like manner, there were relatively fewer arrivals. At Dior Marc Bohan had succeeded Yves Saint Laurent, who opened his own house in 1962, the year young

Jean-Louis Scherrer also inaugurated his in the discreet, elegant manner that would always distinguish him. Philippe Venet also opened in 1962. In 1963 Jules-François Crahay moved to Lanvin after several years with Nina Ricci, where he had enchanted Paris in 1961 with his *Les Années Folles* collection. With brio Michel Goma — following Bohan, Pipart and Lagerfeld — took over Patou, a Lesage customer since the closing of its embroidery ateliers.

There were, however, some events that riveted the attention. They were devised by avant-garde haute couture designers who came forth to bulwark the youth-quake. While the most startling of these did not employ hand embroidery either because they lacked the money to do so or because their styles denied it, they cannot be ignored in a view of Paris fashion of the times.

Pierre Cardin came into his own with his structural garments for women when they were promoted by marvellous Jeanne Moreau. He also reflected non-objective Op (optical) Art and Science Fiction. (In a few years other art movements — colour field and minimalism — would become manifest in Paris avant-garde fashion as well.) Especially, Cardin designed clothes anticipating space-age travel, which had been opened up in 1957 by the accomplishments of the Soviet Union's Sputnik.

Paco Rabanne, a great innovator of materials, erupted in 1963 with armoured dresses of overlapping hammered metal plates worn over a body stocking enhanced by embroidery without any ground and embellished with crystal beads, cellophane pellets, Rhine pebbles, ostrich feathers, buttons and bits of plastic and celluloid. His designs made of more ordinary textiles were often trimmed with metallic embroidery. In his 'metallicism' Paco Rabanne was followed by Pierre Cardin, Issey Miyake and Thierry Mugler.

André Courrèges exploded in 1964. He stood for health : sun and sea and sky, tennis, swimming, golf, gym. Trained as a civil engineer, he spent eleven years learning to sew, fit and draw with the master, Balenciaga. In 1961 he opened his own house where, soon known as Le Corbusier of Fashion, in 1964-5 he brought modernism to its limits in haute couture. (At the time Orwell's *1984* was still far distant.) Five years before the first astronauts landed on the moon, Courrèges presented fitted, sculptural space-age models stripped to a streamline construction. In them the young and carefree could run and jump and show their tanned legs in miniskirts, their tanned arms freed of sleeves, their midriffs bared below unencumbered breasts and their backs nude. They skipped about in metal bikinis, rainbow-hued wigs, space hats, goggles, little square-toed boots worn over short white socks, and short white gloves. Courrèges's trousers denounced traditional

Summer 1966, Pierre Balmain. Real straw cut outs in relief serve as motifs to embroider a corsage along with coral beads and rhinestones.

Summer 1966, Hubert de Givenchy. Inspired by Venetian blinds, this embroidery is composed of plastic bands in two colours, guipure braid and opaque pink rhinestones.

Summer 1967, Cristóbal Balenciaga. Typical sixties sheath of rhodoid feathers on a ground of pear-shaped sequins and mother-of-pearl beads designed to lend relief and movement in a pink ombré (shading).

Winter 1963-4, Hubert de Givenchy. Detail of a corsage embroidered like a painter's palette with ostrich feathers, coloured rhinestones and coloured beads. The edging is finished with multi-coloured ostrich-feather fringe.

masculine forms. Narrow, they were cut erotically low at the waist and, under boleros or square-cut tunics, were meant to be worn anywhere at any time of the day or night.

Emanuel Ungaro, who had replaced Courrèges in Balenciaga's studio, came to him for several seasons, until in 1965 opening his own house. Along with Cardin and Courrèges, he reflected Sputnik, robot and world-of-tomorrow looks, while also bringing strongly coloured eroticism into women's lives. Then he eschewed topicality to offer constantly simple, sprightly, youthful clothes that reflected him — enthusiastic, sincere and happy.

Which, at last, bring us to Yves Saint Laurent. Accustomed as we are to thinking of *Monsieur* Yves as the ultimate defender of what is the nec plus ultra of elegance, taste and refinement, we may forget that — not twenty-five at the dawn of the sixties — he perfectly understood youth and, in anticipating and then mirroring its needs, broke many age-old rules to introduce his own youthful spirit into haute couture. While still with Dior, he had introduced motorcycle jackets in alligator, mink coats with sweater sleeves, turtleneck collars under finely cut suits. As he said later, 'Those street inspirations all seemed very inelegant to a lot of people sitting on the gilt chairs of a couture salon... Social structures were breaking up. The street had a new pride, its own chic, and I found the street inspiring, as I would often again. We must never confuse elegance with snobbery.'

It was in 1962, having just opened his own house, that YSL started bringing out his first fun clothes: the Cowboy Look, the Sailor Look, stylized beatnik numbers, the British Mods and Rockers Look, the Gypsy, Rich Hippie and Robin Hood styles. His checkerboard dresses of 1965 were reminiscent of Mondrian, who viewed everything as square blocks. In 1966 *Monsieur* Yves introduced Pop Art into Paris fashion. He sent leather out on the runway as never before in haute couture, made brass studs for jackets smarter than emeralds and boots a fashion necessity. YSL never used embroidery simply to adorn. He took inspiration from it, and his liking for the exotic found expression in it, despite his knowing that its opulence had little place in the harsh light of the street and everyday life.

Yves Saint Laurent was the first designer to realize how fully women had been liberated and how deeply they knew it. He understood that individually and collectively they had come to feel more important than the clothes they wore. He perceived that women no longer needed garments in which they felt inviolable, or as instruments to entice men and arms to fight them. In 1966 he introduced an adaptation of a man's tailored dinner jacket, in 1967 his trouser suit with a gangster look, and finally the first 'uniform' to be adopted far and wide since the Chanel suit — the trouser suit. Indeed, to support older women as well as the young in their increasing determination to exercise responsibilities on the same level as men, he encouraged them to adopt trousers, that symbol of masculine authority introduced so sexily by Courrèges. YSL's trousers, without any trickery, were ultimately more durable. He designed them to be worn with tailored jackets, blouses, sweaters and tunics. After 1965 more trousers were manufactured for women than skirts — three million pairs were sold in France by ready-to-wear interests in 1971 alone. Delighted by the ease that trousers lent to movement, women took increasingly to masculine attire, which had scarcely changed over a century, as adapted and promoted by *Monsieur* Yves Saint Laurent.

Summer 1964, Lanvin (Jules-François Crahay). 'Teheran'. For a corsage, a rhodoid imitation of lophophore (beetle) wings coloured with transparent yellow beads and fancy iridescent rhinestones.

Summer 1967, Jean Patou (Michel Goma). Various geometrical orange rhodoid motifs placed in strips on a chalk-white sequin background.

Summer 1970, Christian Dior (Marc Bohan). Detail. A sheath entirely embroidered with various applications of coloured organza, multi-coloured glass, coloured beads and fancy gold sequin flowers.

15 · MAY · 1968 · AND · MONSIEUR YVES · THE · EARLY · SEVENTIES

The crisis that exploded in Paris in the torrid May of 1968 originated in the tide of discontent swelling in the ranks of students. Most of these, like the youngsters from the labour class who joined them, had been born four or five years after the end of the Occupation. The unions and Leftist groups came surging forward to stand at their sides behind the hastily erected barricades in the Latin Quarter and to defy the police with projectiles and grenades. Strikes were declared everywhere, transportation broke down, deliveries of food to the capital became hazardous, public buildings were occupied and besmirched, the country verged on paralysis.

Haute couture was not spared. In that month of May, Dior recorded a sixty-nine per cent drop in business. As to Balenciaga, the last — save Chanel and Grès — of the old guard, at seventy-three he knew he would not be able to cope with the swirling currents that were certain to transform the desires of the modern affluent society. When late in 1969 Charles de Gaulle withdrew as the head of the French Government and Cristóbal Balenciaga retired from fashion, an old world came to an end, a new one was born.

Balenciaga's departure dealt a blow to the activity of all the adorners, but particularly to Lesage et Cie, which had largely geared its collections towards the Spaniard's tastes. Fortunately, in Balmain and Givenchy, François still had strong supporters, and he was gradually able to work more with Marc Bohan chez Dior, steadily rising Jean-Louis Scherrer, Michel Goma (Patou) and Jules-François Crahay at Lanvin. Too, *Monsieur* Yves Saint Laurent, striding across the throne room now, initiated a deepening phase of his collaboration with François by asking for special themes: motifs of barbaric jewels embroidered on short leather tunics.

Summer 1969, Hubert de Givenchy. A pair of sleeves inspired by a thorn bush. Detail. A jumble of tightly twisted drake feathers and coloured rhinestones.

· 115 ·

Summer 1969, Jean Patou (Michel Goma). 'Joy', a 'mini' named for the famous Patou perfume and celebrating the moon landings in advance... Detail. Rhinestones and opaque and transparent rhodoid, cabochons dyed pink.

Summer 1971-2, Jean Patou (Michel Goma). Detail of a 'mini' with tapestry-like 'point de Hongrie' of spangles underlined by black sequins.

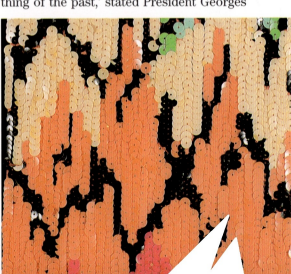

The effects of May 1968 persisted. Gala soirées and charity balls disappeared. Sumptuous gowns were no longer in demand. François refined his motifs to produce more discreet effects, such as silk-fringed gowns adorned with stones rather than jewels. For Dior (Bohan) he adapted painted wallpaper designs, somewhat, though in reverse, as his father had used embroidery motifs for the textile designs he had tried to sell during the Depression. Still, to relieve the gloom with a little gaiety, he gradually phased out the backgrounds filled in with a jumble of materials, introducing stylized flower motifs and thus, with a little bow to *La Garçonne*, reviving the carefree spirit of the years 1925-9. The grounds were of chiffon, with the embroidery — sweet peas, poppies, apple-tree branches — adapted to the renewed *robe-chemise* trend, itself a development and modification of the straight, short dresses persisting from Courrèges. As led by *Monsieur* Yves, all the couturiers took up the revival: pointillism à la Pissarro in art deco motifs for Dior (Bohan) and Givenchy, painters' palettes for Patou (Goma).

Inspired by the recent moon landings, François explored the possibilities of lunar motifs. Again borrowing from textiles, he used a style of drawing which interpreted warp and woof, generally of geometric motifs: squares, bands, patchwork, houndstooth check and '*berlingots*', an opaque background of one colour striped with another opaque colour, inspired by humbug sweets.

'The France of high fashion and champagne is a thing of the past,' stated President Georges Pompidou as the seventies rose above the clouded horizon. 'The France of Concorde and nuclear power plants is replacing it.' Happily, he was not altogether right, but it took several years to prove that he had been somewhat wrong.

During the sixties modern culture had advanced with giant steps in the direction of dehumanization. People had begun to forget what emotions were. Would they ever remember, or learn all over again? On both sides of the Atlantic the year 1968 marked the culminating point in the destruction of modern society as it had been. The very pillars were undermined. Parents — permissive, otherwise occupied — did not bring children up the same way any more. Indeed, they no longer

wanted to be parents, but rather pals, very often divorced, who sought to be understood and supported by their children rather than offering them understanding and protection. Young people lacked the old values of respect, honour and honesty to prepare them for life as it was going to have to be lived. The teenage years of this seventies generation would become notorious for hard drugs, sexual promiscuity, desertion of families and churches, muggings, theft and suicides. Love, the gift of oneself — what was that? Did anyone have anything to give? If so, who wanted it? Violence was de rigueur.

The outlook on life in the early seventies was sober. The mood in Europe as well as in the

Winter 1969-70, Hubert de Givenchy. A 'maxi' with open-work stitch (fagoting) of pink mother-of-pearl and rhinestones with marabou pompoms.

Winter 1969-70, Yves Saint Laurent. For a suede tunic, a Merovingian-inspired necklace of baroque mother-of-pearl, rustic coral blown beads ('pebbles'), emerald rhinestones, and filigree of gold thread as in medieval techniques.

Summer 1972. 'Monsieur Yves' butterfly. Schiaparelli drawing style. Of mat metallic sequins for a yellow georgette crepe blouse. The butterfly's shadow is cast by gold sequins and silk thread.

Details of necklace top of the page.

States (the dollar had been devalued in 1969 and again in 1971) was more realistic than during the sixties, no longer propitious to dreaming, exhibitionism and anarchy. The fantasy fashion of the preceding decade evaporated, rendered outmoded by harsh economic facts. Styles became more practical, easier to wear and less extravagant. Indeed, they reflected a levelling-off process of which the theme was democratic uniformity as supported by the anti-fashion Women's Lib and evinced by the blue denim look that bridged generation gaps and classes, as well as racial and monetary barriers.

In the sixties art movements had come and gone. In the seventies art stagnated. This decade marked the end of avant-garde, and without avant-garde nothing is new, no matter how preposterous. For want of reaction, no action. In short, the dynamic of modernism was giving way to a communications culture in which appearance and credibility were replacing substance and truth. Modernism, as a movement, started turning into a historical period like the Renaissance, Romanticism, Impressionism.

The age of plastics materialized with the early seventies. As this period was grounded in the youngsters' lack of a sense of permanence about what society was producing by way of material goods, they were fascinated with what plastic objects could do for them in their lives. Everything had become expendable. If you broke a plastic article, you just threw it away without any of the regret and remorse your mother or father would have felt for, say, china. The young people also went in for outrageous psychedelic colours — orange, purple, red and green — to set themselves apart as a new generation. 'We are young, daring and courageous,' was their message.

Of the styles that started on the street at this time, predominant was the embroidering, befeathering, befurring and beading of blue denim. The idea was to reflect American and Asian Indians rather than the Victorian Lady, nobility or débutantes. These modes did not mount into the august climes of the haute couture houses, perhaps only because they were so transient. Indeed, changes in styles increasingly accelerated. The young needed new stimuli faster and faster — and ever quickening responses. They were not looking for permanence in their personal possessions. Along with them, older people now believed that whatever one man created this season another man would improve on the following year. In our age of electronics and nuclear science we saw each of the new mechanisms and their application in our daily lives replaced by more sophisticated techniques before we had learned to use the preceding ones. This was reflected in our choice of architecture, interior design, clothing design, hairdos and makeup.

Despite M. Pompidou's predictions, as the early seventies progressed haute couture rose phoenix-like from the ashes, however painfully. Fashion, whether it liked it or not, had been liberated. Each woman was free to choose for herself, according to her figure and taste, at whatever house offered a garment that

Summer 1968, Yves Saint Laurent. Over a dark brown bermuda, a tunic entirely embroidered in a geometric drawing style with plastic rings and white plastic cabochons on a chalk-white sequin background.

appealed to her. Because of the prices, she began to eschew haute couture itself in favour of the couturiers' vastly improved *prêt-à-porter*, which permitted her to go on wearing great name clothes. Indeed, henceforward the couture collections in January and July were planned to maintain the prestige and lustre of the world-renowned labels so that these would attract customers to their *prêt-à-porter*. The couturiers repeated their shows in New York, Milan and Tokyo, as well as in Paris, and presented their wares the world over in their boutiques and department-store corners. Little by little the two types of garments, haute couture and its *prêt-à-porter*, would come closer to one another.

Yves Saint Laurent was the one couturier to keep haute couture designing and *prêt-à-porter* designing separate and straight in his head. Whereas, in general, haute couture treated *prêt-à-porter* like a poor relative, *Monsieur* Yves respected both and designed seriously for each. Moreover, in his Rive Gauche boutiques, inaugurated in 1966, he launched models that were unisex. This signified that women had reached the culminating point of integration into modern times.

In 1971, YSL was attracted to the strength of the themes, the force of the embroidery drawing style and the theatricality of Elsa Schiaparelli, one of his regular customers and a fanatical admirer. Thus he again brought back fun and games. Who still turned around to goggle at 'costumed' people on the streets? *Monsieur* Yves' collaboration with François — steeped in Schiaparelli — now became positively conspiratorial.

In 1972 Yves Saint Laurent's ascension turned into a reign. The coronation was marked by the couturier's distinctive long embroidered cardigan, which would resist the passing of the years. This out-datable separate went with everything: flannel trousers, evening skirts, even the 'mini'. (*Monsieur* Yves often asked François to repair one for a customer who had lived in it and could not bear to think of being without it.) The embroidery of YSL's cardigans gave rise to a school, while the originator renewed it continually with new embroidery styles: imitation Irish sweaters, houndsteeth in trompe l'œil, imitation lizard, turtle shells, crocodiles, tree bark and so on. The Saint Laurent cardigans — to became beaded evening sweaters ten years later — had one immediate effect: the emergence of knit fabrics on knit grounds and body-hugging sheaths. These became part of the seventies look along with minis and midis, and François' unprecedented additions of embroidery to such grounds.

From 1973 François worked more closely with young Jean-Louis Scherrer, a couturier uniting grace and restraint, whose talent had continued to blossom over the eleven preceding years. The embroiderer appreciated the couturier's concept of

Winter 1971-2, Christian Dior (Marc Bohan). Using a pointillist technique à la Pissarro, 'cups' (concave sequins) stitched upside down like tiny cabochons on a flaring fuchsia silk chiffon sheath which weighed only a few grams.

Winter 1970-1, Jean Patou (Michel Goma). 'The Tulips of Hyde Park'. 'Charlotte' (seed) pearls on black velvet to imitate tapestry.

Detail. Lesage et Cie stocks.

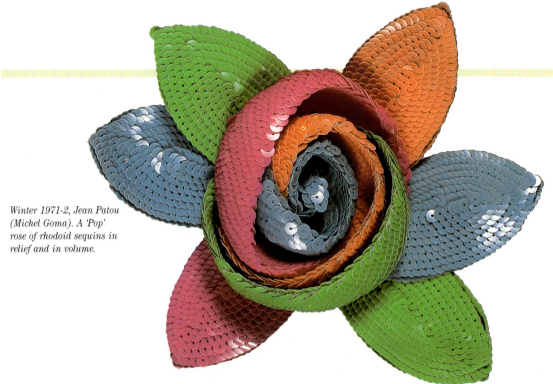

Winter 1971-2, Jean Patou (Michel Goma). A 'Pop' rose of rhodoid sequins in relief and in volume.

haute couture as oriented towards a discreet, refined woman. The Lesage style perfectly suited the elegance of Scherrer clientele, which included Anémone Giscard d'Estaing, who, beside her distinguished husband, so superbly represented France abroad in Scherrer creations.

No longer at present was François deemed a supplier by the couturiers. He walked up the grand staircase of a house or took the lift and, the door being held open for him, entered straight into the office of a couturier, who, to greet him, would rise and come round his desk, hand outstretched. Indeed, some couturiers — Hubert de Givenchy, Jean-Louis Scherrer and Rome-based André Laug — began taking the pains to go to rue Grange to see the samples.

François Lesage was now the most artistically inspired and technically sure master hand embroiderer in the world.

Winter 1971-2, Yves Saint Laurent. Inspired by the Schiaparelli Commedia dell'arte Collection. A patchwork of silk velvet half-moons with coloured rhinestones, coloured sequins and real pink pearls.

Summer 1971, Jean-Louis Scherrer. Afghanistan inspiration. For a navy blue linen bolero, opaque coloured beads and wooden cabochons and beads set in real straw sequins, and gold silk-thread cord.

Winter 1970-1, Pierre Balmain. 'Versailles', a flaring coral faille evening sheath edged above and below with Japanese rooster feathers and esparto cabochons in relief covered by hammered gold-plated strips, coloured rhinestones and motifs of real coral.

16 · OF · ARAB · OIL · AND · PRINCESSES: THE · LATE · SEVENTIES

The first oil crisis in 1973 hurled the Western World into a recession, while events in the Lebanon started to move towards tragedy. In Paris, haute couture, still not recovered from the effects of 1968, and its embroidery, that gauge of prosperity, went drab and boring. But not for long: ironically, the historical circumstances soon affected French fashion favourably.

In the late sixties and early seventies the oil-rich Arab princesses had dressed mainly in Beirut, a corner of paradise for its banking interests as well as for its natural setting. For these ladies Lebanese dressmakers procured French haute couture models and also samples of embroidery. When the political scene in the Lebanon darkened, the dressmakers took flight. Then, in January 1974, the French Government devalued the franc. As a result, the princesses headed for Paris, where the men in their lives were buying up anything that was hellishly expensive, apartments on Avenue Foch being a priority.

The 1975-6 winter collections proved that the couturiers had become fully conscious of the new manna from Muslim heavens. With the help of Lesage et Cie they went all out on evening gowns recalling Farah Diba's imperial gowns, Queen Sirikit of Thailand's lamés, Princess Grace of Monaco's sheaths and the jewelled jackets in which Yves Saint Laurent had swathed every rich *élégante* in the world. Khalid, just crowned King of Saudi Arabia, ordered magnificent wedding gowns for his daughters, while other Arab potentates vied to please their princesses. Each gown represented 2,500 hours of work for twelve embroideresses over two months. (The nouveaux riches did not hand these gowns down to their sisters, nieces or daughters, as was the wont of France. The creations were worn only once.) Undoubtedly some kind of a record for lavish embroidery was set in 1977 at Lanvin (Crahay) by Emperor Bokassa, and his Empress, for their coronation. Another peak was reached when once François's girls had to do a train twenty metres long. François invented a frame measuring five metres. The embroidery for that gown cost one million dollars.

Over the past ten years or so many of the *stylistes* had not only survived, they had improved their talents and extended their businesses. Special recognition has to be paid to Sonia Rykiel, originator of the body sweater, and Emmanuele Khanh, both of whom moved up into the couture ranks, to be joined by Kenzo, who made his first splash in 1972. Another *styliste* keeping haute couture in mind was Karl Lagerfeld for Chloé. While producing in quantity, he did not industrialize altogether. He paid couture-like attention to finish, which he ensured by having it executed partially by hand. Of the wholly industrialized houses, Cacherel, Hechter and Celine maintained high quality in their fabrics.

Despite the growing eminence of foreign designers, Paris remained the magnet for budding talents. Designers still felt that a name and reputation had to be established in the City of Light. Some of the American, Italian and Japanese luminaries opened branches there and later imported their perfumes to compete with the French, but the only durably successful foreigners

1977, Lanvin (Jules-François Crahay). For Emperor Bokassa's coronation. Detail. The Empress' cape: high on the back, a medallion of 18-carat gold bugles and sequins.

Winter 1974-5. André Laug's butterfly.

Detail of the cape train, sprinkled with 18-carat gold sequins and bugles and cut crystal rhinestones.

Detail of the gown embroidered with 18-carat gold bugles and beads and cut crystal mirrors.

were those who based their houses in Paris.

*T*he Chambre Syndicale de la Couture Parisienne measured with intelligence and clairvoyance the *prêt-à-porter* of the couturiers and the ready-to-wear of the *stylistes*. In view of the growing prominence of these latter, it dignified them with a more distinguished appellation, *créateurs*, creators. In 1973 it assembled both elements in an expanded organization — the Fédération Française de la Couture, du Prêt-à-porter des Couturiers et des Créateurs de la Mode — which represented and protected the interests of all their members.

*D*espite the political and economic situation, some newcomers had found ways and means to come forth. At all events, they could not have been contained. They were immensely gifted, raging young lions who — through ambition, creativity and technical know-how — thrust themselves as *créateurs* into the hierarchy above the former *stylistes*. They might easily have aimed at the top haute couture level but found that ready-to-wear, upgraded according to their lights, offered them greater liberty and wider scope of expression while freeing them from the financial constraints of haute couture. Thierry Mugler (1974), Jean-Charles de Castelbajac (1976), Claude Montana (1977), Jean-Paul Gaultier (1979) and Azzedine Alaia, who attracted wide public notice in 1984 — they all had messages to transmit about what women wanted to wear just as strong as those of the couturiers, and they were soon setting trends. To establish their individual images, they were to be seen extravagantly dressed wherever their customers (actual or prospective) went: discos, pavement cafés, popular bistros, avant-garde theatres. They put on shows that had sheer gall. Out for them were the magnificent overheated and overcrowded drawing-rooms with great crystal chandeliers and hard gilt chairs in sumptuous mansions. At first they presented their collections in almost bare locales, sometimes frenziedly illuminated, with reporters huddled together on the floor and propped up by the walls.

*T*o keep the Arab princesses content and reply to the menace of the *créateurs*, particularly the latest ones, for the couturiers François designed samples largely based on jersey for the summer collections shown in January 1976. This could have been a foolhardy undertaking, for jersey was a fabric hitherto hostile to embroidery. François had to accomplish technical miracles to place beads and rhinestones on such a profoundly unstable and elastic ground, while resisting all temptation to add the reinforcement which would have destroyed the fluid character of the material.

Full view of the cape: scarlet velvet edged with ermine — five-meter long train. Weight 85 pounds.

Full view of the gown and train. Weight 45 pounds.

Cape, gown and trains: 12,000 hours of embroidering.

Winter 1978-9, Christian Dior (Marc Bohan). For a corsage, a hand-painted bouquet of violets embroidered with tiny veined-glass beads.

At Dior, Marc Bohan, particularly appreciative of this new technique, designed some entrancing, embroidered jersey evening gowns.

*F*ashion was continuing to express a desire for escape through the exotic which designing for the Arab princesses had stimulated. Now it added romance. Yves Saint Laurent, as had become habitual, showed the way. For his staggering Russian collection (winter) shown in July 1976 he drew his inspiration from the Ballets Russes and in seasons to come from balls in Venice and the Commedia dell'arte beloved of Madame Schiaparelli. As to his Thai jackets, they were wondrous. Thenceforward, year after year, the couturiers were to offer their customers journeys into the past and guided tours of museums and far distant lands. In 1977 YSL followed up a Spanish collection with an exquisite Chinese collection intended to promote his new scent 'Opium'. The embroidery that François correspondingly designed was delicate, pastel and clear, featuring gossamer chiffon enhanced by hand painting. Not only *Monsieur* Yves but all the couturiers were enchanted.

*N*ow the second oil shock blasted the Occident. The Arabs and their princesses were so rich that they started buying up the most prestigious Paris hotels, the couturiers were fighting over them tooth and nail, and François was designing ever more opulent embroidery to suit the increasingly Westernized tastes of this new clientele.

*A*ll of a sudden, with a fresh infusion of money, world conditions improved, and once more partying and jet-setting became the order of the day — and night. In 1979 embroidery at last went really glitzy. For the summer presentations in January François, pursuing his idea of fashion unity through embroidery, developed some particularly exciting themes, adapted by the ensemble of his customers to their needs. First were trompe l'œil scarves and draped belts on flowered grounds, then a return to the Hollywood thirties of Jean Harlow and Busby Berkeley with entirely embroidered suits, shoulder corsages in relief, tuxedo lapels formed by lakes of bugle beads and chiffon tulles embroidered with geometric motifs.

*D*uring a trip to Brazil in February 1978, François

acquired a large number of hard stones : fine-grained and variegated agates with colours arranged in stripes or blended into clouds and mosslike forms; olivine; chrysotile, a kind of asbestos consisting of a fibrous silky serpentine; coloured quartzes, including a clear purple or bluish-violet variety of amethyst; hematite, red

Summer 1979. For Christian Dior, Marc Bohan's butterfly above a trompe-l'œil draped belt and pin.

Summer 1979, Hubert de Givenchy's butterfly.

earthy iron ore; red cinnabar. For the winter collections presented in July 1978 he reproduced these stones in embroidery as if he had cut them into thin cross sections and polished them.

*T*he expression a false 'trompe l'œil' is a pleonasm. Nevertheless, this is what François now produced to the satisfaction of Marc Bohan at Dior, followed by others. He made evening-dress dickeys, folds for skirts and furs, tropical motifs treated with taffeta or shantung, flowered or vegetative straw sequins. He also introduced another technique: motifs cut out one by one and applied to a fabric by means of new thermopasted films. From there on this technique, derived from industry, would make possible miracles that could not have been envisaged with the old collage techniques, such as the 'film Guta', a thin rubber sheet which stuck too fast and left spots. In the years to come François was to develop this thermopasted film process in all possible forms, including real gold sheets and velvet on chiffon.

*I*n her native Japan, Hanae Mori had designed costumes for a thousand films, including those of Misoguchi and Kurosawa. Her great international adventure started in 1962 with a trip to Paris. After meeting Gabrielle Chanel, she gave up the cinema for dressmaking in Tokyo. Yet her goal remained Paris. It took her fifteen years to return. In 1977, preceding Norwegian Per Spook and thus becoming the first foreigner to be accepted by the Fédération, she opened her own house, adding, with Kenzo, an exotic Oriental look to French fashion. In January 1980 Hanae Mori initiated her collaboration with François by requesting a flight of stylized butterflies. The emblem of her family, butterflies would become thematic to her work. And henceforward with her François refined his Oriental inspiration.

Summer 1979, Christian Dior (Marc Bohan). Trompe-l'œil belt and cord of bugles and small mirrors.

Winter 1977-8, Yves Saint Laurent. Scottish plaid effect. Detail. An evening jacket entirely embroidered with gold bugles in various harmonies, the lapels formed by raised embroidery (soulevé) of very fine jet bugles.

*M*ore and more François diversified through using sources provided by great artists, and the couturiers fell into step with him. For July 1980 Hubert de Givenchy requested him to interpret the drawing style typical of Douanier Rousseau in his jungle scenes while multiplying varied coloured applications of taffeta and faille. Six months later several couturiers — Givenchy, Scherrer and Balmain — had an enormous success with variations of the Fortuny theme presented to them by François.

*M*ariano Fortuny (1871-1949) was born in Grenada and lived and worked in Venice. An inspired designer who did fashion collections and interior decorations in his own fabrics, he dreamt of an imaginary Orient and its fanciful cities. He produced fabrics inspired by fifteenth-century Venetian stuffs and sixteenth-century dalmatics and became well known the world over for his silk Knossos scarves, pleated Delphos dresses and cloaks, robes and dresses in his wrinkled and stencilled velvet. François, as inspired by him, was able to use the new thermopasted film technique to adorn chiffon with appliquéd gold leaf, panne cutouts and Fortuny's wrinkled velvet.

*F*or several years François had been increasingly adding to all his samples the finishing touches that so enhanced his best work. In 1980 he presented a Tartar theme that greatly appealed to romantic

Winter 1978-9, Yves Saint Laurent. From Lesage themes inspired by Brazilian stones, brown and blue sequins and bugles imitating polished agate.

Jean-Louis Scherrer. It featured braid of jet or sparkling (glass) jewels according to the season and edgings of *plissés bijoux*, numerous minute pleats snuggling together. *(Mon bijou* here means not a gem but 'my little darling'.) He also edged many samples with mink bands which lent a look very 'Empress Catherine of All the Russias'. In addition, he embroidered bayadères — fabrics with horizontal or oblique strips in strongly contrasted colours used for the costumes of Hindu dancing girls — with arabesques or brocade designs, modifying the bayadère by varying the colours per strip.

So it went on. Never had François's talent been more creative. Coincidentally, new legislation came into force that greatly helped the visualization of what had become genius. In 1980, for the first time in the history of fashion photography, an embroiderer was officially authorized, during the parades, to take photographs of the couturiers' creations to which he had so marvellously contributed.

Summer 1979, Hubert de Givenchy. A trompe-l'œil bow and flap end of silver thread and bugles and a 'camaieu' (shading within the range of one colour) of transparent blue sequins — all sprinkled with a vermicelli of blue micro-beads.

Summer 1981. Indian Collection. Cashmere drawing style. Left: 18-carat gold lamé applications on a background of mat olive-green sequins and motifs in gold thread and chalk-white sequins. Right: shantung and appliquéd 18-carat gold lamé, silk thread and gold bugles.

JEAN-LOUIS SCHERRER
Winter 1977-8. Woof effect. A jacket entirely embroidered in a gold-thread woof with jet and gold bugles enhanced by touches of coral beads. The lapel is of raised jet bugles edged with gold and coral bugles.

Winter 1980-1. An entirely embroidered corsage: a ground of transparent and gold bugles, appliquéd panne, gold-thread passementerie braid and white ermine edging.

Detail.

• 126 •

HANAE MORI
Winter 1985-6. Detail. A butterfly for a blouse.

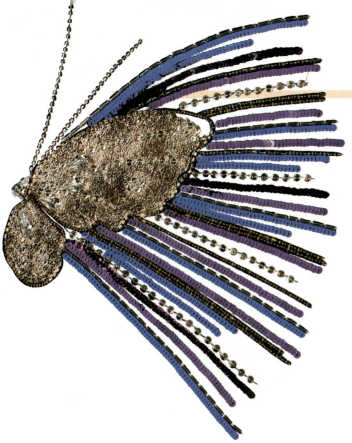

Winter 1985-6. A bolero of night blue satin embroidered with 'snow crystals' of variously shaped rhinestones, aquamarine rhinestones and silver thread.

Summer 1986. A long jacket entirely embroidered. On a ground of a black sequin 'forest', butterflies of 'camaieux' (shading within the range of one colour) of blue and mauve semi-transparent sequins.

Summer 1986. Motif for a suit. A zebra of jet beads, small mirrors and chalk-white bugles.

JEAN-LOUIS SCHERRER
Winter 1986-7. Evening gown with taffeta skirt. The corsage entirely embroidered with sequins and bugles in shaded peacock hues to imitate feathers. On the edges, real feathers. The ensemble sprayed with gold powder.

17 · A · GOLDEN · AGE : THE · EARLY · EIGHTIES

Historians and sociologists observing contemporary manners in 1980 were gloomily predicting the decadence to engulf us all by the end of the century. They saw expressions of its sleazy eroticism in advertising, in the violent theatre and TV films and serials, in the ingenue-sirens Nastassja Kinski and Isabella Rosselini, and in the macho muscle-men, Burt Reynolds, Sylvester Stallone, Arnold Schwarzenegger, Gérard Depardieu.

*F*or the oracles, in France the end-of-the-century decadence was submerging us fast. Who could be called a great living French writer? No one. Unity of style? It no longer existed, just a confusion of distant ages and ways of living. Alone *Monsieur* Yves Saint Laurent represented the eternal genius of France. Thus it is perhaps not so ironic that the predictors of doom found their one positive element in French fashion, which — still, as always, a gauge of world conditions — did not agree with them at all. Indeed, the dawn of the eighties ushered in a golden age in haute couture. The oil crises were to subside, but the coffers of Arab potentates would continue to brim over and their princesses to dote on Paris. The dollar began its rise to vertiginous heights, bringing in its wake Texan oil millionaires' wives and daughters straight out of *Dallas* and *Dynasty*, and Mexican and South American oil heiresses.

HUBERT DE GIVENCHY Winter 1980-1. Fortuny Collection. Left, a jacket; right, jacket and gown. Various appliquéd grey and bordeaux-red velvet pannes with gold-thread stitching.

*A*nother factor contributed to these halcyon days: the Executive Woman. More and more women were rising to positions of responsibility: between 1972 and 1983 their ranks in US firms rose from 1.4 million to 3.5 million. The increase of women in the work force was one of the most significant developments that had ever taken place in American business. Moreover, these women, whose numbers continued to increase, kept moving to higher positions in government, engineering and publishing companies, banks, manufacturing firms, retail companies and service corporations on the basis of their brains, application to their studies and talent, not their connections. The importance of women executives in other countries of the Western World also grew. All these ladies wanted to force the recognition of their achievements and status. One major way was through their clothes and accessories, luxurious, of excellent fabric, fine workmanship — and bearing a great Paris designer label rather than that of an exclusive shop.

*T*he desire to escape through the exotic and find romance had persisted in Paris haute couture over the years. Nymphets, with Valenciennes on chiffon printed with polka dots, appeared chez Dior (Marc Bohan). Yves Saint Laurent offered Valenciennes-enhanced silk embroidery, black lace roses appliquéd on shantung and coloured silk flowers embellished by rococo ribbon. Jean-Louis Scherrer, however, was the designer who expressed the romantic mood most resolutely. His entrancing 'Indian Hour' (January 1981) featured gowns resembling those worn by the wives of British viceroys in India under Queen Victoria.

*F*or the winter collections shown in July 1981, Paris went Asian. Sumptuous Chinese and Japanese kimonos triumphed everywhere. François embroidered satin shantung in a stylization of Ming, often edged with a mat gold frieze of braiding or passementerie à la Chinoise.

Detail of the jacket to the left.

PIERRE BALMAIN (Erik Mortensen) Summer 1985. For Queen Sirikit of Thailand…

… a corsage embroidered with real lophophore (beetle) wings supplied by the Thai court and 18-carat gold blown beads.

Scherrer took off for Manchuria, then turned round to visit *Les Petites Anglaises*, little English girls, with a combination of tulle and *point d'esprit* lace embroidered with silk à la Romantic Age in England. English patchwork materialized chez Dior (Bohan). *Monsieur* Yves went Turkish and also evoked Morocco (he had a castle at Marrakech). Visits to foreign climes continued. For January 1984 Lagerfeld at Chanel requested Chinese blue; six months later Yves Saint Laurent did Scottish jackets. In January 1985 Scherrer featured Japanese motifs, whereas Chanel-Lagerfeld stressed white china and Chinese-teapot images and some extraordinary embroidery reminiscent of the ceramics used for late nineteenth-century flower-pot holders.

By now young Christian Lacroix (Patou), who had prepared to be a curator, was — with the assistance of his 'godfather' (sponsor), François Lesage — a figure to be reckoned with. Early in 1985 he presented Texan shirts and American-type suspenders, followed the next seasons by Dior (Marc Bohan) in Bali, Givenchy reviving Saracen art and then an ancient Turkish style of drawing revived in the nineteenth century by the Japanese, Scherrer rediscovering Venice and then leaping over to nineteenth-century Spain as it had been viewed by Napoleon III's court in honour of Empress Eugénie.

Yves Saint Laurent in 1980 paid tribute to the greatest of the early twentieth-century poets by means of Lesage embroidery: Guillaume Apollinaire, who expressed his way of living *'Tout terriblement'* (Everything, terribly); Louis Aragon, who immortalized his love for Elsa Triolet with a collection, *Les Yeux d'Elsa* (Elsa's Eyes); and Jean Cocteau, one of whose most famous verses began, *'Soleil, moi je suis noir dedans* (Sun, I am black inside).

Soon *Monsieur* Yves asked François to interpret the Pheobus Apollo that Albert Lesage had created for Madame Schiaparelli some forty years before. When, in 1981, YSL presented blouses embroidered à la Matisse, together with François he launched a vogue for creations inspired by great artists. Chanel (Lagerfeld) asked François for baroque themes recalling Boulle furniture for his tailored suits and Gobelin tapestries for fur jackets. Art deco returned in July 1983, especially chez Scherrer, who next reminded those who knew of Chyperus, a sculptor very active during *Les Années Folles*. In July 1984 Marc Bohan (Dior) paid tribute to the modern Czech-born artist, Polok, and then recalled the great Viennese turn-of-the-century painter, Gustav Klimt. Six months later Karl Lagerfeld at Chanel asked François for silk embroidery featuring little roses in relief reminiscent of the paintings of Vlaminck, and in January 1986 he recalled Kandinski in sequins and Miró edged with jewelled braid. The following season he presented a trompe l'œil that was a game of chess designed by Salvador Dali. Meanwhile, Lacroix at Patou had embroidered pullovers à la Bakst. YSL followed up a season

A bolero also embroidered with the real lophophore (beetle) wings and 18-carat gold-plated bugles. Erik Mortensen sketches.

CHRISTIAN DIOR (Marc Bohan)
Winter 1984-5. Balinese folklore inspiration. Detail. A jacket entirely embroidered like a patchwork with various applications of coloured fabrics embroidered with multi-coloured sequins and chenilles and enhanced by gold bugles.

later with little bows in the style of wonderful Christian Bérard.

At this juncture it is to be noted that, significantly, Yves Saint Laurent, Chanel (Lagerfeld), Givenchy, Dior (Bohan) and many of the other couturiers, defending themselves against the inroads of the *créateurs*, had improved their *prêt-à-porter* so successfully that they could afford to ask François to begin to provide embroidery for it.

For the winter showings in July 1982, Paris was beginning to take advantage of the mounting dollar. The Arab princesses were still indulging their taste for luxury. The Mexicans and South Americans ordered showy things, whereas the North American ladies were more restrained: they just bought up everything in sight that was not too flashy. François duly tuned down his glitz. Fifty years after Callot Sœurs had asked his father in vain to adapt embroidery to sportswear, he now succeeded to do so, while remaining luxurious and refined. Notably, he beaded mohair for YSL and Givenchy.

It must not be thought that Paris was becoming muted. In fact, the couturiers had rarely been so jewellery-conscious. At Chanel, Lagerfeld asked François for an embroidery of trompe l'œil jewels recalling Coco's renowned *sautoirs*, or waist-long necklaces, and had the famous quilted Chanel bag embroidered à la Schiaparelli. He featured blue porcelain, as well as white porcelain by itself or on a Lesage 'Afghan rug'. At Dior, Bohan brought out embroidered broken mirrors lacquered black or combined with jade, Mauboussin vanity cases with embroidered diamond clasps, and braiding that resembled white and gold ceramics. Scherrer embroidered cashmere with fine mosaics and lace with mat silver sequins in relief, and ventured into the jungle with embroidered Lalique crystal. YSL fancied an embroidery of cameos enhanced by baroque arabesques, then rock crystals and opaque pampille for tunics. Lacroix for Patou beaded an unusual harlequin-patterned pullover and had a wedding gown embroidered with angora and pearls.

Yves Saint Laurent, for his showing in January 1983, ordered fish-scale embroidery that required thousands of hours of work. For him François also did a series of trompe l'œil in relief fancifully representing hides of leopards and black and white tigers. When François revived exoticism with an African touch in jungle plants, flowers from the savannas and animals, *Monsieur* Yves ordered lizards and crocodiles for his evening

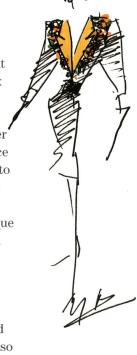

Winter 1985-6. For the theme 'Harlequin Broken Mirror', a corsage entirely embroidered with large, differently arranged silver bugles and a necklace of rhinestones and turn-of-the-century jet motifs.

Winter 1985-6. Art deco inspiration. Trompe-l'œil lapels with appliquéd satin over garlands of tiny coloured spangles. Mark Bohan sketch from a François Lesage sample.

sweaters. The theme was also adopted by Patou (Lacroix), Bohan at Dior and Scherrer.

In 1981, although less than twenty fashion houses were still in business, a twenty-five per cent increase from 1980 in haute couture turnover reached 5 billion francs ($833 million). With *prêt-à-porter*, the turnover in 1982 was almost ten billion francs ($1 billion 600 million).

Since licensing had been launched by Jacques Rouët for Christian Dior, couture houses had exploited the idea to the nth degree — and kept their names alive and glowing. The 320 Dior licenses now included cocktail and evening dresses, scents, luggage, spectacles, baby clothes, crystal, dinnerware — worth in all $7 million. Through his 860 licensing deals (1987), Pierre Cardin sold everything from vacuum flasks to repasts, de luxe delicatessen, hotel rooms and cruises bearing the Maxim label that he had acquired. With 180 licenses, Givenchy sold clothes, sheets and towels, and the interior of Lincoln Continentals. Ungaro had signed 120 licenses. Yves Saint Laurent had an $80 million or so company — royalties and couture sales only.

The difference between American and Paris designers at the beginning of the eighties was still as sharp and clear as it always had been: the Americans designed the way they understood their clients wished to be dressed, whereas the couturiers — each knowing he had his own slice of the cake and wisely refraining from trying to grab it all — obstinately continued to design the way they pleased. 'If you want my dresses, this is how they are, or go somewhere else.' Over the years François had become increasingly impressed by the gifts of American designers, as well as by the expanded embroidery market that they might represent. In September 1982 he returned to the States after having obtained an appointment with Calvin Klein, who, at the sight of his samples, reacted like 'a child in a pastry shop'. The American dashed over to Paris to see more and ordered a mountain for his collection to be shown at the end of October — that is, in six weeks.

CHANEL (Karl Lagerfeld) Summer 1984. Chinese blue theme.

Micro-mosaics of transparent Chinese blue glass and opaque white glass. Modelled by Inès de la Fressange.

Chinese blue silk-thread motifs and mosaics of Chinese blue glass and opaque white glass. 1800 hours of embroidering. 200,000 micro-beads.

Detail.

Lesage et Cie worked day and night, and Mr Klein's assistant jumped on to Concorde every three days to pick up the pieces that had been finished in the interval. François went back to New York to see the collection, which was received very well for both himself and the designer. Encouraged, he paid visits, 'a bit timidly', to Bill Blass, Oscar de la Renta and Geoffrey Beene. They welcomed him so warmly that he was taken aback. He had never imagined that the name of Lesage was known on Seventh Avenue. Duly, he took orders from these American designers for the following season. Carolyne Roehm, Mary

1937. Marlene Dietrich gowned by Travis Banton as Ernest Lubitsch's 'Angel'.

McFadden and Carolina Herrara soon joined the ranks.

It was upon returning to Paris to prepare the 1983 summer collection, to be shown in January, that François learned that Karl Lagerfeld had just signed with Chanel. François had not worked for ready-to-wear Chloé when Lagerfeld was with them, but Lagerfeld — who was with glee to unite the old enemies Coco and Shiap in his designs for Chanel — requested François at once to supply him for the imminent first show.

Their relationship was an easy one based on mutual respect and admiration. Although highly independent and determined to follow his own convictions about themes, Lagerfeld soon came to listen to François. The first thing he asked the embroiderer to do was improvise on the famous Coromandel screens in Chanel's salon. This initial collaboration suited both men perfectly. It opened up a pleasant and exciting concerted action, for the autocratic, mischief-loving Lagerfeld was (and is) most witty and engaging. Indeed, François came to feel so confident with him that when the couturier proposed this or that theme, he dared to tell him if it had already been treated.

The high jinks in fashion continued undiminished. For the winter showings in July 1986 François presented themes based on real gold or bronze wrinkled leather cutouts and animal, bird and plant motifs. Sometimes these were combined — by Givenchy with a panther on a blue background, by Christian Lacroix for Patou with petrified wood motifs. Marc Bohan (Dior) developed a kaleidoscope of gold leather on white satin for a wedding gown and designed a bird's body in gold leather feathers ending in real feathers; Scherrer showed gold leaf leather undergrowth and silk fern, and combined trompe-l'œil feathers and a representation of a bird of paradise. At Chanel, Lagerfeld chose silk birds and feathers in an embroidery inspired by an eighteenth-century fan. Yves Saint Laurent earned wild applause for a bronze 'bark' sprayed with gold and adorned with 'sculptured' embroidery edged with Chinese cock's feathers highlighted with gold.

This golden age undoubtedly came to a climax with a garment entailing 280,000 three-millimetre black sequins

Winter 1981-2, Yves Saint Laurent. Cashmere drawing style. Jacket and long skirt embroidered with gold sequins, beige chenille and coloured rhinestones.

• 133 •

1935. Marlene Dietrich costumed by Travis Banton in Josef von Sternberg's 'The Devil is a Woman'.

romantic leads like Kevin Costner, Tom Hanks, Matt Dillon, Matthew Broderick, Tom Cruise and Michael J. Fox, Lambert Wilson and Anthony Delon, Rupert Everett.

*F*rench haute couture was at a crossroads. On the one hand, the dollar had dropped forty per cent. On the other, few of the Arab princesses, Texas millionnairesses and Mexican and South American heiresses were continuing to be faithful. Yet François was encouraged by an unprecedented number of orders placed for the *prêt-à-porter* shows in March 1987, a significant trend.

*R*eflecting the impact of Aids, fashion returned to mystery and charm. Clothes, even those of the often over-bumptious *créateurs*, ceased to be aggressive. They became pretty and flirty again. A sprayed with fine gold, 300 metres of silk chenille embroidered with petit point, 200,000 sticks of grey glass, 150,000 bugle beads on braid — all adding up to one million stitches, 624 hours of work. The result was No. 76 in the Karl Lagerfeld-designed Chanel collection, July 1986: an evening sheath embroidered in trompe l'œil inspired by the world famous quilted Chanel bag.

*A*s 1987 came into view, it disclosed a number of arrows that were pointing in a direction contrary to the dire predictions of end-of-the-century decadence. Aids was perhaps the major factor. Having started on its terrifying march, it actually began doing a lot to clean up the world of drugs and easy sex and renew morality, love and fidelity. In the cinema the machos and their violence were being ousted by clean and tidy, courteous and

Summer 1987, Jean-Louis Scherrer. Spanish Collection. A long bustier adorned with shocking pink sequin and silk-thread roses and tiny black bugles in various stitches.

new mood certainly, but was it a new look? At all events, in the spring of 1987 the sixties were revived, not with macrame belts and pillbox hats, but with mini-skirts replacing the billowing ankle-length skirts popular in the preceding years. The minis in the sixties suited a rebellious, sex-free youth. Now, coming from the young trend setter Christian Lacroix (Patou) in feminine flounces, tiers and bubbles, they were designed especially for young and middle-aged American women who, following the diets and exercises prescribed by Jane Fonda and Raquel Welch, were proud of what these had done at least for their legs.

JEAN PATOU (Christian Lacroix)

Summer 1985. A 'Texan' shirt of lemon yellow organza embroidered with hearts of jet and mirrors on a background of transparent yellow sequins.

Summer 1986. Leon Bakst inspiration. For a bustier, spirals of mat gold-plated bugles on a background of mat black sequins. Skirt hand-painted from a design by Mr Lacroix.

YVES SAINT LAURENT requests Surrealism, Winter 1980-1.

'Sun, I am black within and pink without, work the metamorphosis...' The request in this line from a Jean Cocteau poem (in 'Monsieur' Yves' handwriting) is fittingly answered by appliquéd black suede underlined by rhinestones on a Shocking pink silk satin jacket with a rhinestone collar and gold-braid sun beams.

Poet Aragon's signature in rhinestones in relief on the back of a black velvet jacket with rhinestone edging.

'Monsieur' Yves' handwriting in gold-plated strips and rhinestones underlined with jet on the Nattier-blue velvet front of the jacket...

*I*t is not to be concluded that haute couture was finished. Far from it. On Sunday 26 July 1987, in a superb eighteenth-century mansion on rue du Faubourg Saint Honoré, a new house was inaugurated — the first in many years. It bore the name of Christian Lacroix. The opening had been preceded on both sides of the Atlantic by an indescribable publicity campaign. How could this charming, modest, very cultivated young man live up to it? Prudently, he did not try. Rather than hurl bombs which might not have exploded, he chose to use his Provençal origins and fond Camargue memories as a backdrop and, following the lines which he had already traced with such success at Patou, continued his 'fresh follies' (admirative Georgio Armani) from where he had left them off. The result was screaming, foot-stamping ovations and rhapsodic notices — 'genius', 'Messiah', 'new chapter in fashion history'.

*N*aturally, the couturiers had for years been eyeing Lacroix's growing challenge. A young man who announced that he intented to bring 'clean' romance, glamour and fun back into fashion and who was being given limitless financial backing to do so? Too much attention was being paid to him, and they would prove it. So, during the days following the opening, business went on as usual, apparently — for Yves Saint Laurent's collection was more sumptuous than ever, Jean-Louis Scherrer's, Vienna-inspired, romantic with a capital R, and Karl Lagerfeld's for Chanel a positive *jamais-vu* for showstopping Lesage embroideries. Because of the Lacroix Effect, Paris was more alive and kicking than it had been in years.

*A*nd beyond that? Young people will be eternally attracted by fashion in Paris and go there to absorb the magnificent French cultural heritage that it represents, especially now that the Institut Français de la Mode has opened its doors to students. An already huge field will, as it always has done, offer ever wider expanses to the young seekers of adventure and creators of tomorrow.

... 'Les Yeux d'Elsa' (Triolet) are of silk, the eyebrows of gold braid and a dust of tiny silver bugles.

The Crocodile Cardigan. A wholly new François Lesage technique to achieve the effect of scales through relief and volume: on a diagram of bugles, sequins are placed like roofing tiles and sprayed with dye to produce a turquoise 'camaieu' (shading within the range of one colour) for greater realism.

CHANEL (Karl Lagerfeld). Winter 1986-7

A sable-edged bustier featuring a Dali designed trompe-l'œil chess game. Marquetry of turtle-shell, real mother-of-pearl and mat black sequins, and cream and red porcelain bugles.

Inès de la Fressange models a two-piece wool suit embroidered with black sequins recalling through trompe-l'œil motifs the famous Chanel quilted bag and enhanced with a trompe-l'œil chain. Each square is sprayed with gold powder to accentuate the effect of relief.

Based on an eighteenth-century fan, embroidery representing flowers and birds with plumage enriched by coloured rhinestones. A cane-bottom background of black micro-beads.

Winter 1984, Oscar de la Renta. A stylized Chinese-inspired yellow wool jacket: gold passementerie, flowers and leaves in black bugles and black chenille.

October 1982, Calvin Klein. Mat gold sequins.

Winter 1984, Bill Blass. For the lapel of a Shocking pink wool jacket, revives Elsa Schiaparelli's watermelon in jade-green porcelain bugles, mirrors, pink sequins and jet seeds.

• 140 •

Summer 1987, Carolyne Roehm. Admiral style. A woollen jacket and dress: leaves and roses in 18-carat gold-plated wrinkled leather, tiny gold beads and gold thread.

Summer 1987, Bill Blass. Trompe-l'œil W(omen's) W(ear) D(aily) head: tiny chalk-white sequins and jet micro-bugles, sprayed with grey ink to create shadow (an exclusive Lesage technique).

Summer 1984, Bill Blass. Stylized coral branches of chalk-white sequins in relief for a yellow crepe dress.

18 · THINGS·OF·BEAUTY, JOYS·FOREVER

1932. Brigitte Helm in G.W. Pabst's 'l'Atlantide'. Cretan inspiration.

Why does an artist progress from watercolours and gouaches to oils, from sketches to lithographs? Because, to give expression to his developing gifts, he needs to widen his horizons. So it was with François Lesage. With the advent of the eighties he became restless, felt impelled to break out of the confines of embroidery for clothes, no matter how imaginative, varied and exciting his creativity continued to be, especially now that he had reached heights of success that undoubtedly no other embroiderer had ever attained. Moreover, it also had to be admitted that haute couture was manifestly going over the top, golden age or no, and a new clientele had to be found.

In order to diversify without vulgarizing his product, François conceived a new venture: embroidered jewellery and accessories. To accompany him on this undertaking, he invited Gérard Trémolet to join Lesage et Cie. This gifted young designer had, in art classes throughout his early schooling, sketched women's styles. He also drew much of the time he attended a business school imposed by his father. When one observes Gérard calculating his prices and balancing his accounts, one sees that M. Trémolet *père* was not mistaken. After that, higher level business school?

Mais non! He enrolled in a private art school in Montparnasse but departed after six months because, in putting his ideas for fashion designs on to paper, he was chided by the teachers for going too far his individual way.

Jean-Louis Scherrer, on seeing the sketches Gérard submitted with fear and trepidation, did not agree with the art school teachers. He hired the lad, scarcely twenty years of age, to assist him with his accessories. Scherrer is a fine gentleman; he is also a taskmaster. For Gérard this was a finishing school where he learned the spirit of couture and Parisian elegance. After several years he was wooed away from Scherrer by a manufacturer of accessories: he was to be responsible for the articles from beginning to end — that is, the designing, supervision of manufacturing, distribution and sales, and checking of invoices. Little wonder that François, hearing of him, in 1985 brought him in as head of the new department.

In the Lesage sense, embroidered jewellery and accessories were unknown. Yet the accessories in particular had historical predecessors. From the earliest of recorded times to the great outburst in the eighteenth century and the insensate apogee in the nineteenth century, many attempts were made to associate embroidery, ornamentation and adornment. During Oriental antiquity, shawls were embellished with metallic embroidery. Immortalized in the Louvre by a bronze statue dating from 1500 BC and unearthed in Susa, the ancient city of Elam in southwest Iran, Queen Shou Bad wears a kind of breast shield covered with tubular beads held in place by two gold pins.

For a short period (1350-40 BC) during the XVIII Dynasty, Egyptians affected sandals embroidered with beads or appliquéd with variously coloured leather cutouts. Excellent examples were found in 1922 when King Tut's tomb was opened.

During the Iron Age, from 900 to 700 BC Syrian costumes featured a white woollen 'Sumerian' scarf embroidered in red and blue (anticipating present-day plaids), worn over a linen loincloth and fastened on the shoulder. Rich and prominent Cretans in the ninth

Circa 1730. A lady's damask shoe embroidered with gold thread. Gérard Trémolet drawing.

1987, Lesage. Egyptian inspiration. Bracelet and earrings made of chalk-white and opaque coloured mosaic beads of different rectangular sizes, taken from late nineteenth-century stock.

century BC loaded embroidery on their dress, while court dignitaries paraded about in bead-embroidered sandals tied to the calves with embroidered laces.

Brocaded headbands covered with gold- or silver-plated rosettes were fashionable with the Assyrians in the seventh century BC. Their arms and wrists were clasped by bracelets usually embroidered with rosettes.

For almost a thousand years, from 300 BC to AD 600, Egyptian civil and religious masculine dress included fabric or leather leg-guards with embroidered motifs.

Not to be outdone, from the second century AD the Romans added embroidery to women's clothes and then embroidered their accessories: handkerchiefs, fans, parasols and brilliantly coloured shawls.

Tight-fitting trousers enclosed by embroidered trompe l'œil bracelets were all the rage for six hundred years up to AD 1000 in Eastern Europe and Byzantium. During the reign of Henri IV in France these would be revived as garters for hose.

At the height of the Gothic period in the thirteenth century bishops' mitres were embroidered with gold thread and silk. Competing with the magnificence of the Church, princely and ducal courts of the fifteenth century tried to ape royal courts and outdo one another in splendour. The walls of great rooms were hung with embroideries containing images to be compared favourably with those in tapestries. Embroidery, adorning everything in dress from coifs down to slippers, spread to accessories: fans, ribbons, purses, scarves, shawls, dressing cases, not to mention caparisons, trappings, saddles and harnesses. In Burgundy during the time of Duke Philippe le Bon headdresses were embroidered with beaded fringe.

The following century embroidery increased in importance. This can be accounted for by the development of new techniques: coloured silks, combinations of metal threads, stylized designs. Upon Francis I's ascension to the throne of France in 1515, the liking of Anne de Bretagne, widow of the two preceding kings, for bead-embroidered gold or silk snoods worn with a bonnet became a vogue. Linen bonnets were soon being embroidered, while passementerie-embroidered hats flourished.

It is little wonder that embroidery prospered during Elizabeth I's glorious reign. Richly embroidered stockings became fashionable, as did men's hose, notably with the emblematic motifs that attracted the eye to the Count of Dorset's legs. Sir William Playters launched a vogue when he appeared with a passementerie-embroidered tassel fastened to his left ear.

Gloves were imported into France under Louis XIII (1601-43). They came in soft kid with large flaring cuffs similar to gauntlets called 'crispins'. Many were embroidered and often scented. Another mark of luxury was the embroidered shoulder belt. Over one's jerkin one tied with studied negligence a scarf embroidered with filet lace and later silk adorned with fringe. That same period saw re-embroidered lace cut-outs placed on slippers and the silver-thread

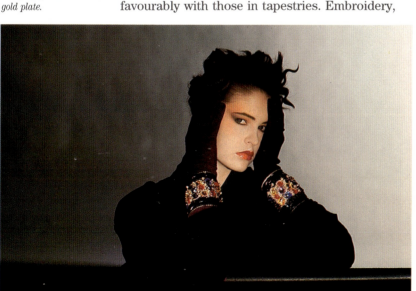

1987, Lesage. Medieval stained-glass window inspiration. Bracelets of coloured glass cabochons set in gold beads and edged with marquetry motifs of jet mounted on gold plate.

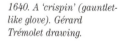

1640. A 'crispin' (gauntlet-like glove). Gérard Trémolet drawing.

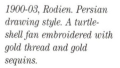

1900-03, Rodien. Persian drawing style. A turtle-shell fan embroidered with gold thread and gold sequins.

embroidered felt hat that Frederick III, King of Denmark and Norway from 1648 to 1670, wore with his brocaded 'crispins' at the Rosenborg Castle in Copenhagen. Towards 1680 women's leather shoes were adorned with silk embroidery, while carmine velvet shoes for both women and men were embroidered with silver thread in relief. This vogue would continue into the eighteenth century: towards 1730 in metallic-thread embroidered green damask ladies' shoes with red heels, and twenty years later silk slippers with buttoned straps and high heels.

Under all the Bourbons, stones were greatly used to embroider leather. Men's waistcoats were also, sometimes magnificently, embroidered with silk, paillettes, silver thread. At this time fabrics became more fanciful — brocaded wool moiré, velvet taffeta. So did embroidery materials — gold, silver, paillettes, chenille, lace, feathers. The master embroiderers were François Bouy, Ranson and Charles-Germain de St Aubin. The latter, one of Madame de Pompadour's protégés, received the title of 'King's Costume Designer' and in 1770 wrote the *Art of the Embroiderer*, the first treatise of any consequence on the subject.

1987, Lesage. Belt, bag and watches. Gold-plated strips in relief with tiny chalk-white sequins and small black and gold bugles.

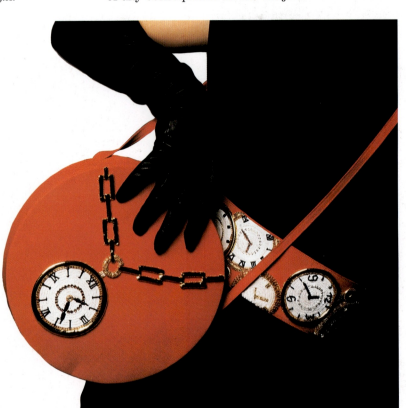

With the arrival of Marie-Antoinette, Rose Bertin and her rival *marchands de modes* (style merchants) reached the height of their power, popularity and fortune. Not only did they shower trimmings on their customers, they sold them endless bonnets, flounces, hoods and mantillas, all ornamented, adorned and embroidered.

Shoes, purses, belts, hose and sleeves were, during the Directoire (towards 1795), still being richly embroidered. This tradition continued into Napoleon I's Empire with embroidered boots, fans embellished with gold paillettes and particularly shawls embroidered with spiral-twisted gold thread. This was a technique reserved for the mighty of the period and represented an arrogant imperial flaunting of the 'simple' silk and gold thread of the Ancien Régime.

Throughout the Bourbon Restoration (1815), the Romantic Age (1830-48) and the short-lived Second Republic (1848-51) rich women clamoured for embroidered *frivolités* that were more and more refined and increasingly dissociated from gowns: veils, coin purses, bags, parasols embellished with sequined lace and edged with little pompoms, open-worked white stockings and stockings of golden yellow silk embroidered with red roses, evening booties, house slippers and so on.

Now embroidered accessories were in demand as never before in history. Throughout the Second Empire and the early days of the Third Republic, this demand was fired as much by nostalgia for former times as by the desires of the moment. Women wished to enrich everyday objects by bestowing upon them an appearance of luxury and refinement: bags, belts, shawls, scarves, bathing scarves and bathing costumes, combs, handkerchiefs, gloves, fans, lanyards, screens, and even a timid attempt at jewellery with necklaces and brooches. For over sixty years jet played an important role in embroidery for gowns. No smart woman would be seen without it liberally splattered all over her. Nor were

1987, Lesage. For a cashmere scarf, appliquéd silk satin, silk-thread cord, 18 carat gold bugles and silk-thread bullion tassels with heads of coloured beads.

men overlooked; they had embroidered waistcoats, cuff links, braces (suspenders), belts and much more.

Although styles and quantity changed, embroidered accessories and adornments remained in vogue until the First World War. Immediately afterwards, as the new twenties styles in clothes appeared, so did diversified uses of embroidery for accessories. Little by little jet was abandoned in favour of richer and more agreeable materials such as sequins and spiral-twisted silver thread. Embroidery was employed for shoe buckles, little silk coin purses, evening fans and bags, Hermès gloves, men's wallets. Elsa Schiaparelli placed an accent on embroidered accessories with Albert Lesage from 1935 to 1940 as never before or after in the history of haute couture. With the end of the Second World War a few embroidered articles were still to be seen, particularly chez Roger Vivier, the great shoe designer, but in the sixties embroidered accessories all but vanished.

It remained for François Lesage to inaugurate a mode of embroidered jewellery and bring back to life embroidered accessories. Thus he renewed with consummate French refinement and artistry a tradition that had sought its plenitude since prehistoric times.

1987, Lesage. A lanyard of gold-plated bows embroidered with gold beads and gold thread, the chain composed of mother-of-pearl and gold-plated beads.

1987, Lesage. A 'sautoir' in antique jet and late nineteenth-century jet beads, the clasp embroidered with antique jet beads and antique cut rhinestones mounted on gold-plated metal.

Circa 1830. A silk stocking embroidered with red silk-thread roses. Gérard Trémolet drawing.

19 · RUE · GRANGE

With the upswing in the mid-seventies François Lesage had taken over the second apartment on the fifth floor of rue Grange and extended his ateliers. Little by little he also acquired most of the maids' rooms on the attic floor. To link this to the fifth floor below on the interior, he had a stairway built leading down from the studio he reserved for himself up there. This was composed of two maids' rooms with the dividing wall removed. As these cubicles had only tiny windows, he increased the light by placing large mirrors facing one another on the opposite window-less walls and training on them a bank of spotlights suspended from the ceiling.

This is the room in which he works today. On the walls all about he hangs framed samples of which he is particularly proud and pins photographs of family and friends, letters of some significance or

Finishing touches on a sketch for 'Monsieur' Yves Saint Laurent.

other and sketches by famous couturiers. Against one wall is a filing cabinet full of embroidery materials. In low shelves are his reference books, albums of drawings of embroidery, tapestry and carpeting throughout recent centuries in various countries, illustrated books on the arts, crafts and fashion, black-bound tomes on the turn-of-the-century theatre inherited from M. Michonet. Atop the shelves is his laboratory corner — dyes, varnishes, spirits, acetone, an air compressor used in drawing and drying, the telephone and a minitel practically covered by paraphernalia. Over there, piled high with empty cardboard boxes full of tissue paper, is a photocopying machine. In the middle of the room two great white enamel-topped tables are pushed together. Here M. Lesage — no one addresses or speaks of him otherwise — does his conceiving and designing amid swatches of fabrics, cheese boxes full of embroidery materials, kilometres of ribbons and piles of notes left during his absence for his attention.

The Lesages were friendly with another Versailles family, the Dieuleveults, of noble Breton descent. A very young, unusual son, Gaël, had, along with his fine eighteenth-century manners and moral elegance, a gift for maths that oddly enough found a place at Lesage et Cie, where he came to work. In starting to learn the business, Gaël classified the stock in plastic bags often containing millions of units according to type, substance and colour — bugle beads, 'charlotte' or seed pearls, 'lice' or black seed pearls, 'tops', beads tinted or coloured in silver and gold, mother-of-pearl and iridescent beads, soutache braid, gimp, chenille, 'bigoudis', rhinestones,

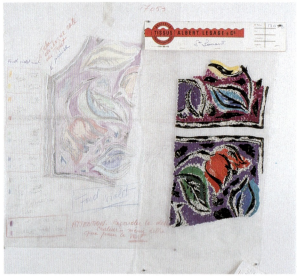

An Yves Saint Laurent sketch, the drawing of the embroidery and the sample as executed.

spangles, sequins, paillettes, metallic strips, cabochons, jet and so on. He labelled each box in which he placed the bags, taping one item next to the label to show what the contents were. This job was all the more heroic for François's recent acquisition of forty tons of goods from a defunct French embroidery house. With this purchase he made sure that generations of successors would have enough stocks to carry on. What is more, to keep enriching his Ali Baba caves of treasures and renewing his ideas, he constantly buys up discarded experiments of embroidery and passementerie, pieces of theatre jewellery which he has unmounted piece by piece, and model garments often centuries old and sometimes representing needlework techniques other than embroidery.

For all his stocks, over the years François has had to face changing conditions in availability of embroidery materials. Suppliers are increasingly going out of existence. Glass blowers and enamellers have almost entirely disappeared. The traditional suppliers of rhinestones in Austria and bugle beads in Czechoslovakia (Bohemia) can no longer guarantee quantity and delivery dates. Moreover, quality has declined. The Czech beads now tend to expand with heat or contract with cold. The situation is complicated by the growing necessity of resorting to plastic, a substance not really pleasing to a master hand embroiderer. On the other hand, new substances to which developing procedures in decalcomania (transfers) and collage can be applied make renewal possible.

At the same time that Gaël was sorting out the materials, Sophie, a young art history student at the Ecole du Louvre and the Université de Paris, was classifying by year and by season, winter or summer, all the samples and models in the Lesage archives, over a hundred thousand from the days of Michonet to the present, including the entire collections of many couturiers. They represent more than eight million work hours.

The procedure leading from the conception of an idea to the embroidered garment emerging on a couturier's runway during a fashion show is well structured, but within the confines of each phase it is not cut and dried, for modifications can be made all along the way. In conceiving the themes of a new embroidery collection, François asks himself the same question as do the couturiers — what are women going to want in the short term? Again like the couturiers, he sniffs the wind: what grounds (organza, tulle, velvet, satin, chiffon) and what colours are likely to be in vogue? Obviously, other considerations come into play. A popular film about a period or a country, a great star strikingly dressed, world events or street fashion: all have their effect on the designs of motifs of clothing and trim, and of course on embroidery.

M. David, the chief draughtsman, and his assistants are installed in an erstwhile drawing room and former bedroom. They have their own fully equipped kitchen and a storeroom filled from top to bottom with shelves groaning under rolls and rolls of classified drawings.

When François wishes to develop an original idea — or, it may be, one submitted by a couturier — he goes down the stairs from his studio to consult with M. David. He gives him an exact description of what he wants — trompe l'œil, imitation lace, flowers, arabesques. On tracing paper M. David and his team do full-size charcoal drawings to which, with soft coloured pencils, they add hues associated in François's mind with the particular embroidery material envisaged.

After François has approved a drawing, possibly requesting slight alterations, M. David, again on tracing paper, does a replica using a hard pencil, a more precise medium than charcoal. Next he proceeds to perforate the tracing paper by means of a stitching machine, following the outlines of the drawing. Then he stencils the design on to the specified ground, using a fine powder, or pounce — lamp black and crushed resin for pale colours, calcium carbonate (whiting) for dark ones. Finally, he fixes the powdered design on to the fabric with methylated spirits.

The time has now come to choose the embroidery materials to be incorporated into the

Completion of a drawing.

M. David calculating a geometric drawing.

Various materials.

design. François, basket in hand, goes to market, as he puts it — that is, he visits the storerooms and selects the elements according to their availability and his inspiration.

The drawing will now be transformed into a sample. François takes the pounced ground and the materials to an embroideress and gives his instructions. As she works, he checks the progress. He may ask for improvements in form and volume, and often changes materials en route. 'It's like adding seasoning while you're cooking a dish,' he says.

Once a sample is finished, François can present it to a couturier. Having accepted the sample, the couturier does a sketch of his own of the garment in question. This stipulates the fabric and the colours that he has chosen, often inspired by François's original conception. Fabrics determine

A study of the positioning of a sample for a corsage.

the shapes of his forthcoming collection, and shapes decide the position of embroidery. In outlining the form of a bodice, jacket sleeve or belting in the sketch, the couturier indicates this positioning.

The couturier also furnishes a full-size toile, always flat, stitched to show the outlines of the part to be embroidered. M. David reproduces this toile on tracing paper with a hard pencil, taking into account measurements intended to add the concept of the garment's volume to the flat form, never a simple technical task. François submits this tracing-paper drawing to the couturier. When it has been approved, M. David adds a note for the embroideress stipulating the materials, form and colours to be used. He places this drawing on the ground specified by the couturier, perforates it, then pounces it and sends it to the atelier.

Over the years dyeing of materials had become an increasing problem in the field of hand embroidery. Many suppliers went out of business, and those who remained could no longer be bothered with small quantities and, at that, limited themselves to basic colours. Little by little the Lesage girls learned to use and improve the methods of basin-dyeing which had been devised by Albert, thus being able to create ombré (shading) from the lightest to the darkest hues. They dilute a powder of a frank, basic colour with methylated spirits, add acetone to lighten it or varnish to darken it, mix it with another powder to obtain the desired hue, then dip the parts of the material in the mélange the number of times required to achieve the specified range. Only since 1985 have they used an airbrush to dye feathers, thread and plastic sequins: the atomizer process enhances

M. Lesage and M. David consulting.

iridescence. To render brilliance to seed pearls and braids, they soak them in pure water before adding tea or common dye powder pastilles. Once François bought a mass of beads among which the white ones had changed colour because of the heat of a fire. The girls restored them with a good wash in a detergent generally used for doing the dishes. (A little household hint: your jet will scintillate much more after being steeped in vinegar.)

Hand embroidery facilitates the bold treating of materials and combinations of them. Some of Lesage's most spectacular work in terms of design has been adapted to ermine, mother-of-pearl, cork and eighteen-carat gold bugle beads. Once the girls plucked white hairs from a colleague's head to embroider seed pearls on a white background so that the thread would be invisible. One day Elsa

Schiaparelli rang up. 'François! Shells!' Lesage et Cie ate mussels all winter.

At rue Grange the two embroidery ateliers, supervised by the *premières* Madame Michèle and Madame Gisèle, are illuminated by lamps suspended from the ceiling above the embroideresses and their frames. They are grouped close to the stockrooms filled with shelves and tables laden with classified bags of materials. These are run by Annie, a former embroideress, with the advice of Ginette, also formerly an embroideress, the oldest member of the company. In the renovated maids' rooms under the eaves each atelier has its own little bathroom and dining room as well as a fully equipped kitchen. For lunch they are often joined by Madame Françoise, head of fabrication, responsible for distributing work to them as it returns from the couturiers for final execution.

The perforation of drawing paper.

Although the two basic work methods remained unaltered, *La Main* and *Lunéville*, the education and training of embroideresses had improved along with industrial progress. The practice of hiring promising adolescent apprentices had declined greatly after the First World War and was abandoned altogether before the Second. An embroidery house such as Lesage began recruiting from the three technical schools in the Paris area.

How does an embroideress now develop? First, as a little girl participating in the life of the family at home, she perhaps shows an aptitude for sewing and darning, washing and ironing lingerie and layettes, and removing spots from fabrics. During grammar school, she feels a predilection for the art courses. When she is twelve or thirteen, she enrols for three years in a *college d'enseignement technique* (technical training school). On the first day the teacher asks new students to draw the objects that they saw on display when arriving. On the basis of these drawings, which demonstrate faculties of observation, the staff gain from the outset an idea of the individual differences between the girls.

Classical academic schooling continues: French and a second language (now generally English), maths, history, geography, and rudimentary physics and chemistry. Meanwhile instruction in sewing, embroidery, ironing and cuisine proceeds. (The girls have to eat what they cook, so it had better be tasty.) Very soon each starts intensive training in the discipline she has chosen — for bourgeoning embroideresses this may mean eight hours a day. The most difficult exercises are not those designed to improve speed but rather

Stencilling with black powder.

written texts on technique. At the end of the three years the successful student, trained in both *La Main* and *Lunéville*, receives a Certificate of Professional Aptitude.

Considerable change and renewal took place at Lesage et Cie in the seventies. Marie-Louise, Countess since her mother's death, came to rue Grange every day — designing, advising on colour, checking output — until she was seventy-five, in 1970. Over the ensuing five years she progressively slowed down. The embroideresses were not, for the most part, young women at the time either. Some, even older than herself, had been with her for half a century, others forty years. They had stayed on for several reasons. They loved the quiet atmosphere and their beautiful work and greatly appreciated the unusual feeling of family, for despite her severity

Sample reference cards.

and insistence on output per hour, Marie-Louise was humane. She watched over her employees, took care of them when they or theirs fell ill or encountered problems. Nor did she neglect embroideresses in the Paris area working at home. She visited each one regularly, not only to check production. On the other hand, these women were far from being rich. They had not always benefited from legislation governing purchasing power and retirement, and Marie-Louise would never have dreamed of forcing one to leave. Still, understandably, after she had withdrawn at the age of eighty in 1975, and despite François's continuation of her policy, sooner rather than later they bade farewell.

*I*n refraining from coming to rue Grange every day, Marie-Louise did not neglect Lesage et Cie. From Chaville she kept herself abreast of the daily

The sample, the Yves Saint Laurent sketch and the technical drawing.

activity by telephone and through François's firsthand reports until but a few days before her death at ninety-one. While devouring history books she continued to design embroidery. One year she embroidered a belt for each of her granddaughters. Then she undertook to redecorate the entire drawing-room — divans, armchairs, straight chairs. For rugs in *point de croix* she sent her motifs to rue Grange to be embroidered. Obviously, when everyone was wildly busy, which was (*Dieu merci!*) generally the case, the partially completed pieces were put to one side. If a girl happened to be free for an hour or two, François would pull one of his mother's designs out of a drawer, sometimes having to dust it before it was fitted into a frame. Often three or four years were needed to complete a design, and 'to pull the carpets out of the drawers' came to mean filling in unoccupied time.

*B*y his first marriage to Colette, a gifted designer, François had a son, Jean-Louis, so named for his late brother, and two daughters, Martine and Marion, also a talented designer. His sister Christiane, married to an eminent neuro-surgeon and psychiatrist, had five children. As with Bidul and Titane, Marie-Louise gave books rather than toys to her grandchildren, who called her 'Mamita', and regularly conducted them to museums and churches. She was closest to Jean-François, François's son by his second marriage, to the lovely, charming and chic German-born Gisella. Jean-François was only nine when his Mamita retired, and this fine boy spent much of his time with her, becoming imbued with her natural good taste and refinement as well as her knowledge of

Madame Michele working on a part of a corsage for Jean Patou (Christian Lacroix).

art and technical know-how. At twenty-one not only was he enrolled in the Ecole du Louvre, he was running his own antique shop with success.

*I*n 1975 François had been the head of Lesage et Cie for over twenty-five years. Supported by his mother, he had grown more and more master of all he surveyed. He kept several horses in a stable in Versailles, though he had little time to ride them. He had a house in the south of Corsica that he could take advantage of only a few days a year.

*T*here is nothing flashy about François Lesage. Like all good executives, he is unassuming and always available. Contrary to many men in fashion and fashion-related fields he dresses like a businessman, albeit successful and natty, and eschews jewellery save for his wedding ring and a pipe-lighter suspended from a short cord around his neck. Ordinarily, he works fourteen hours a day six days a week and, extraordinarily, twenty hours a day seven days a week, loving every minute. A quiet man, he never becomes flurried no matter how hard-pressed or tired he may be and never raises his voice, however annoyed. He does not have to insist on his authority: he selects employees of such quality that there is rarely any need. Never in the ateliers does one hear any of the gossiping or twitting that might be expected of women working closely together. François perpetuates the family spirit that he inherited from his parents, but never does it have a hint of forced paternalism, for he is benign and trusting by nature.

*E*very year François designs two haute couture collections of from 250 to 300 samples each and increasingly large collections for the expanding couture *prêt-à-porter*. As executed by his embroideresses, every sample represents between

'La Main': placing chenille.

forty and sixty work hours. Each bead and each strip, sequin, cabochon and so on requires a single stitch. Every year the embroideresses use 300 kilos of beads and one hundred million sequins, often stringing 10,000 with one needle. Some articles involve 100,000 stitches. All told, a single collection necessitates from 18,000 to 25,000 hours of preparation and an outlay of from $200,000 to $300,000.

*W*hy not send work to China, North Africa, India or Hong Kong, where embroidery traditions go back to pre-recorded times? After all, an hour's work in these places costs one-twentieth what it does chez Lesage. The answer is simple. The techniques of those regions where labour is cheap have not developed, drawing styles have scarcely evolved, materials bear no comparison.

*F*rançois introduces three or four themes into each of his collections, following his policy of avoiding a hodgepodge of a little of everything. Obviously, the couturiers occasionally inform him as to what they specifically desire, and he has to be familiar enough with them to grasp what they are after. One day Yves Saint Laurent rang up from his castle in Marrakech. 'M. Lesage, I am thinking about mice.' Another day Karl Lagerfeld called: 'Please do graffiti.' As to Lacroix (Patou) he once slipped François a note: 'Sioux?' Sioux it was. Nevertheless, if one is surprised to sense more and more a kind of overall unity in the haute couture presentations, it can be partially explained by the Lesage Effect. The couturiers derive ideas from the samples of embroidery. Though each couturier is hyper-secretive about his designs, the Lesage themes seep deeper and deeper into the substrata.

A part of Madame Michele's atelier.

*G*enerally speaking, for the haute couture collections the couturiers buy fifty per cent of the samples offered — that is, between 120 and 150 pieces from each lot. (François sells the rest to them for their *prêt-à-porter* and to private customers the world over.) At the end of December and the end of June Lesage et Cie has only from twenty-four to twenty-eight days to execute the embroideries ordered. During these periods, everyone works night and day seven days a week and certain corners of the ateliers are transformed into dormitories. Yet never is François too busy to escort student groups or professionals in fashion-related fields on a tour of the premises, even during these peak periods.

*F*rom time to time, on a late Friday afternoon, François will call the embroideresses together for a little drink and chat, and he never fails to

organize a gathering on the afternoon of Christmas Eve. Partywise, the highlight of the year is St Catherine's Day, 25 November, traditionally reserved to young unmarried women of twenty-five or over and their fanciful hats. Several years ago François opened out the fête: everybody could participate. He set the new tone by appearing costumed as Caesar (an earlier boss man), then encouraged general dressing up by announcing themes. For 'La Mer' he entered as Neptune (god of all he surveyed) amidst herrings (smoked), shrimps, sardines, turtles and dolphins. For 'Planètes' he was the Sun (shades of Louis XIV, another top executive) illuminating heavenly bodies. During the autumn of 1986 he stipulated barnyard animals. A few weeks after his announcement Marie-Louise died. He had lost his guide, companion, friend and confidante as well as mother – and was deeply affected. Spontaneously, all the employees suggested that only a simple and subdued get-together be scheduled for the St Catherine. 'Thank you but no,' replied François. 'We'll carry on as we always have done. Traditions must be maintained. My mother would want that. And it will give her joy to see us all together as usual — and happy. That will not prevent us from thinking about her too.' The affair was unusually inventive and merry, with François as Chantecler (the famous rooster from the Rostand play) leading his secretary, Nadine, Chantecler's mate, and various chickens, geese, ducks and even a caterpillar up and down the streets and boulevards and in and out of the passages of the area. After lunch, served personally by Chantecler, there was a raffle for which everyone drew a chance (that he had not paid for). Calling out the numbers, François, now a *vicomte*, dipped into boxes full of packages and distributed them as gifts. No one was overlooked. Then he started opening bottles of champagne and led the dancing in the ateliers.

During January and July, as you will remember, Lesage et Cie works non-stop preparing the fashion collections. If, around one o'clock on a Sunday afternoon during these particular months, you happen to pass by rue Grange, take the lift to the fifth floor. Upon entering, you will see Nadine's desk and reception table covered with wrapping paper taped to the wood, like the huge tables pushed together for lunch in the adjoining atelier. Since everybody takes a hand in almost anything chez Lesage whenever necessary, you may find M. Raymond, the company secretary, measuring out arms-lengths of swansdown, used as stuffing to add soft relief to certain embroideries, while Emmanuel, a 'family' friend, M. Scherrer's assistant, registers sales in the ledgers of Lars, the Danish-born ready-to-wear designer, another 'family' friend, whose premises are on the fourth floor. Lars will probably be setting the tables — paper plates and cups but real cutlery. Gaël will be

'Luneville': positioning braid right side up.

Jean-Louis Scherrer. A part of a corsage in the process, the sample as presented to Mr Scherrer, his sketch from the sample and the technical drawing.

transporting the bottles of Sauvignon and Bordeaux with the help of the trainee Sophie. Patrice Stable, the photographer, will be preparing to take embarrassing shots of everyone in unguarded moments.

Just inform whoever greets you that you have heard so much about Lesage et Cie that you simply couldn't stay away, and you will be shown to François's kitchen. Here you will find that preparations are being made to serve lunch to thirty-five people. Gérard composes tasty salads that are extremely well tossed. His beauteous assistants, Brigitte, who handles press relations, and Christine, cut sausage and slice tomatoes with exquisite finesse. Charles, the chauffeur-delivery man, a young ladykiller who works on theatre sets in his spare time, shoves stools and chairs around the tables. Madame Françoise unwraps the cheese and places it on platters, while M. David and Nadine cut the apple tarts for dessert. François's assistant for sales, Madame Monique ('Moumou'), will be helping François, wearing an apron, see to his roast veal and mashed potatoes, roast beef and green beans, or *bouchées à la reine* and rice.

A technical drawing and the execution of a sample.

Sitting quietly to one side Jennifer, Monique's royal-blue cocker spaniel, the most famous dog in Paris fashion and as lovable as her mistress, observes the preparations with undisguised interest.

Certainly, François will ask that an extra plate be set for you. And why not? There is always more than enough (the leftovers are finished off on Monday). He never turns away an unannounced visitor from Chanel or Balmain, so why not you? Now, if you plan your schedule carefully, you will come along on the first Sunday in January, the *Fête des Rois* (Twelfth Night). For dessert there are *galettes* filled with marzipan. The one finding the *fève*, in olden days a bean and later a porcelain image, now a little cardboard figure, has the right to designate the king to rule throughout Epiphany by placing a gold cardboard crown on his head. (Usually, François receives this distinction.) The embroideresses may finish the hilarious meal singing, but soon their merriment subsides and they return to the silence and precision of their work. You will, I am sure, offer to help clear the tables...

Summer 1985, Chanel (Karl Lagerfeld). Inspired by 19th century ceramic flower-pot holders. An evening gown wholly embroidered in chalk-white sequins and bugles. 2000 hours. Photographed on the famous Chanel staircase.

Winter 1984-5, Jean-Louis Scherrer. Persian rug drawing style. A fringed shawl corsage entirely embroidered with tiny glass mosaic beads in harmonies of fifteen different colours modified according to model. 1500 hours of beading.

Summer 1986, Christian Dior (Marc Bohan). A corsage of sequins — turtle-shell brown on white and white on turtle-shell brown — so blended with tiny beads as to produce a 'sponge' relief effect. 400 hours.

Summer 1987, Hubert de Givenchy. 'Sarazakit', or ancient Turkish, drawing style as revived by the Japanese during the nineteenth century. On chalk-white sequins, different coloured porcelain sequins with a touch of chalk-white jet and bugles. 600 hours.

Summer 1987, Christian Lacroix. For a brocade toreador bolero, chenille and silk-thread carnations with gold braid and bold bead arabesques.

Winter 1984-5, 'Monsieur' Yves Saint Laurent. On a velvet jacket, the likeness of cameos is achieved by coral and ivory beads amidst baroque arabesques in relief of bulging gold-thread cord, simple and wrapped gold-plated strips and 18-carat gold bugles.

· E P I L O G U E ·

***I**t is a most agreeable task to salute the talent, love of one's work, creative qualities and pursuit of a distinctly Parisian activity that contributes to expanding, glorifying and propagating French fashion.' Thus began a speech by the Deputy Mayor of Paris in charge of cultural affairs, tracing the life and career of Marie-Louise Lesage and addressed to her son François in her absence. The occasion, on 28 February 1985, was a reception inaugurating 'De la Mode et des Lettres', an exhibition at the Musée de la Mode et du Costume, Palais Galliera, arranged by its Curator-in-charge, Guillaume Garnier. 'Surely you will find the proper words to express to your mother all our sincerest admiration for the unflagging energy and devotion she has consecrated to cultivating the virtues of creativity and haute couture...' the speech concluded, 'and tell her how sensitive we are to the great-heartedness and constantly renewed inspiration that make of Marie-Louise Lesage a personage inseparable from Paris fashion in what is most savoury and exciting about it.'

With this François was handed the Gilded Silver Medal that the City of Paris was awarding to his mother.

On 14 October 1985 the French Minister of Culture named François Lesage Chevalier of the Order of Arts and Letters.

During the twentieth semi-annual reception given on 30 January 1986 for the 'Dé d'Or' (Gold Thimble), whereby a jury of prominent fashion editors honours couturiers and members of haute couture-related activites, Madame Jacques Chirac, wife of the Mayor of Paris, presented M. Lesage with the Medal of the City of Paris.

When you walk down rue de la Paix from the Opéra or up rue Castiglione from the Tuileries, you come to Place Vendôme. At No. 21, Elsa Schiaparelli's mansion, you will find that her boutique has, since its inauguration on 28 July 1987, been a showcase for the jewellery and accessories of recently renamed Lesage SA. As you go in, listen closely. You will hear some music : heroes are being sung.

·APPENDIX·FRAUDULENT·COPYING·

Author's Note:

To my knowledge, the subject of copying French fashion designs has not been treated in detail in any 'commercial' book. If I am mistaken, I beg the pardon of those who have indeed covered it and will take whatever steps are necessary to acknowledge that I stand corrected.

Over the years the copying of clothes came to involve suppliers of accessories, adornment and embroidery. I feel that I owe a résumé to them, as well as to the French fashion authorities and couturiers who have lent me assistance for so long and will undoubtedly welcome seeing a statement made for an international audience.

'Being copied is the
ransom of success.'
Gabrielle Chanel
'When you cease being
copied, you cease
to be news.'
Elsa Schiaparelli
'Copying is to be judged
according to resemblances,
not according to differences.'
French Jurisprudence

During his pioneer trip to the United States with his wife Denise in 1913, Paul Poiret was shocked and enraged to see his name, unauthorized, on labels for clothes and hats in a shop on Fifth Avenue. He was further incensed when he learned from a New York lawyer that there were no laws in America to protect him from piracy. Upon returning to Paris, he called together his most important competitors and with them proceeded to draw up a set of rules and regulations which, when made official, would enable the couturiers to riposte to wanton copying. Nothing in fact came of his efforts, but an impetus had been given.

One need only contemplate French artistic achievements across the ages and the added impact of the Industrial Revolution to understand why the French, on the threshold of the modern era at the end of the nineteenth century, came to value works of periods past more deeply than ever. The need to protect them, and those to come, from being copied was paramount.

The French State took the initiative to have the right to 'industrial property' recognized on an international level with the Convention de Paris, signed in 1883, and revised in 1900, 1911, 1925, 1934, 1958, 1967 and 1980 to adapt it to the development of the industrial world. It confers upon any member the right to industrial property in the signatory countries — now ninety-two — as, however, subject to local rules and regulations.

For the French, the Convention was not very satisfactory. They did not have easy recourse to the laws of each country, which differed greatly and were less protectionist than French laws. Experience proved that suits introduced by the French abroad required considerable expenditure in return for disappointing results.

If the means to fight fraudulent copying in foreign countries remained almost inaccessible, it was not the same in France. (French legislation, it is to be noted, is as simple as it is effective.) The Law of 14 July 1909, more specific than the 1883 Convention, was meant to protect designs and models on the condition that they be registered at the Institut National de la Propriété Industrielle.

Unfortunately, like protection outside France continued to be nil. Finally, by the Hague Agreement of 1 July 1928, an international instrument of protection — the only one ever — was promulgated. It covered all designs and models registered with the Organisation Mondiale de la Propriété Intellectuelle in Geneva. Cynically perhaps, few members of national fashion organizations could be bothered to proceed to any such registration.

Embroidery was always fraudulently copied, but the practice did not become intolerable until just after the First World War, when Paris modes were being popularized and rendered desirable and available on a worldwide scale. The changes and innovations intrigued copyists more and more. In the early twenties Madeleine Vionnet reacted to the increasing piracy. She fought for the implementation of a workable procedure governing the registration of designs and models under the Law of 14 July 1909, and improvements were made early enough to protect the *Garçonne* styles as well as her own bias-cut garments.

Madame Schiaparelli was greatly copied, much for her Lesage embroidery and especially the use of metal-plated strips. These were produced by means of special needles: the eye was horizontal rather than vertical. Albert Lesage bought them secretly from a British supplier from whom he exacted the promise not to sell them to anyone else.

Copying involved two aspects: the idea and the registered trademark. Since its initiation in the nineteenth century, the latter had come to represent excellent protection. Pirates could be brought to court all over the world. But the idea?

With the revival of French fashion after the Second World War, the French and the Germans, in 1947, signed the Berne Agreement, a remarkable document which included the important 'resemblances' ruling: if the desire to usurp an idea which underlies a creation is to be found in a copy, this is a fraudulent copy. The penalty was not monetary but penal. The offender could be sent to prison. Also since 1947 French law has been such that if the precedence of a creation can be proved by means of archival samples, classified and referenced day by day (which was and is the case at chez Lesage), there is no further need for registration according to the provisions of the Law of 14 July 1909. Visual examination is all that is required.

A new method of selling was launched by Christian Dior as early as his second collection (August 1947) and quickly adapted by his competitors: toiles, or muslin models of a garment. This created a conflict between the couturiers and their suppliers of adornment. Take the case of embroidery. The couturiers wanted to consider that they had both the commercial and artistic rights to a model which they had bought and used. The embroiderers denounced such a concept. If, by a gentlemen's agreement, Lesage, for example, granted a couturier the exclusivity of a model, in his mind the original embroidery remained his sole property.

When the couturiers started to sell toiles and later paper patterns, some of their customers wished to copy the embroidery that sometimes went with the garment. Respecting the gentlemen's agreement, the couturiers would ask Albert to sell them the design and model outright. He always replied, 'Non!' And so does his son.

The Lesage principle has never varied. 'I give you, the couturier, the exclusive right to a model, but I remain the sole owner of it. I have promised not to sell that model to anyone else without your permission. When a dress-shop owner asks us to do the embroidery for this or that haute couture gown, we always check that he has bought the toile or paper pattern for it and has obtained your permission to reproduce it.'

When, after the Second World War, haute couture, becoming increasingly international, reigned supreme before the arrival of *prêt-à-porter*, Christian Dior (or, rather, Jacques Rouët) exacted a year's contract for many Dior products from a buyer in return for his right to sell a toile or paper pattern to dressmakers in his country. It does not come as a surprise to learn that the dressmakers secretly exchanged them with colleagues in other countries. Yet how could a Greek dressmaker be stopped from trading models with a Portuguese colleague? This also went for embroidery. The piracy was already fearful when sales were authorized. Unauthorized, it became sheer madness and could not be countered even by the offer of rewards for the denunciation of copyists. It was high time for fashion to be protected by tough legislation.

Law No. 52-300 dated 12 March 1952 represented a giant step forward. Hitherto 'industrial property' alone — trademarks — had been protected. Now the *idea*, artistic and intellectual property, was defended. The Law was designed to repress the fraudulent copying of the 'Seasonal Industries of Clothing and Adornment'. By 'seasonal' was meant those industries which frequently renewed the form of their products: couture, fur, lingerie, shoes, gloves, morocco-leather goods, novel fabrics, furnishing materials and special fabrics for haute couture and embroidery. 'A reproduction disguised even under a deformation of a secondary nature,' reads the Law, 'is sufficient to be considered as an offence from the moment the creative originality of the model copied is found to be usurped.' Echoes of the 1947 Berne Agreement.

That was not all. Five years later came the Law of 11 March 1957. This protected the most humble object. Moreover, it annulled the imperative of registering a design or a model with the Institut National de la Propriété Industrielle, although such registration might be made according to the Law of 14 July 1909, still in force, if so desired.

The March 1957 Law was a tribute to the very French principle of the unity of the arts. The sensible attitude which it embodied served the interests of all creators. A refusal to protect accessories, household furnishings, even watches, not forgetting clothes, on the assumption that their function took precedence over their artistic aspect, would have denied protection to almost the totality of the articles of the applied arts.

Progressively an efficient juridical organization was set up in France to fight copying. This organization, however, still had no effect in foreign countries. Such a situation is unfortunate, for copying abroad is most detrimental to the de luxe French exports. It is true that *prêt-à-porter*, as it advanced, greatly purged copying, since the famous names were affixed to cheaper, more widely accessible products. Nevertheless, the cost of foreign copying can still be conservatively estimated at an annual two billion francs ($350 million), corresponding to 25,000 jobs that, as a result, cannot be created.

In a letter dated 3 March 1982 addressed to the Conseil Economique et Social, the French Prime Minister wrote:

> Trademarks, models and designs play an important role in French export.
>
> **O**n the one hand, they represent a great part of the royalties received by France in our international commercial exchanges under the heading of patents and licenses; on the other, they protect a large number of our exportations.
>
> **I** would like the Conseil to... draw up proposals to reduce the importance of fraudulent copying.

The Conseil submitted 'The Problem of French Copying' in the report on its findings of 14 and 15 June 1983. This report was published in the *Journal Officiel* on 8 July 1983. Action is yet to come.

'It is desirable,' stated François Lesage in 1987, 'for so-called Western industrialized countries to recognize the terms of the 1947 Berne Agreement. True, people who are going hungry in India, South Korea, China replacing Hong Kong, etc. can be pardoned for "taking their inspiration" from the creativity and dynamism of the Western culture. Yet, it is not normal for clothes manufacturers, wherever they may be, to continue to indulge in fraudulent copying.'

· S H O R T · B I B L I O G R A P H Y ·

Since this book does not pretend in any way to be a manual on the technique of embroidery, the author has confined himself to books which, though they may illustrate the multitude of stitches, contain references to the history of needlework.

Antrobus, M., *Needlework Through the Ages, A Short Survey of its Development in Decorative Art*, London, Hodder and Stoughton, 1928.

Boucher, F., *Histoire du Costume*, Paris, Flammarion, 1965

Campbell-Harding, Valerie and Watts, Pamela, *Bead Embroidery*, Berkeley, Calif., Lacis, 1993

Caulfield, S. F. A. and Sayward, B. C., *The Dictionary of Needlework, an Encyclopedia of Artistic, Plain, and Fancy Needlework*, London, Upcott Gill, 1885.

Dean, B., *Ecclesiastical Embroidery*, London, Batsford, 1958.

Edwards, Joan, *Bead Embroidery*, Berkeley, Calif., Lacis, 1992.

Fukuyama, Yusai, *Tambour Work*, London, Dryad, 1987.

Gostelow, M., *A World of Embroidery*, London, Mills & Boon, 1975.

Jones, Julia, *The Beading Book*, Berkeley, Calif., Lacis, 1993

Jones, M. E., *A History of Western Embroidery*, London, Studio Vista, 1961.

Kendrick, A. F., *English Embroidery*, New York, Charles Scribner's Sons, 1905.

Montano, Judith Baker, *The Art of Silk Ribbon Embroidery*, Lafayette, Calif., C & T Publishing, 1993.

Pike, Kaye and Landy, Lynne, *Elegant Embroidery*, Australia, Allen & Unwin, 1991

Schuette, M. and Muller-Christensen, S., *Domestic Needlework, Its Origins and Customs Throughout the Centuries*, New York, Charles Scribner's Sons, 1926.

Thompson, Angela, *Embroidery With Beads*, Berkeley, Calif., Lacis, 1992.

· P I C T U R E · A C K N O W L E D G E M E N T S ·

The photographs of models being presented during fashion parades were furnished amicably by the houses represented, unless otherwise specified.

All the photographs of Lesage samples, sketches and rue Grange activities were taken by Patrice Stable, unless otherwise specified.

The photographs related to the Lesage family and other personal matters were provided by François Lesage. While every effort has been made to give correct acknowledgement wherever due, this has proved difficult. Where insufficient credit has been given the publishers will be pleased to make amendments in any future edition. Archives Chanel : 132 up left and down centre; Collection Cinémathèque Française : 18 up, 19 up, 20 up, 142 up centre; the New York Fashion Institute of Technology, Design Laboratory : 36 left; Archives Hubert de Givenchy : 106, 129 left; Calvin Klein : 140 down left (photo Bruce Weber); Archives Lesage : 21 up, 22-3 margins, 102 down right, 187 down left; Roxanne Lowit : 135 down right, 141 up left, 154, 156, 164; Le Musée de la Mode et du Costume, Palais Galliera, Paris : 143 down (photo Jean d'Alban); the Metropolitan Museum of Art, New York, a gift of Mrs. Harrison Williams, Lady Mendl, Mrs. Ector Munn 1946: 53 (photo Cindy Sirko); Collection National Film Archives London : 21 left down, 32 up left, 56, 58, 134 left, 135 left; Collection *l'Officiel*, Paris : 61 down right. 100 centre, 66 up, 75, 78, 80 left up and down, 97, 154 up left, 99 down right, 143 centre (photo Francis Giacobetti and maquillage Fabienne Sevigne 1986); Archives Jean Patou (Mr Jean de Mouÿ) : 43 right, 44; Collection Laurent de Teto and Raymonde Zehnecker : 76 right, 79, 80 right; 'Monsieur' Yves Saint Laurent : 117 centre right, 119 down right, 133 right, 136; Musée des Arts de la Mode 16 up : American *Vogue :* 71 - Copyright © 1936 (renewed 1974) by the Condé Nast Publications Inc, 107 left — Copyright © 1964 by the Condé Nast Publications Inc, and also by the courtesy of Miss Audrey Hepburn. 106, photo Raymond Voinquel.

·INDEX·

Page numbers in *italics* refer to illustration captions; pre-modern historical details and technical embroidery terms are not listed.

Adrian, *21*, 89
Agnès, 39
Alaia, Azzedine, 122
Alix (cf Grès)
Années Folles, 38, 42, *42-3*, 44, 51, 58-9, 116, 130
Arab princesses, 121-2, 129, 131, 134
Aragon, Louis, 130 *136*
Arletty, *18*
Arts Décoratifs, École Nationale Supérieure des, 34, 36-7, *39*, *40*, *45-6*, *52*, *54-5*, *131*; history, 34; Exhibition (1925), 45; Vionnet's reflection of, 47

Bachelor girl (cf also Garçonne, La), 39, 44, 59
Baker, Joséphine, *42*, 44
Bakst, Léon, 34, 131, *135*
Balenciaga, Cristóbal, 66, 73, *73*, 76, 78, *78*, 80, 84, *92*, 96, 100-2, *104-5*, 107, *108-9*, 109-11, *112*, 115
Ballets Russes, 34, 38
Balmain, Pierre, *21*, 78-9; New-look, *80*, 84; 'Jolie Madame', *93*, 96, *98-9*, *101-4*; *104*, *107-11*, *120*, *130*
Banton, Travis, *56*, *58*, *133-4*
Barioz, Jean, *77*, 77, 84, 96
Bauhaus, 42, *45*
Beat generation, 106
Beatniks, 106
Bechoff, David, 39, 47
Bérard, Christian, 61, 92, 131
Bias cut (Vionnet), 47-9, 51
Black African art, 39
Blass, Bill, 133, *140-1*
Bœuf sur le toit, 38, 56
Bohan, Marc (Dior), *54-5*, 110-1, *114*, 115, *118*, 122-3, *123-4*, 124, 129-30, *131*, 131,133, *158-9*
Bokassa, Emperor and Empress, 121, *121-3*
Boulle furniture, *20*, 130, 151
Boussac, Marcel, 79-80
Bouvet-de Lozier, Simone, 29-30, 40, 52, 82, 85, 87, 90
Boyer, Charles, 88-9
Breton, André, 39
Brokers (cf Commissionnaires de Commerce Extérieur)

Cacharel, 108, 121
Callot (Sœurs), 25, 40, 47, 56, 96
Cardin, Pierre, 100, 107, 111, 132
Castelbajac, Jean-Charles de, 122
Castillo, Antonio del, 76
Catherine, Sainte (celebration), 43, 152
Chambre Syndicale de la Couture Parisienne (later Fédération Française de la Couture, du Prêt-à-Porter des Couturiers et des Créateurs de la Mode, q.v.), 59, 61, 71, 100, 121
Celine, 108, 121
Chanel (cf Lagerfeld, Karl), *20*, 39, 59, 71, 76, *81*, 100, 110, 115, 124, 130-1, *132*, 133, *138*, *154-5*,
Chaumont, Marcelle, *96*, 96
Chaville, 52, 71-2, 75, 83, 90
Chicago, 31, 33, 84, 87
Chloé, 121, 133
Churchill, Winston 61, 71
Cocteau, Jean, 25, 38, *59*, 61, 63, 130, *136*,
Colcombet (Bucol), 57
Colonial Exhibition (1922), 39
Commissionnaires de Commerce Extérieur (brokers), 29-30, 38, 39
Courrèges, André, 111-2
Crahay, Jules-François, 111, *112*, 115, *121*
Créateurs (formerly *stylistes*) (q.v.), 122, 131, 135
Cubists, 34

Daché, Lily, 86
Dali, Salvador, 61, 63, 65, 130
Dépression (1929), 56, 58
Déssès, Jean, 96, *97-8*, 99, 110

Diaz, Elsa, 89-90
Dietrich, Marlene, *56*, 89, 107, *133-4*
Dieuleveult, Gaël de, 146
Dior, Christian, *54-5*, *76*, 78, *79*, 79, 80, 92, 96-100, 102, 107, 110, *114*, 115-6, *118*, *123-4*,130, *131*, 131-3, *158-9*
Doeuillet, 39
Dormoy, Marcelle, *74*, 96
Dorothée bis, 108
Douanier Rousseau, 124
Doucet, Jacques, 25, 40, *42*, *45*, 47
Drôle de guerre, 71, 83
Drécoll, 39, 66, 96
Dress: basic form, 19, 24; sportswear, 39, 108; change after First World War, 42; in the twenties, 45; early thirties, 59; Occupation 77; post-Second World War, 77: youth movement effects, 106
Dufy, Raoul, 57
Duncan, Isadora, 34
Duse, Eleonora, 38

Edward VII, 39
Eiffel, Gustave, 52
Embroideress, modern training, 149
Embroidery: history, 16, 27, 78; twenties development, 42; Vionnet, 48, 51; effects of Depression (1929), 56; Schiaparelli, 62, 66; Nazi Occupation, 72, 76; post-Second World War, 77; history of jewellery and accessories, 142, 145
Exodus (1940), 72

Farah Diba, Shabannou, 121
Farida, Queen of Egypt, *66*
Fashion (Paris and the French industry): 38, 45; effects of Depression (1929), 56; led by Schiaparelli, 61-2; during Drôle de Guerre (1939-40), 70-2; during the Occupation (1940-5), 75-6; post-Liberation, 77; effects of baby-boom and youth movement, 106; effects of oil crises and Arab princesses, 121-2, 129, 131; turnover early eighties, 131; high eighties times, 133; mid-eighties crossroads, 134; Lacroix Effect, 137
Fath, Jacques, 73, 76; New Look, *80*, 84, 92, *94*, 95, 96, *97*, 99-101, *101*, 102
Fauves, 34
Fédération Française de la Couture, du Prêt-à-Porter des Couturiers et des Créateurs de la Mode (former Chambre Syndicale de la Couture Parisienne (q.v.), 122, 124
Féraud, Louis, 96
Flapper, 39, 42, 44
Flower Children, 106
Folie, 52
Fortuny, Mariano, 124, *129*
Fressange, Inès de la, *132*, *138*
Futurists, 34

Garçonne, La, 42 *42-4*, 48,
Gaulle, Charles de, 107, 115
Gaultier, Jean-Paul, 122
Giacometti, 61
Givenchy, Hubert de, *99*, *100*, 102, *106*, 107, 109, 110, *113*, 116, 119, 124, *124-5*, *129*, 130-2, *160-1*
Gobelins (tapestry), 130
Goma, Michel, 111, *112*, 115, *116*, *118*
Grace of Monaco, Princess, *104*, 121
Grès (formerly Alix), 37, 76, 100 *110*, 110, 115
Griffe, Jacques, 84, 100
Gropius, Walter, 42

Harlow, Jean, 123
Haute couture : 23-4, 45; the Lesage key, 78; post-Liberation, 92, 108, 111; effects of May 1968, 115; early seventies and revival, 117-8; 121-2; eighties, 129, 132
Hechter, Daniel, 108, 121
Heim, Jacques, 84, 96, 110
Henry à la Pensée, 96
Hepburn, Audrey, *106*
Herrara, Carolina, 133
Hitler, Adolf, 66, 70, 72, 77

*I*mpressionism, 117

*J*ean-Louis (designer), 89, *90-1*
Jenny, 40, *43-4*, 51, 66

*K*andinski, 130
Kennedy, Jacqueline, 107
Kenzo, 121, 124
Khanh, Emmanuele, 108, 121
Klein, Calvin, 133, *140*
Klimt, Gustav, 130

*L*acroix, Christian, 130, 131, 133, *135*, 137, *150*, *162-3*
Lafaurie, Jeanne, 96
Lagerfeld, Karl, *20*, *81*, 100, 108, 111, 121, 130, 131, *132*, 133-4, 137, *138*, 151, *154-5*
Lanvin, 25, 38-40, 96, 110-1, *112*, 114-5, *121*, 121, 126
Lapeyre, 83
Laroche, Guy, 96
Lars, 153
Laug, André, *121*, 132
Lecomte, Germaine, 96
Le Corbusier, 111
Lelong, Lucien, 39-40, *43*, 51, 61, *64*, *66*, 66, 71, *72*, 72-3, 75-6, 79, 92, 96, 101
Lesage, Albert: family history, 29; infancy, adolescence and employment with *commissionnaires*, 29-30; captivity in Germany, 30; return to civilian life, 30; in Chicago with Marshall Field, 31, 33; return to Paris, 38; meeting with Michonet and Marie-Louise, 40; marriage, 40; working with M. Vionnet, 48, 51; early married life, 51-2; rue Grange, 57; Depression (1929 ff) efforts, 56-7; accessories and jewelry, 58; work for Elsa Schiaparelli, 62, 66; trip to New York (1939), 70; return to Paris, 70; in Mont-Dore during drôle de guerre, 71; move to Thonon-les-Bains, 72; in Paris during Nazi Occupation, 72, 75; post-Second World War efforts, 77-8; work with Balmain, 82; death of Jean-Louis, 83; his own death, 90
Lesage, Albert: *29*, *33*; Occupation textile designs, *57*; Schiaparelli belts, *58*; designs for the King and Queen of Egypt, *66*; in New York (1939), *71*; with his son, *84*; sample for Jean-Louis, *91*
Lesage, Colette, *98*, *101*, *103*
Lesage, Christiane, 52, 71, 82, 83, 150
Lesage, François: birth, early education, 52, 71, 82-3, during Nazi Occupation, 83; with Jean-Louis, 83; return to Paris, adolescence, rue Grange instruction, art excursions, 83-4; trip to USA, 84, 90; return to France, 95; taking over Lesage et Cie, 95; change in clientele, 95-6; learning fashion in the fifties, 96, 104; company development in the sixties, 108, 109; effects of 1968, 115; master embroiderer and the seventies, 119, 125; the eighties, 129, 133; American clients, 132-3; accessories and jewellery, 142, 145; life and work rue Grange, 146, 153; family, 150; personality, 150-1; attitude toward copying, *85-7*
Lesage, Jean-François, 150
Lesage, Jean-Louis, 52, 58, 71, 72, 75, 82-3, 87, 89
Lesage, Marie-Louise, née Favot: family history, 34; infancy, adolescence, interest in painting, 34; enrollment in l'École Supérieure des Arts Décoratifs, 36; learning to make dresses, 36; employment with Vionnet and assignment at Michonet's 37; meeting with Albert and marriage, 40; raising her children, *34-6*, *38*, 82, 87, 95-6, 98, 101, 149, 150, 152,
Licensing, 80, 132
Lunéville and lunévilleuses, 43, *43*, *49*, 52, 56, 62, 149

*M*ad Carpentier, 96
Main, La, and mainteuses, 42-3, *43*, 62, *96*, 149
Mainbocher, 71
Marie-Martine, 108
Marshall Field, 31, *33*, 33, 87
Martial et Armand, 40
Martine, 36, *46*
Media, the, 45, 75, 92, 106
Michelangelo, 83

Michonet, *22-8*, 25, *35*, *37*, 37, *39*, 39-40, 48, 110
Miyake, Issey, 111
Modelistes, 108
Modernism, 111, 117
Molyneux, 39, 51, 71, 78-9
Montana, Claude, 122
Montmartre, 56-7, 92
Montparnasse, 44, 56, 92
Mori, Hanae, 124, *127*
Mortensen, Erik, 78, *130*
Mugler, Thierry, 111, 122

*N*ew Look, 78, 80, 92, 97

*O*ccupation (1940-1945), 72, 77, 83, 115
Oil crises, 121, 123

*P*aquin, 25, 39, 51, 76, 100
Paris: twenties, 38-9, 44; 1939, 70; during Nazi Occupation, 73; post-Liberation, 77, 92, 94; seventies, 115, 121
Patou, Jean, 39, 40, *43*, 44, 59, 111, *112*, 115, *116*, 116, *118*, 130-1, 133, *135*,137, *150*
Piguet, Robert, 66, 73, 76, 96, *96*, 101
Pipart, Gérard, 108, 111
Plastics, 101, 117
Poiret, Paul, 24-5, 27, 29, 34, 36-9, *40*, *46*, 47, 52, 58-9, 78, 80, 92, 145
Pompidou, Georges, 116-7
Prêt-à-porter, 100, 108, 118, 122, 131-2, 135, 152

*R*abanne, Paco, 111
Ready-to-wear, 107, 121-2
Rebé, 78-80, 94, 96, 98, 110
Redfern, 25, 39
Renta, Oscar de la, 133, *140*
Ricci, Nina, 96, 107-8, 111
Robe-chemise, (short straight dress), 42, *43*, 45, 47, 116
Rochas, Marcel, 84, 96
Rodier, 57, *143*
Roehm, Carolyne, 133, *141*
Rouët, Jacques, 80, 132
Rouff, Maggy, 40, 96
Rykiel, Sonia, 108, 121

*S*aint Laurent, Yves, *18*, *94*, 98, 100, 110-12, 115-19, 121-5, 129-34, *136-7*, 137, *146*, 151, *164-5*
Scherrer, Jean-Louis, 111, 115, 119, *119*, 124, *126*, *128*, 129-31, *134*, 137, 142, *151*, *156-7*
Schiaparelli, Elsa, *15-6*, *19*, 31, *52*, 58-66, *58-65*, *67-9*, *72*, 73, 78, 80, 84, 92, *92*, *94*, 95-6, 99, 100, *102*, 102, 107, 122, 124, 130, *138*,
Seventies, the: 117; plastics, 117, 121, 123
Sirikit, Queen of Thailand, *21*, 121, *130*
Sixties, the, 137
Spook, Per, 139
Street inspiration, 106, 108, 117
Stylistes, (later *créateurs*, q.v.), 108, 121-2

*T*hirties, the, 61, 73
Thomass, Chantal, 108
Trémolet, Gérard, 142 ff, *143*, *144*
Twenties, the, 38-9, 45

*U*ngaro, Emanuel, 112, 132

*V*amp, 39, 42, 44
Van Dongen, 44, 61
Vionnet, Madeleine, *17*, *35-6*, 37, 39, *39*, 40, *41*, 45, 47, *47-9*, 48-9, *51-61*, 56, 58, 63, *64*, 66, 71, 78-9, 96, 100

*W*omen: American, 32-3, 56; changes in attitudes, status and tastes, 23, 25-6, 39, 59, 77-8, 97, 107, 117-8; executives, 129
Worth, Charles Frederick and successors, 25, 25, 39, 51, 61, 66, *70*, 96

*Z*ehnacker, Raymonde, 79-80

Art Director:
François Huertas

Book Designer:
Chantal Garrard - Influences

Publisher's coordinator:
Jean Arcache

Composition:
Bussière A.G., Paris

Photoengraving:
Actual, Bienne

Printing:
Weber, Bienne

Binding:
AGM, Forges-les-Eaux